Disability Policy in China

Without access to a public social welfare system in parts of China, some families face invidious decisions about the lives of their children with disabilities. In other places, children with disabilities can now expect to participate in their families and communities with the same aspirations as other children. Understanding how Chinese policy has changed in the places that have addressed these stark situations is vital for the rights of the children and their families who still struggle to find the support they need.

This book examines family experiences of child disability policy in China, and is the first to compile research on this area. It applies a child disability rights framework in four domains – care and protection, economic security, development and participation – to investigate families' experiences of the effectiveness of support to fulfil their children's rights. Questioning how families experience the interrelationships between these rights, it also considers what the further implications of the policy are. It includes vivid case studies of families' experiences, and combines these with national data to draw out the likely future policy directions to which the Chinese government has said it is committed.

Bringing together a wealth of statistical and qualitative data on children with disabilities, this book will be of great interest to students and scholars of Chinese social welfare, social policy, society, disability and children's studies, as well as policy-makers and nongovernment organizations alike.

Xiaoyuan Shang is a Professor, Beijing Normal University, and Associate Professor, Social Policy Research Centre, University of New South Wales, Australia. She is a leading international expert in the research of children welfare and protection in China.

Karen R. Fisher is an Associate Professor, Social Policy Research Centre, University of New South Wales, Australia. She is a social policy researcher on the organisation of social services, including disability policy, in Australia and China.

Routledge Contemporary China Series

For a complete list of titles in this series, please visit www.routledge.com.

92 **The Chinese Corporatist State**
Adaption, survival and resistance
Edited by Jennifer Y.J. Hsu and Reza Hasmath

93 **Law and Fair Work in China**
Sean Cooney, Sarah Biddulph and Ying Zhu

94 **Guangdong and Chinese Diaspora**
The changing landscape of Qiaoxiang *Yow Cheun Hoe*

95 **The Shanghai Alleyway House**
A vanishing urban vernacular
Gregory Bracken

96 **Chinese Globalization**
A profile of people-based global connections in China
Jiaming Sun and Scott Lancaster

97 **Disruptive Innovation in Chinese and Indian Businesses**
The strategic implications for local entrepreneurs and global incumbents
Peter Ping Li

98 **Corporate Governance and Banking in China**
Michael Tan

99 **Gender, Modernity and Male Migrant Workers in China**
Becoming a 'modern' man
Xiaodong Lin

100 **Emissions, Pollutants and Environmental Policy in China**
Designing a national emissions trading system
Bo Miao

101 **Sustainable Development in China**
Edited by Curtis Andressen, Mubarak A.R. and Xiaoyi Wang

102 **Islam and China's Hong Kong**
Ethnic identity, Muslim networks and the new Silk Road
Wai-Yip Ho

103 **International Regimes in China**
Domestic implementation of the international fisheries agreements
Gianluca Ferraro

104 **Rural Migrants in Urban China**
Enclaves and transient urbanism
Fulong Wu, Fangzhu Zhang and Chris Webster

105 **State-Led Privatization in China**
The politics of economic reform
Jin Zeng

106 **China's Supreme Court**
Ronald C. Keith, Zhiqiu Lin and Shumei Hou

107 **Queer Sinophone Cultures**
Howard Chiang and Ari Larissa Heinrich

108 **New Confucianism in Twenty-First Century China**
The construction of a discourse
Jesús Solé-Farràs

109 **Christian Values in Communist China**
Gerda Wielander

110 **China and Global Trade Governance**
China's first decade in the World Trade Organization
Edited by Ka Zeng and Wei Liang

111 **The China Model and Global Political Economy**
Comparison, impact, and interaction
Ming Wan

112 **Chinese Middle Classes**
China, Taiwan, Macao and Hong Kong
Edited by Hsin-Huang Michael Hsiao

113 **Economy Hotels in China**
A glocalized innovative hospitality sector
Songshan Sam Huang and Xuhua Michael Sun

114 **The Uyghur Lobby**
Global networks, coalitions and strategies of the World Uyghur Congress
Yu-Wen Chen

115 **Housing Inequality in Chinese Cities**
Edited by Youqin Huang and Si-ming Li

116 **Transforming Chinese Cities**
Edited by Mark Y. Wang, Pookong Kee and Jia Gao

117 **Popular Media, Social Emotion and Public Discourse in Contemporary China**
Shuyu Kong

118 **Globalization and Public Sector Reform in China**
Kjeld Erik Brødsgaard

119 **Religion and Ecological Sustainability in China**
Edited by James Miller, Dan Smyer Yu and Peter van der Veer

120 **Comparatizing Taiwan**
Edited by Shu-mei Shih and Ping-hui Liao

121 **Entertaining the Nation**
Chinese television in the twenty-first century
Edited by Ruoyun Bai and Geng Song

122 **Local Governance Innovation in China**
Experimentation, diffusion, and defiance
Edited by Jessica C. Teets and William Hurst

123 **Footbinding and Women's Labor in Sichuan**
Hill Gates

124 **Incentives for Innovation in China**
Building an innovative economy
Xuedong Ding and Jun Li

125 **Conflict and Cooperation in Sino-US Relations**
Change and continuity, causes and cures
Edited by Jean-Marc F. Blanchard and Simon Shen

126 **Chinese Environmental Aesthetics**
Wangheng Chen, translated by Feng Su, edited by Gerald Cipriani

127 **China's Military Procurement in the Reform Era**
The Setting of New Directions
Yoram Evron

128 **Forecasting China's Future**
Dominance or Collapse?
Roger Irvine

129 **Chinese Migration and Economic Relations with Europe**
Edited by Marco Sanfilippo and Agnieszka Weinar

130 **Party Hegemony and Entrepreneurial Power in China**
Institutional change in the film and music industries
Elena Meyer-Clement

131 **Explaining Railway Reform in China**
A train of property rights re-arrangements
Linda Tjia Yin-nor

132 **Irony, Cynicism and the Chinese State**
Edited by Hans Steinmüller and Susanne Brandtstädter

133 **Animation in China**
History, Aesthetics, Media
Sean Macdonald

134 **Parenting, Education and Social Mobility in Rural China**
Cultivating dragons and phoenixes
Peggy A. Kong

135 **Disability Policy in China**
Child and family experiences
Xiaoyuan Shang and Karen R. Fisher

Forthcoming

The Politics of Controlling Organized Crime in Greater China
Sonny Shiu-Hing Lo

Inside Xinjiang
Space, Place and Power in China's Muslim Far Northwest
Edited by Anna Hayes and Michael Clarke

China's Strategic Priorities
Edited by Jonathan H. Ping and Brett McCormick

China's Unruly Journalists
How Committed Professionals are Changing the People's Republic
Jonathan Hassid

Disability Policy in China

Child and family experiences

Xiaoyuan Shang and Karen R. Fisher

Routledge
Taylor & Francis Group

LONDON AND NEW YORK

First published 2016
by Routledge
2 Park Square, Milton Park, Abingdon, Oxon OX14 4RN

and by Routledge
711 Third Avenue, New York, NY 10017

Routledge is an imprint of the Taylor & Francis Group, an informa business

British Library Cataloguing in Publication Data
A catalogue record for this book is available from the British Library

Library of Congress Cataloging in Publication Data
Shang, Xiaoyuan.
Disability policy in China : child and family experiences / Xiaoyuan Shang and Karen R. Fisher.
pages cm. -- (Routledge contemporary China series ; 137)
Includes bibliographical references and index.
1. Children with disabilities--Government policy--China. 2. Children with disabilities--Services for--China. 3. People with disabilities--Government policy--China. 4. Family policy--China. 5. Child welfare--China. 6. Public welfare--China. I. Fisher, Karen R. II. Title.
HV890.C5S447 2016
362.4'045610951--dc23
2015023553

ISBN: 978-1-138-93247-0 (hbk)
ISBN: 978-1-315-67884-9 (ebk)

Typeset in Times New Roman
by Saxon Graphics Ltd, Derby

Contents

List of illustrations   xi
Acknowledgements   xiii

1 Introduction to child disability in China   1

Children with disabilities 1
Policy context 2
Research methods 4
Structure of the book 8
References 8

2 Rights of children with disabilities in China   11

Families of children with disabilities in China 11
Children's rights 12
Care and protection 14
Economic security 16
Health and disability support 18
Education right 19
Social inclusion 20
Summary of the rights of children with disabilities 22
References 22

3 Profile of children with disabilities and families in China   25

Geographical distribution of children with disabilities 25
Demographic characteristics of children with disabilities 28
Household status of children with disabilities 30
Summary of the profile of children with disabilities in China 32
References 32

4   Welfare provision of children with disabilities   33

Chinese welfare system 34
Role of the family in child disability support 37
*Laws, regulations and policies of welfare provision to children
    with disabilities 38*
Government child disability support structure 39
Government child disability support services 43
Non-government sector 44
Social security provision to children with disabilities 45
Care and protection for orphaned children with disabilities 48
Conclusions about child disability welfare policy 49
References 50

5   Right to life and protection   53

Children born with disabilities 53
Cases to analyse the right to life 55
Deciding to abandon the life of a child with disabilities 58
Decision processes about the children's lives 59
Reasons parents decide to abandon their children's lives 65
Conclusion about right to life 69
References 70

6   Right to care and protection: support for mothers   73

Parenting responsibilities for children with disabilities 73
Family case studies 74
Children with disabilities and their families 76
Mothers' responsibilities to children with disabilities 77
Shared responsibility in the community 81
Conclusion about support for mothers 85
References 86

7   Right to care and protection: alternative family care   88

*Greentown State Child Welfare Institution foster care
    project 88*
Research methods 89
Management of the foster care programme 91
Family-based care 93
Health and therapy 95
Social inclusion and education 96
Conclusion about alternative care protection 98
References 99

8 Right to economic security 100

Relationship between economic security and disability 100
Incidence of poverty 102
*Absolute and relative poverty in households of children with
 disabilities 104*
Housing security 106
Access to social security 107
Impact of the costs of disability 110
Employment status of young people with disabilities 111
Conclusion about the right to economic security 113
References 114

**9 Right to children's development: health and therapy
 services** 115

Medical, health and therapy service system 115
Family experiences of access to services 117
Services used or needed by children with disabilities 119
Information obstacles 120
Availability of services 124
Disability support and poverty 125
Conclusion about access to health and therapy services 126
References 128

10 Right to children's development: education policy 130

Education policy for children with disabilities 131
Mainstream state schools 135
Special education schools 137
Non-government special schools 142
Conclusion on education policy and development 144
References 144

11 Right to children's development: education experiences 147

School conditions 148
Social attitudes 154
Socio-economic factors 155
Positive impact of quality education 157
Conclusion on education and development 158
References 159

12 Right to social participation: social institutions of support   160

Social participation and an ecological model 160
Life history case studies 161
Communication 165
Social relations 167
Interest representation 173
Conclusion about social institutions 175
References 178

13 Interrelated rights and social exclusion   180

Social exclusion and discrimination 180
Right to care and protection 181
Right to economic security 183
Rights to developmental support 184
Social participation rights 186
Impact on children's development 187
Impact on families 188
Impact on the community 189
Conclusion about interrelated rights and social exclusion 189
References 190

14 Child and family disability policy in China   191

Social policy reform 191
Right to care and protection 192
Right to economic security 193
Right to child development 193
Right to social participation 194
References 194

Appendix: Articles relevant to child disability in the UN Conventions   195
Glossary   201
References   203
Index   214

Illustrations

Figures

1.1 Research sites for fieldwork about children with disabilities in China   6
3.1 Proportion of children with disabilities aged under 18 years by
location in China   27
8.1 Incidence of absolute poverty in households with children by
number of members with disabilities, per cent   105

Tables

1.1 Sample case studies of children with disabilities   5
3.1 Rural, urban distribution of children with disabilities aged
under 18 years by sex   25
3.2 Regional distribution of children with disabilities aged under 18 years
by location in China   26
3.3 Age of children with disabilities by sex and location, per cent of
all children   28
3.4 Disability type by children's age compared to all people with
disabilities   29
3.5 Household size by age of children, disability and location,
per cent within age group   30
3.6 Households with children by number of people with disabilities,
per cent   31
3.7 Households with children and people with disabilities by child
disability and number of members with disabilities, per cent   31
4.1 Provincial and regional financial revenue and expenditure, 2011   35
4.2 Provincial population structure of China   36
4.3 National child and total dependency ratio   37
4.4 Administrative structure in China   40
4.5 Functions of government organized child welfare organizations
relevant to disability   41
5.1 Case studies for right to life analysis   55
5.2 Internet survey – what is your opinion of the case of Mother Han?   63

5.3	Citizens' opinions about how to solve child abandonment	64
6.1	Sample case studies of mothers of children with disabilities	75
7.1	Children with disabilities in the guardianship of the Greentown State Child Welfare Institution	89
7.2	Motivations for fostering a child	94
7.3	Children's measures of development from Institution staff observations	95
7.4	Type of support foster families said they needed	96
8.1	Living standard and income of households of children with disabilities, per cent	102
8.2	Living standards in families of children with disabilities	103
8.3	Incidence of poverty for households with children by number of people with disabilities, per cent	105
8.4	Absolute and relative poverty in rural and urban households of children with disabilities, per cent	106
8.5	Housing type of rural and urban children with disabilities, per cent	107
8.6	Proportion of children with disabilities who have a disability certificate by age, sex and location	108
8.7	Economic activity of young people not in paid work by disability, sex and location, per cent	112
8.8	Young people in paid work by disability, sex and location, per cent	113
9.1	Case study children for access to health and therapy services	118
9.2	Children's use of services by disability and location	119
9.3	Service types by need and received, per cent	120
10.1	Education levels of school-age children by disability, sex and location, per cent	132
10.2	Level of school enrolment of children with disabilities in Gao'an City	138
12.1	Case study children for social participation	162

Acknowledgements

Thanks to the research participants who shared their stories.

The research was funded by the Australian Research Council and Right To Play China and conducted by researchers from UNSW Australia and Beijing Normal University. Ethics approval was from UNSW. Thanks to Wei Wei, without whose support and participation this research would not have been possible; and to Dr Jiawen Xie, who organized and managed the fieldwork collection; and to the team of field researchers from Beijing Normal University. Thanks too, for translations by Beijing China-En Translation and research assistance from Ruan Zhiling, Xi Liangping, Zhang Guozhen, Song Weiguo, He Wanting, Lu Weijing, Wu Ping, Xia Tian, An Qiongying, Zhang Hua, Xu Hao, Zeng Lin, Xi Liangping, Yang Zhenzhen, Lin Yutao, Yin Shanshan, Zhang Min, Zhang Min, Pi Sanrong, Zhang Peng, Zhan Chengcheng, Jia Naer, Zhaoxin, Gao Xiaodan, Chen Si, Liu An and Ryan Gleeson.

Chapter 2 and the Appendix include extracts from the United Nations Convention on the Rights of Persons With Disabilities © (2006) United Nations and the United Nations Convention on the Rights of the Child © (1989) United Nations. Reprinted with the permission of the United Nations.

Chapter 3 and 8 data analyses were by Ruan Zhiling.

Chapter 5 is adapted from an earlier version of the chapter in Fisher, K.R. and Shang X. (2014) Protecting the right to life of children with disabilities in China. *Journal of Social Service Research* 10.1080/01488376.2014.922521. Additional cases were added to the analysis in this chapter.

Chapter 6 is adapted from a related publication, Shang, X. and Fisher, K.R. (2014) Social support for mothers of children with disabilities in China. *Journal of Social Service Research* 10.1080/01488376.2014.896849.

Chapter 7 is adapted from Shang, X. (2012) Looking for best practice in caring for disabled children: a case of socialized foster care in China. *Asia Pacific Journal of Social Work and Development* 22(1–2): 127–138.

Chapter 9 is adapted from Fisher KR and Shang X. (2013) Access to health and therapy services for families of children with disabilities in China. *Disability & Rehabilitation* 35(25): 2157–2163.

Chapter 10 and 11 fieldwork was conducted by Xi Liangping, Zhang Guozhen, Pi Sanrong and Song Weiguo in 2010.

Chapter 12 is adapted from Fisher, K.R., Shang, X. and Xie, J. (2011) Support for social participation of children and young people with disability in China, in Carrillo, B. and Duckett, J. (eds) *China's Changing Welfare Mix: Local Perspectives*, Routledge, London and New York.

Chapter 13 is adapted from Shang, X., Fisher, K.R. and Xie, J. (2011) Discrimination against children with disability in China: a case study in Jiangxi Province. *International Journal of Social Welfare* 20(3): 298–308.

1 Introduction to child disability in China

Without access to a public social welfare system some families of children with disabilities in China face invidious decisions. The director of a large State Child Welfare Institution told us of a four-year-old girl who was found at the railway station on a winter evening in Tianjin, a large wealthy city in northern China. The health check at the institution found that she had already had two major operations and needed more surgery to survive. When the director, doctor and nurses were discussing how to organize another operation for her, the girl interrupted, 'How much would it cost?' She clearly understood the financial costs that had kept her alive to that point. The director said to us,

> I could imagine how many times the little girl had heard her parents discussing the costs of her operations, and how desperate they were when they were faced with the dilemma of abandoning their beloved child or seeing her die without treatment because they had run out of money and could not afford more operations. I never blame parents who abandon their children with disabilities, after I heard what the little girl said.

Understanding how policy has changed in the parts of China that have addressed these stark situations is vital for the rights of other children and their families who still encounter them. In some places, children with disabilities can now expect to participate in family and community life, with the same aspirations as other children. Examining the places where such changes have occurred will inform the remaining policy gaps for the rights of others.

Children with disabilities

This book is the first to bring together research about family experiences of child disability policy in China. It applies a human rights framework for children with disabilities in four domains – care and protection, economic security, development and participation – to investigate families' experiences of the effectiveness of support to fulfil their children's rights. The book uses the terms child or children with disabilities to be consistent with the person-first language adopted in the United Nations Convention on the Rights of Persons with Disabilities (CRPD 2006).

As a result of its immense population, the number of children with disabilities in China is as large as the entire populations of some countries. China has five million children with disabilities (Chen and Chen 2008). This is more than 6 per cent of all people with disabilities in China and 1.7 per cent of children in China (Chen and Chen 2008; Lu 2005). Most children with disabilities are younger than fifteen (3,870,000; CDPF 2007). About 10 per cent of Chinese families have a child born with disabilities (30 million families; Yang 2010). While these are the official estimates, the exact numbers of children with disabilities are not available because of the size of the Chinese population and diverse circumstances, and questions about how disability is defined (WHO 2011; Kohrman 2005).

Chinese children with disabilities, as in other countries (Goodley and Runswick-Cole 2011), are over-represented in disadvantage measures, including poverty, education and living conditions (Shang and Wang 2012; CDPF 2008). Eighty per cent of families of children with disabilities live in rural areas in impoverished conditions, with few or no services (PED JICA 2002). These disadvantages affect not only the immediate quality of life of these children, but also their life trajectories and opportunities in adulthood. They are disadvantaged in access to education (McCabe 2007; Ellsworth and Zhang 2007; Deng and Holdsworth 2007), specialist disability support (Hampton 2001; McCabe 2008b), social networks and basic physical needs (Hernandez 2008); poverty (PED JICA 2002); and inadequate health and disability services (Chan, Ngok and Phillips 2008; Deng, Farnsworth and Poon-McBrayer 2001) and access to other welfare support (Shang, Wu and Wu 2005).

The current child disability support system in China was developed before China's transition to a market economy, which began in 1978. It remains based on the premise that the primary source of protection for children with disabilities is the family (Fisher and Li 2008; Chan, Ngok and Phillips 2008). This premise is also supported by Chinese cultural norms that view the family as a microcosm of society (Holroyd 2003). Family experience of caring for children with disabilities is an accepted way of examining child disability because it seeks to understand children's experiences in the context of their families (Ryan and Runswick-Cole 2008; Goodley and Runswick-Cole 2011). It follows the ecological approach to childhood and recognizes that child disability affects the entire family. This book extends that international approach to child disability studies to the experiences of families supporting their children in the Chinese context.

Policy context

In recent years, international and domestic attention has focused on the protection of disadvantaged children in China. National and international nongovernment organizations, such as Right To Play China, Plan International, UNICEF and Save the Children, have contributed to a Chinese government focus on child wellbeing and child rights. In 2005 and 2006, the United Nations Committee on the Rights of the Child formally raised concerns about child rights in China, the vulnerability of children with disabilities and the limited information available about these questions (UNCRC 2006a, 2006b).

In contemporary China, prioritizing children with disabilities and their rights is marginalized by other public policy agendas perceived to be more immediate (Hernandez 2008). Yet for families of children with disabilities in China and internationally, the protection of their children's rights has immediate importance and is measurable through their access to support for child development relative to the support available to other children (Stein 2010). Policy goals to achieve that access include changing attitudes, supporting children and families, community based therapy, assistive technology, universal design, access to health and education, and protection from abuse and neglect (UNICEF 2013).

In this context, understanding families' experiences of child disability policy is needed to inform policy change and to support the rights of children, families and people with disabilities. Previous research on child disability in China has focused on institutionalized children (Shang 2001a), service provision (Pearson, Wong and Pierini 2002) or child protection (Johnson, Huang and Wang 1998; Shang 2002; Shang and Wu 2003; Shang, Wu and Li 2005). It has not examined families' experiences of whether social policies in practice actually address the rights of children with disabilities as citizens of China.

The research framework in the book is based on the United Nations human rights model of child rights (Funder 1996; Quinn and Degener 2002; CRPD 2006; UNICEF 2006, 2013; UNCRC 2005), explained in Chapter 2. This model holds that children with disabilities 'should enjoy a full and decent life, in conditions which ensure dignity, promote self-reliance and facilitate the child's active participation in the community' (UNCRC 2006b). In a rights framework, meeting the support needs of children with disabilities is required in order to fulfil their rights as children (CRPD 2006). The UN Convention on the Rights of the Child (CRC 1989) and the more recent UN Convention on the Rights of Persons with Disabilities (CRPD 2006) do not provide benchmarks for interpretation or measurement of these rights. However, the dire situation of disadvantaged children in China (Shang, Wu and Li 2005) indicates that a relevant standard is whether families experience support similar to that available to other children in their community and at least basic social support to fulfil their children's rights. This standard provides a measure by which to address questions such as whether more children with disabilities are abandoned at birth; which families of children with disabilities do not live in relative poverty; and which children with disabilities receive any education. This book applies these standards.

Nationally, China adopts a rights framework in children's and disability law. China is a signatory to the CRC and CRPD. Its domestic legislation also reflects a commitment to equal participation and access to support (Law on the Protection of Persons with Disabilities 2008; Stein 2010). The Chinese government has not contested the application of rights-based policy within the Chinese cultural context (Bickenbach 2009; Fisher, Shang and Blaxland 2011), although, in practice, international disability support models are adapted to the local context (Chung, Packer and Yau 2011). Like other countries, research on child disability in China indicates gaps between government commitment and family experience of policies and consequent support required to fulfil their children's rights.

In light of these international and Chinese concerns about child disability policy (Ali *et al.* 2001; Kohrman 2005; Miles 2000), it is timely to publish research on the experience of families of children with disabilities about the support they receive to fulfil their children's human rights. The findings in this book support the efforts of policy makers, agencies and researchers to assist the Chinese government to establish effective child disability policy in order to realise the rights of children with disabilities.

Research methods

The research for the book applied mixed methods. The analysis draws on the children's data in the 2006 Second China National Sample Survey of Disability (SCNSSD). The China Disabled Persons' Federation (CDPF) conducted the survey in April 2006, as a repeat of the 1986 survey (CDPF 2007, 2008; Chen and Chen 2008). The survey used stratified, multiple phase and cluster probability sampling in all 31 Chinese provinces, autonomous regions and municipalities directly subject to the central government. The sampling units were a national random selection of villages, households and people with disabilities. It included three surveys – a random sample of villages (community survey) and in each village, all households (household survey) and all people identified as having disabilities (people with disabilities survey). The sample was 771,797 households, with 2.6 million people from 5,964 communities in 2,980 townships (and streets and districts) in 734 counties. The total number of sampling areas was 5,964, averaging 420 persons in each area. In this survey, 2,526,145 people in 771,797 households were included, with a sampling ratio of 1.93 respondents per thousand. Variables included all services available; household living arrangements and housing; demographic and socio-economic data on household members and people with disabilities; and disability type, cause, needs, support used, and support requirements.

Nearly one in five households surveyed (18.4 per cent; 142,112) included at least one person with disabilities. People with disabilities were 6.4 per cent (161,479) of all respondents. Survey doctors checked the disability type and level according to definitions from the CDPF (CDPF 2007, 2008). Data available for academic analysis were a 10 per cent subsample, with a sample size of 252,969 people in 77,240 households, including 61,555 children aged under eighteen years (24.3 per cent of total respondents) and 1,002 children with disabilities (1.63 per cent of total children).

The benefit of using the survey data in the research was the large national sample, enabling analysis across different locations. Limitations of the survey for the purpose of this book were the constrained definition of disability, which follows an exclusive categorization (physical; emotional, including behaviour and psychosocial; vision; multiple; speech; intellectual, including learning and developmental; and hearing), rather than a social model of disability (Kohrman 2005); and the lack of qualitative data about reasons and experiences to explain the data.

We critically interpreted the SCNSSD data and addressed the gaps in the SCNSSD about family experiences by conducting national interviews with 52 families (Table 1.1) and relevant officials throughout China (Figure 1.1) and by analysing secondary policy data referred to throughout the book.

The interviews were organized using a case study approach. Case studies offer an opportunity to intensely observe, record and analyse data relating to the social relationships in a relevant research site (Yin 2003; Miles and Huberman 1994; Stake 2000). From this experience, the data can be analysed for patterns of action to address the research question. More generally, the analysis can also inform exploration of the case or theory.

Fieldwork interviews were conducted by Dr Shang and students from Beijing Normal University from 2009 to 2011. The fieldwork researchers were chosen to conduct the research because they were qualified in social science research and the recruitment could build from their contacts within their local communities in fifteen provinces, as necessary for sensitive in-depth interviewing. These methods were the most suitable for understanding the social relations within the family and community. The researchers received two sessions of training on interview methods and techniques specific to the project, and carried out the research in their hometowns during their winter vacation in 2010.

The sampling frame for the interviews was families of children with disabilities living in the local community. The two sampling methods were random selection, supplemented with convenient selection. First, the interviewers visited the local Disabled Persons Federation (DPF, responsible for disability policy adminis-tration), or special education schools in their hometown. They asked these officials to randomly select the families of children from their list of registered children and students with disabilities. They called the families first to ask for voluntary agreement to participate. If this recruitment method was not feasible in the location, the researchers also sought voluntary, confidential participation from

Table 1.1 Sample case studies of children with disabilities

Child*	Sex	Number of children (n=52)
Sex	Boys	36
	Girls	16
Age	Under school age (0–7 years)	10
	Compulsory educational age (8–14 years)	19
	Above compulsory educational age (15–18 years)	18
	Young people (19–23 years)	5
Registered as having a disability	Yes*	38
	No	14

Source: Fieldwork 2010

Notes: * higher than national average (Table 8.6)

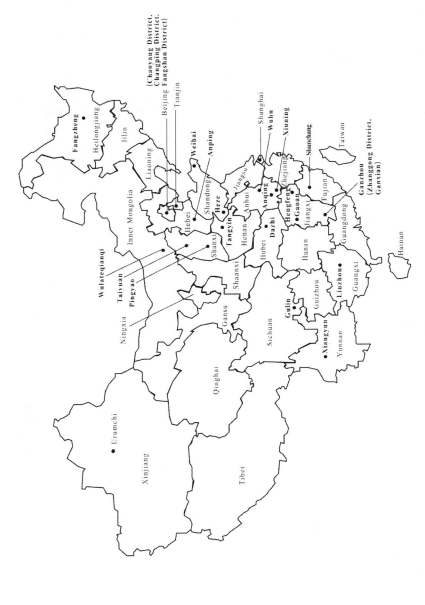

Figure 1.1 Research sites for fieldwork about children with disabilities in China

Note: Bold indicates city or district research site

families in the communities or villages through their local contacts. This combination mitigated sampling biases from each sampling method. The local rate of DPF registration was likely to include people more actively seeking government support. The convenient selection relied on prior relationships.

The fieldworkers received a research handbook for the semi-structured interviews that covered the topics in the research questions. Questions included the economic situation of the household, child care, access to health, therapy and educational services and social exclusion. The interviews were conducted mainly in the family home and were recorded if the interviewee consented. The voluntary consent and withdraw forms informed the family of the purpose of the research and the confidentiality of the interview materials, including the use of aliases. The fieldworkers also wrote investigation diaries and transcribed their fieldwork notes. The interview handbook included an observation form for the interviewer to complete about their observations and impression at the interview, including the conditions in the household and the emotional atmosphere. Children were not interviewed for ethical reasons, although the researchers observed their interactions with the family members during the research activities and some young people with disabilities also directly participated in the interviews. Most interviewers wrote vivid observation notes.

Officials of the local DPF, directors of residents' or villagers' committees, neighbours and teachers (48) were also interviewed to gain local context data for the case studies. The local officials were interviewed in their offices about the statistical profile of children with disabilities in their areas, support policies and how the organizations worked with families. The teachers were asked about school performance of children with disabilities, special support arrangements and child protection questions about abuse and violence towards children with disabilities at school.

Supplementary interviews were conducted with people who provide services to families of children with disabilities or to children with disabilities in other parts of China. The interviewees included staff of local civil affairs departments and directors of State Children's Welfare Institutions (SWCI). These interviewees were from Beijing, Yunnan, Guangdong, Ningxia, and Henan. They were attending the National Forum of Directors of State Children's Welfare Institutions in Luoyang and a training course in Tianjin in 2008. We asked the interviewees about the common problems facing their clients in order to compare the data with that of the families in the case study sites.

Guided by research questions, the findings were coded according to the research questions, adding new topics as they appeared in the investigation. When new topics appeared, further investigations were conducted to develop relevant theories. Some cases were investigated up to five times within two years to validate the findings and emerging theories. The material was analysed against the research questions to understand the differences in service use identified in the quantitative analysis, using this modified form of grounded theory.

Structure of the book

Chapter 2 introduces the human rights theoretical framework, particularly in reference to the relevant UN Conventions and their application in China. The research addressed the following questions, which guide the structure of the book.

- What is the current profile of children with disabilities and their families in China? (Chapter 3)
- What is the formal welfare policy system for children with disabilities? (Chapter 4)
- What are the experiences of families of children with disabilities in realizing their children's rights to life (Chapter 5), protection and care within a family (Chapter 6 – mothers and Chapter 7 – alternative family care)?
- What are families of children with disabilities' experiences of economic security? (Chapter 8)
- Do families of children with disabilities experience effective support to realize their children's development rights to access health services and disability support (Chapter 9) and education (Chapter 10 – policy; Chapter 11 – experiences)?
- How do the experiences of these rights by families affect their children's rights to social participation (Chapter 12)?
- How do these rights interrelate (Chapter 13) and what are the implications for policy (Chapter 14)?

The structure is designed to explore variation of experience, including location (urban/rural), age, sex, socioeconomic status, family structure and support needs, adding nuance to these broad questions.

References

Ali, Z., Fazil, Q., Bywaters, P., Wallace, L. and Singh, G. (2001) Disability, ethnicity and childhood: a critical review of research. *Disability & Society* 16(7): 949–968.

Bickenbach, J. (2009) Disability, culture and the UN Convention. *Disability & Rehabilitation* 31(14): 1111–1124.

CDPF, China Disabled Persons' Federation (2007) *Handbook of Main Data from the Second National Sampling Survey on Disability (2006-2007)*, Office of the Second China National Sample Survey on Disability, Beijing: Huaxia Press.

CDPF, China Disabled Persons' Federation (2008) *Data Analysis of the Second China National Sample Survey on Disability*, Office of the Second China National Sample Survey on Disability and the Institute of Population Studies (IPS) Peking University, Beijing: Huaxia Press.

Chan, C.K., Ngok, K.L. and Phillips, D. (2008) *Social Policy in China: Development and Wellbeing*, Bristol: The Policy Press, University of Bristol.

Chen, X. and Chen, Y. (2008) *The Status Analysis and Strategies of Children with Disabilities in China*, Beijing: Huaxia Press.

Chung, E.Y.-H., Packer, T. and Yau, M. (2011) When East meets West: community-based rehabilitation in Chinese communities. *Disability & Rehabilitation* 33(8): 697–705.

CRC, United Nations Convention on the Rights of the Child (1989) www.ohchr.org/en/professionalinterest/pages/crc.aspx [2 May 2015].

CRPD, United Nations Convention on the Rights of Persons with Disabilities (2006) www.un.org/disabilities/default.asp?id=150 [1 February 2012].

Deng, M., Farnsworth, E. and Poon-McBrayer, K.F. (2001) The development of special education in China. *Remedial & Special Education* 22(5): 288–298.

Deng, M. and Holdsworth, J.C. (2007) From unconscious to conscious inclusion: meeting special education needs in West China. *Disability & Society* 22(5): 507–522.

Ellsworth, N.J. and Zhang, C. (2007) Progress and challenges in China's special education development. *Remedial and Special Education* 28(1): 58–64.

Fisher, K.R. and Li, J. (2008) Chinese disability independent living policy. *Disability & Society* 23(2): 171–185.

Fisher, K.R., Shang, X. and Blaxland, M. (2011) Review Article: Human rights based social policies – challenges for China, *Social Policy & Society* 10(1): 71–78.

Funder, K. (ed.) (1996) *Citizen Child: Australian Law and Children's Rights*, Melbourne: Australian Institute of Family Studies.

Goodley, D. and Runswick-Cole, K. (2011) Problematising policy: conceptions of 'child', 'disabled' and 'parents' in social policy in England. *International Journal of Inclusive Education* 15(1): 71–85.

Hampton, N.Z. (2001) An evolving rehabilitation service delivery system in the People's Republic of China. *Journal of Rehabilitation* 67(3): 20–25.

Hernandez, V.T. (2008) Making good on the promise of international law: the Convention on the Rights of Persons with Disability and Inclusive Education in China and India. *Pacific Rim Law and Policy Journal* 17(2): 497–527.

Holroyd, E. (2003) Chinese cultural influences on parental caregiving obligations toward children with disabilities. *Qualitative Health Research* 13(4): 4–19.

Johnson, K., Huang, B. and Wang, L. (1998) Infant abandonment and adoption in China. *Population and Development Review* 24(3): 469–510.

Kohrman, M. (2005) *Bodies of Difference: Experiences of Disability and Institutional Advocacy in the Making of Modern China*, Berkeley: University of California Press.

Law on the Protection of Persons with Disabilities (2008) China Disabled Persons Federation www.cdpf.org.cn/english/laws1documents/200804/t20080410_267460.html [2 May 2015].

Lu, S. (2005) *The System of China's Policies on Children and Protecting Minors*, www.china-ccaa.org/site per cent5Cinfocontent per cent5CETFY_20050907113342718.htm [28 July 2011].

McCabe, H. (2007) Parent advocacy in the face of adversity: autism and families in the Peoples Republic of China, *Focus on Autism and Other Developmental Disabilities* 22(1): 39–50.

McCabe, H. (2008b) Two decades of serving children with autism in the People's Republic of China: achievements and challenges of a state-run mental health center. *Disability & Society* 23(3): 271–282.

Miles, M. (2000) Disability on a different model: glimpses of an Asian heritage, *Disability & Society* 15(4): 603–618.

Miles, M. and Huberman, A. (1994) *Qualitative Data Analysis: An expanded sourcebook* 2nd edn, Beverley Hills: Sage Publications.

Pearson, V., Wong, Y.C. and Pierini, J. (2002) The structure and content of social inclusion: voices of young adults with learning difficulties in Guangzhou. *Disability & Society* 17(4): 365–382.

PED JICA, Planning and Evaluation Department, Japan International Cooperation Agency (2002) *Country Profile on Disabilities, People's Republic of China*, Tokyo: Japan International Cooperation Agency.

Quinn, G. and Degener, T. (2002) *Human Rights and Disability: The current use and future potential of United Nations Human Rights Instruments in the context of disability*, United Nations.

Ryan, S. and Runswick-Cole, K. (2008) Repositioning mothers: mothers, disabled children and disability studies. *Disability & Society* 23(3): 199–210.

Shang, X. (2001a) Moving towards a multi-level and multi-pillar system: institutional care in two Chinese cities. *Journal of Social Policy* 30(2): 259–281.

Shang, X. (2002) Looking for a better way to care for children: cooperation between the state and civil society. *Social Service Review* 76 (2): 203–228.

Shang, X. and Wang, X. (2012) *Discovery Report: Emerging Issues and Findings for Child Welfare and Protection in China (2011)*, Beijing: Social Sciences Academic Press.

Shang, X. and Wu, X. (2003) Protecting children under financial constraints: the case of Datong. *Journal of Social Policy* 32: 549–570.

Shang, X., Wu, X. and Li, H. (2005) Social policy, gender and child abandonment in China. *Youth Studies* 4: 1–5.

Shang, X., Wu, X. and Wu, Y. (2005) Welfare provision to vulnerable children: the missing role of the state. *The China Quarterly* 18(1): 122–136.

Stake, R. (2000) Case studies, in Denzin, N.K. and Lincoln, Y.S. (eds) *The Handbook of Qualitative Research*, 2nd edn, Thousand Oaks: Sage Publications.

Stein, M.A. (2010) China and disability rights. *Loyola of Los Angeles International and Comparative Law Review* 33(7): 7–26.

UNCRC, United Nations Committee on the Rights of the Child (2005) Fortieth session Consideration of Reports submitted by states parties under article 44 of the convention Concluding observations: China.

UNCRC, United Nations Committee on the Rights of the Child (2006a) *Excluded and invisible, the state of the world's children 2006*, UNICEF.

UNCRC, United Nations Committee on the Rights of the Child (2006b) *General comment no. 9 the rights of children with disabilities*, Forty-third session, Geneva, 11–29 September.

UNICEF, United Nations Children's Fund (2006) *An Investigation of Families with Children with Disabilities and Relevant Policies.* Unpublished internal document.

UNICEF, United Nations Children's Fund (2013) *The State of the World's Children 2013: Children with disabilities*, www.unicef.org/sowc2013 [2 May 2015].

WHO, World Health Organisation (2011) *World Report on Disability 2011.* WHO Press, Geneva whqlibdoc.who.int/publications/2011/9789240685215_eng.pdf [2 May 2015].

Yang, W. (2010) One child with disability was born in China in every 30 Seconds, can we prevent the disability at birth? *Renmin Daily*, 13 September 2010, http://health.people.com.cn/GB/12703109.html [9 September 2011].

Yin, R.K. (2003) *Case study research*, 3rd edn, Thousand Oaks: Sage Publications.

2 Rights of children with disabilities in China

> Recognizing that children with disabilities should have full enjoyment of all human rights and fundamental freedoms on an equal basis with other children, and recalling obligations to that end undertaken by States Parties to the Convention on the Rights of the Child.
>
> (CRPD Preamble)

This chapter introduces the background to the rights of children with disabilities in China. It sets the context about families of children with disabilities in China and current international concepts about rights of children with disabilities. Children with disabilities in China struggle to share the same citizenship rights as other children in their communities. Seeking socially inclusive policy for children with disabilities is on the political agenda in China and internationally (WHO 2011) and the rights of children with disabilities in China have attracted special attention from the UNCRC (2006b).

Families of children with disabilities in China

As with families throughout the world, disability and parenting in China continues to rely mainly on individual and family responsibility (Shang 2012; Ma 2002). Parenting responsibilities are primarily borne by women, who also bear the additional support needs of their children with disabilities (McCabe 2010). Chinese women in general have a high labour market participation rate (70 per cent) and their earnings are a major part of their family income (Rajivan 2010). Paid work opportunities for mothers of children with disabilities are, however, restricted by their time commitment to care responsibilities, which affects their family income (McCabe 2010).

In China, social services and income support for families of children with disabilities are limited. Except in wealthier cities, support for children with disabilities is mainly provided by their families (Fisher, Shang and Li 2011). Recent national and international focus on the protection of children with disabilities in China has examined the support for these children, such as their access to support within a family context, including education, therapy and health care (McCabe 2008b, 2010; McLoughlin, Zhou and Clark 2005).

For children with or without disabilities, families are their first and most important educators, socializers and providers (Jenks 2005; Banks 2003). Parents are the first carers for their children's physical, emotional and developmental needs and basic rights. The experiences of children with disabilities to achieve their basic rights cannot be explained without use of a framework that first determines the ability of families to support enjoyment of these rights.

The extent of involvement families have in their children's care and development depends on cultural, political, social and geopolitical contexts (Meekosha 2004). This is true also of families living in China, where cultural norms are reflected in the service system they access for their children's care and development and in their children's experience of disability (Chan, Ngok and Phillips 2008; Shang 2008). The family in China is viewed culturally and in the disability service system as an extension of the state in terms of its organization and its responsibility to provide care to its members (Chan, Ngok and Phillips 2008; Shang 2008). This emphasis on family solidarity is mirrored in Chinese service system policies, which state that the duty of care for children with disabilities lies with the family (Shang 2008). Formal disability support programmes for the families of children with disabilities have only recently emerged, and generally provide time-limited training to parents so that they can provide skilled support independent of the service system (Deng and Holdsworth 2007).

Many families face a combination of barriers to caring for their children with disabilities. These include an adequate service system, living in rural or remote areas, poverty, and cultural norms. These are generally not conditions specific to China. Additional factors that exacerbate Chinese families' responsibilities include transition from a state-dominated to a free market economy and associated political developments; the disparity of wealth and services between rural and regional areas; the organization of the family unit and the responsibility of its members to one another; and the social stigma attached to disability as a result of traditional cultural norms and practices (Chiu *et al.* 2013).

Children's rights

The state's responsibility to support the parenting of children with disabilities can be understood in terms of interdependence of three sets of rights – the rights of people with disabilities, the rights of children and the rights of women (Muir and Goldblatt 2011). These rights are recognized in UN Conventions: the Convention on the Rights of Persons with Disabilities (CRPD 2006); the Convention on the Rights of the Child (CRC 1989); and the Convention on the Elimination of All Forms of Discrimination against Women (CEDAW 1979). The most recent of these, the CRPD, recognizes rights in related Conventions and the social interdependence of people with disabilities within their social networks, including the family (Kayess and French 2008).

China is a signatory to these Conventions and the Chinese government is striving to address its policy shortcomings by reforming and implementing policy to meet its international obligations towards its citizens with disabilities (Fisher, Shang and

Blaxland 2011). The official position of the Chinese government on disability policy has been rights-based since the 1980s (Law on the Protection of Persons with Disabilities 1990, 2008), but in practice policy remains within a medical model of individual deficit in all but the wealthier eastern city locations (Kohrman 2005; Fisher and Li 2008). The Chinese government formulates five-year plans, currently the Outline of the Twelfth Five-Year Plan for the Disabled in China (2011–15), to implement its policy on the rights of people with disabilities (CDPF 2015).

The CRC defines children as below the age of eighteen years, and states that every child is both an independent individual, and a member of family and the society, entitled to all the rights of an individual person. In addition, children with disabilities are entitled to the same rights as their peers. They 'should enjoy a full and decent life, in conditions which ensure dignity, promote self-reliance and facilitate the child's active participation in the community' (CRC 1989). The more recent CRPD (2006) seeks to 'ensure the full enjoyment by children with disabilities of all human rights and fundamental freedoms on an equal basis with other children'. Article 3 of the CRPD below, sets out the general principles including those for children, and Article 7 defines rights specific to children with disabilities. Words about children and age in the Articles are highlighted in bold.

CRPD Article 3: General principles

The principles of the present Convention shall be:

a   Respect for inherent dignity, individual autonomy including the freedom to make one's own choices, and independence of persons;
b   Non-discrimination;
c   Full and effective participation and inclusion in society;
d   Respect for difference and acceptance of persons with disabilities as part of human diversity and humanity;
e   Equality of opportunity;
f   Accessibility;
g   Equality between men and women;
h   Respect for the evolving capacities of **children** with disabilities and respect for the right of **children** with disabilities to preserve their identities.

Article 7: Children with disabilities

1   States Parties shall take all necessary measures to ensure the full enjoyment by **children** with disabilities of all human rights and fundamental freedoms on an equal basis with other children.
2   In all actions concerning **children** with disabilities, the best interests of the child shall be a primary consideration.

3   States Parties shall ensure that **children** with disabilities have the right to express their views freely on all matters affecting them, their views being given due weight in accordance with their age and maturity, on an equal basis with other **children**, and to be provided with disability and age-appropriate assistance to realize that right.

The following sections explain the four sets of rights used in this book: care and protection (Chapters 5–7); economic security (Chapter 8); health, disability support and education (Chapter 9-11); and social inclusion (Chapter 12). In practice, these rights are interrelated (as analysed in the final case study (Chapter 13). Children and families do not experience their lives in these convenient categories. The four sets are a merely a framework for understanding the experience of rights of children and their families in China. Extracts from relevant Articles from the CRPD are included in each set. The Articles are summarized in the Appendix.

Care and protection

International rights of children with and without disabilities are grounded in the basic rights to care and protection of life, protection from exploitation, abuse and neglect of needs such as food, shelter and education. Inadequate care and protection is linked with negative life outcomes for children with disabilities, including poor health, social exclusion and marginalization, low personal wellbeing and abuse (Clarke 2006). The experience of families of children with disabilities providing for these basic rights depends on their income status, their access to welfare support and requirements of basic living, and the impacts these have on family life. Care and protection includes two parts that are explored in detail in this book: the right to life and freedom from violence; and family care.

Life and freedom from violence

The right to life and freedom from violence affects children before and after birth (Articles 10 and 16). Chapter 5 conceptualizes right to life in relation to children with disabilities. Depending on the particular context, these rights can be threatened by social, cultural, political and economic norms. This is particularly so in China, where historical and political norms have forced families to make decisions contrary to a child's right to life, sometimes based on disability.

CRPD Article 10: Right to life

States Parties reaffirm that every human being has the inherent right to life and shall take all necessary measures to ensure its effective enjoyment by persons with disabilities on an equal basis with others.

Article 16: Freedom from exploitation, violence and abuse

1   States Parties shall take all appropriate legislative, administrative, social, educational and other measures to protect persons with disabilities, both within and outside the home, from all forms of exploitation, violence and abuse, including their gender-based aspects.

2   States Parties shall also take all appropriate measures to prevent all forms of exploitation, violence and abuse by ensuring, *inter alia*, appropriate forms of gender- and **age-sensitive** assistance and support for persons with disabilities and their families and caregivers, including through the provision of information and education on how to avoid, recognize and report instances of exploitation, violence and abuse. States Parties shall ensure that protection services are **age-**, gender- and disability-sensitive.

5   States Parties shall put in place effective legislation and policies, including women- and **child-focused** legislation and policies, to ensure that instances of exploitation, violence and abuse against persons with disabilities are identified, investigated and, where appropriate, prosecuted.

Family care

The second part of care and protection is the right to live in a family (Articles 18 and 23). This includes the right to registration, care in a family, and support to live there. Family capacity to care for and protect their children depends on their personal, household and community capacity. This might include where they live, such as a city or rural area, access to social welfare support and poverty status. Chapters 6 and 7 discuss the threats to family care from the perspective of the responsibilities of mothers to care and protect their children without adequate state support; and the consequences for alternative care outside the family.

CRPD Article 18: Liberty of movement and nationality

2   **Children** with disabilities shall be registered immediately after birth and shall have the right from birth to a name, the right to acquire a nationality and, as far as possible, the right to know and be cared for by their parents.

Article 23: Respect for home and the family

1   States Parties shall take effective and appropriate measures to eliminate discrimination against persons with disabilities in all matters relating to marriage, family, parenthood and relationships, on an equal basis with others, so as to ensure that:

a   The right of all persons with disabilities who are of marriageable age to marry and to found a family on the basis of free and full consent of the intending spouses is recognized;

b   The rights of persons with disabilities to decide freely and responsibly on the number and spacing of their children and to have access to age-appropriate information, reproductive and family planning education are recognized, and the means necessary to enable them to exercise these rights are provided;

c   Persons with disabilities, including **children**, retain their fertility on an equal basis with others.

2   States Parties shall ensure the rights and responsibilities of persons with disabilities, with regard to guardianship, wardship, trusteeship, adoption of children or similar institutions, where these concepts exist in national legislation; in all cases the **best interests of the child** shall be paramount. States Parties shall render appropriate assistance to persons with disabilities in the performance of their child-rearing responsibilities.

3   States Parties shall ensure that **children** with disabilities have equal rights with respect to family life. With a view to realizing these rights, and to prevent concealment, abandonment, neglect and segregation of children with disabilities, States Parties shall undertake to provide early and comprehensive information, services and support to children with disabilities and their families.

4   States Parties shall ensure that a **child** shall not be separated from his or her parents against their will, except when competent authorities subject to judicial review determine, in accordance with applicable law and procedures, that such separation is necessary for the best interests of the **child**. In no case shall a **child** be separated from parents on the basis of a disability of either the **child** or one or both of the parents.

5   States Parties shall, where the immediate family is unable to care for a **child** with disabilities, undertake every effort to provide alternative care within the wider family, and failing that, within the community in a family setting.

Economic security

Care and protection relies on the family capacity for economic security, either through their own resources or supplemented by the state (Article 28). This right is particularly important for children with disabilities because of the additional costs of disability support (Chapter 8). If a family's resources are insufficient and state social protection is available, they might rely on it to ensure their child's right to care and protection (Clarke 2006). Without this state support, other rights, including the right to life, can be at risk.

CRPD Article 28: Adequate standard of living and social protection

1 States Parties recognize the right of persons with disabilities to an adequate standard of living for themselves and their families, including adequate food, clothing and housing, and to the continuous improvement of living conditions, and shall take appropriate steps to safeguard and promote the realization of this right without discrimination on the basis of disability.

2 States Parties recognize the right of persons with disabilities to social protection and to the enjoyment of that right without discrimination on the basis of disability, and shall take appropriate steps to safeguard and promote the realization of this right, including measures:

   a To ensure equal access by persons with disabilities to clean water services, and to ensure access to appropriate and affordable services, devices and other assistance for disability-related needs;

   b To ensure access by persons with disabilities, in particular women and **girls** with disabilities and older persons with disabilities, to social protection programmes and poverty reduction programmes;

   c To ensure access by persons with disabilities and their **families** living in situations of poverty to assistance from the State with disability-related expenses, including adequate training, counselling, financial assistance and respite care;

   d To ensure access by persons with disabilities to public housing programmes;

   e To ensure equal access by persons with disabilities to retirement benefits and programmes.

Social welfare provision in China has undergone reform since decentralization and privatization from 1978 onwards, discussed further in Chapter 4 (Shang, Wu and Wu 2005; Chan, Ngok and Phillips 2008; Shang and Wu 2004). The aims of these benefits are to ensure that families are free from absolute poverty and are able to protect the rights of its members to care and protection (Braithwaite and Mont 2008). Personal, community and state resources vary widely across China, which affects the level of care and protection families experience (Chan, Ngok and Phillips 2008).

The difficulties facing disadvantaged families to care for and protect their children are compounded by the costs of disability support, which increase the risk of poverty and decrease their capacity to overcome poverty (Clarke 2006; Braithwaite and Mont 2008). Families without access to the basic services and resources for daily living and community participation struggle to protect the rights of their children, as described by some of the mothers in Chapters 5 and 6.

Poverty is an indicator and cause of social exclusion for many children with disabilities and their families (Emerson 2004). Material family resources can play an important role in determining the level of social inclusion experienced by a child with disabilities (Clarke 2006). Through these resources, some families of children with disabilities are able to access specialist disability support and treatment, education, medical care, and the basic necessities of living required to help their children participate as full and active members of their community (SEU 2001; Clarke 2006).

International evidence identifies poverty as one of the barriers to accessing disability services (Braithwaite and Mont 2008). Children with disabilities living in poverty face greater exclusion and marginalization from mainstream and specialist services as a result of their disability and poverty. Poorer families can be reluctant to access services for their children because of time, cost, travel and effort, discussed more in Chapter 9. This impacts on the children's right to development and to becoming active and valued members of their community, leading to diminished outcomes in terms of health, personal wellbeing, education, care and protection.

Health and disability support

The next set of rights is health and disability support (Articles 25 and 26), including rights to general support expected by any citizen and specialist support related to their disability needs. Like care, protection and economic security, these rights enable other rights to a meaningful life in childhood and later in adulthood. When these rights are protected, children are able to experience social inclusion and participate in their community. Chapter 4 describes state welfare policies and Chapter 9 discusses the experiences of children and families trying to access adequate support.

CRPD Article 25: Health

States Parties recognize that persons with disabilities have the right to the enjoyment of the highest attainable standard of health without discrimination on the basis of disability. States Parties shall take all appropriate measures to ensure access for persons with disabilities to health services that are gender-sensitive, including health-related rehabilitation. In particular, States Parties shall:

a   Provide persons with disabilities with the same range, quality and standard of free or affordable health care and programmes as provided to other persons, including in the area of sexual and reproductive health and population-based public health programmes;

b   Provide those health services needed by persons with disabilities specifically because of their disabilities, including early identification and intervention as appropriate, and services designed to minimize and prevent further disabilities, including among **children** and older persons;

Article 26: Habilitation and rehabilitation

1 States Parties shall take effective and appropriate measures, including through peer support, to enable persons with disabilities to attain and maintain maximum independence, full physical, mental, social and vocational ability, and full inclusion and participation in all aspects of life. To that end, States Parties shall organize, strengthen and extend comprehensive habilitation and rehabilitation services and programmes, particularly in the areas of health, employment, education and social services, in such a way that these services and programmes:

   a Begin at the **earliest possible stage**, and are based on the multi-disciplinary assessment of individual needs and strengths;
   b Support participation and inclusion in the community and all aspects of society, are voluntary, and are available to persons with disabilities as close as possible to their own communities, including in rural areas.

Most care and support is from the families themselves, supplemented with professional support from health and disability providers (Banks 2003). Support is either time-limited or life-long to enable children to be active members of their communities. The international experience of families of children with disabilities receiving specialist support depends on the availability and access to services through the state social welfare system. Most families can expect their children to receive some state health and disability support. Actual availability of formal support varies, depending on variables such as the degree of universal or rationed support, urban and rural location (Downing and Peckham-Hardin 2007), the type and level of disability, and the availability of appropriate support.

China's current health and social welfare system is still increasing in response to the economic reforms since 1978 (Chen, Wehmeyer and Zhang 2005; Shang, Wu and Wu 2005). Most children with disabilities living with their families have access to little or no formal support from the service system, and the usual support option available to children without family members is institutional care (Shang and Fisher 2013).

Education right

The next set of rights is to education (Article 24). Equality of access to, and availability of, education is a key right for children with and without disabilities (Hernandez 2008). Inclusive education with adequate disability-specific support can enable children to experience a childhood with their peers and contribute to social and academic skills for social inclusion in anticipation of adult life.

CRPD Article 24: Education

2   In realizing this right, States Parties shall ensure that:

a   Persons with disabilities are not excluded from the general education system on the basis of disability, and that **children** with disabilities are not excluded from free and compulsory primary education, or from secondary education, on the basis of disability;

b   Persons with disabilities can access an inclusive, quality and free primary education and secondary education on an equal basis with others in the communities in which they live;

c   Reasonable accommodation of the individual's requirements is provided;

d   Persons with disabilities receive the support required, within the general education system, to facilitate their effective education;

e   Effective individualized support measures are provided in environments that maximize academic and social development, consistent with the goal of full inclusion.

The gap between formal policies for access to education and the resources to implement the intention of inclusive education (Chapter 10) means that many children remain excluded from the educational opportunities to which they are entitled (Chapter 11).

Social inclusion

The final set of rights is to social inclusion (Articles 8 and 30). Social inclusion in the context of this book means the right of children with disabilities to be recognized and valued members of their communities and society, and to have an active voice in making the decisions that affect their lives (Bell *et al.* 2009). This implies two conditions: that they have opportunities for social participation in their families and community with other children and adults (Chapter 12); and that people do not discriminate against them compared to other children (Chapter 13).

CRPD Article 8: Awareness-raising

1   States Parties undertake to adopt immediate, effective and appropriate measures:

- To raise awareness throughout society, including at the **family** level, regarding persons with disabilities, and to foster respect for the rights and dignity of persons with disabilities;
- To combat stereotypes, prejudices and harmful practices relating to persons with disabilities, including those based on sex and **age**, in all areas of life;
- To promote awareness of the capabilities and contributions of persons with disabilities.

Measures to this end include:

b   Fostering at all levels of the education system, including in all **children** from an early age, an attitude of respect for the rights of persons with disabilities;

Article 30: Participation in cultural life recreation, leisure and sport

5   With a view to enabling persons with disabilities to participate on an equal basis with others in recreational, leisure and sporting activities States Parties shall take appropriate measures:

d   To ensure that **children** with disabilities have equal access with other children to participation in play, recreation and leisure and sporting activities, including those activities in the school system.

Social inclusion is linked to whole of life outcomes, including access to necessary services, education (Clarke 2006), and transition to adulthood (Beresford 2004). Social inclusion can also be understood in terms of the inclusion of the child within the family as a whole in their community, which is experienced in different ways by each of its members (Beresford 2004; Clarke 2006). Clarke (2006: i) states:

Ensuring the protection of human rights and access to entitlements for disabled children involves an understanding of the complexity of the individual and family experiences of impairment and disability in social (including socio-economic) context.

Social attitudes play an important role in determining the level and extent of social inclusion experienced by children with disabilities. Bell *et al.* (2009) state the term 'social inclusion' is used to refer to the extent to which children with disabilities are accepted into their communities and society as valued and active members. Traditionally Chinese cultural norms led parents to believe that having a child with disabilities was a social impediment and a source of shame for the family (Holroyd 2003; Huang, Fried and Hsu 2009). Chapter 13 discusses the impact of social attitudes on social participation in a rural setting.

Economic and social change has the potential to diminish social exclusion of marginalized groups (SEU 2001). In China, changes such as the shift away from rural life present opportunities but also risks to social inclusion. Families of children with disabilities can experience additional risks in these changes due to the additional responsibilities within the family (Clarke 2006). These circumstances are extreme in China with the rapid economic changes, particularly urbanization since 1978 (Shang, Wu and Li 2005), which can undermine family and kinship support. Some families have benefited from the opportunities, particularly in relation to education (Holroyd 2003) and specialist disability support (McCabe 2008b) and exploring their experiences may assist policy development for others. Chapter 12 discusses facilitators and barriers to social participation experienced by some of these children.

Summary of the rights of children with disabilities

The rights of children with disabilities and their families is a useful framework to understand the experience of these children compared to their peers. This chapter presented four sets of rights – care and protection; economic security; child development through health, disability support and education; and social inclusion – which are applied throughout this book to understand the experience of children and their families in China. Addressing the rights of children with disabilities remains a struggle throughout the world. Understanding the Chinese experience within the same framework helps draw implications for change and build on the positive experiences in parts of China and in other countries.

References

Banks, M.E. (2003) Disability in the family: a life span perspective. *Cultural Diversity and Ethnic Minority Psychology*, 9(4): 367–384.

Bell, M., Franklin, A., Greco, V. and Mitchell, W. (2009) Working with children with learning disabilities and/or who communicate non-verbally: research experiences and their implications for social work education, increased participation and social inclusion. *Social Work Education* 28(3): 309–324.

Beresford, B. (2004) On the road to nowhere? Young disabled people and transition. *Child: Care, Health and Development* 30(6): 581–587.

Braithewaite, J. and Mont, D. (2008) Disability and poverty: a survey of World Bank poverty assessments and implications. *Social Protection Discussion Paper 0805*, Washington: World Bank.

CDPF, China Disabled Persons' Federation (2015) *Statistical Communique on the Development of the Work for Persons with Disabilities in 2014*, www.cdpf.org.cn/zcwj/zxwj/201503/t20150331_444108.shtml [3 May 2015].

CEDAW, United Nations Convention on the Elimination of all Forms of Discrimination against Women (1979) www.un.org/womenwatch/daw/cedaw/text/econvention.htm [3 May 2015].

Chan, C.K., Ngok, K.L. and Phillips, D. (2008) *Social Policy in China: Development and wellbeing*, Bristol: The Policy Press, University of Bristol.

Chen, L., Wehmeyer, M.L. and Zhang, D. (2005) Parent and teacher engagement in fostering the self-determination of students with disabilities: a comparison between the United States and the People's Republic of China, *Remedial and Special Education* 26(1): 55–64.

Chiu, M.Y.L., Yang, X., Wong, F.H.T., Li, J.H. and Li, J. (2013) Caregiving of children with intellectual disabilities in China – an examination of affiliate stigma and the cultural thesis. *Journal of Intellectual Disability Research* 57: 1117–1129.

Clarke, H. (2006) Preventing social exclusion of disabled children and their families: literature review. *Research Report RR782*, paper for the National Evaluation of the Children's Fund, Institute of Applied Social Studies University of Birmingham.

CRC, United Nations Convention on the Rights of the Child (1989) www.ohchr.org/en/professionalinterest/pages/crc.aspx [2 May 2015].

CRPD, United Nations Convention on the Rights of Persons with Disabilities (2006) www.un.org/disabilities/default.asp?id=150 [1 February 2012].

Deng, M. and Holdsworth, J.C. (2007) From unconscious to conscious inclusion: meeting special education needs in West China. *Disability & Society* 22(5): 507–522.

Downing, J. and Peckham-Hardin, K. (2007) Supporting inclusive education for students with severe disabilities in rural areas. *Rural Special Education Quarterly* 26(2): 10–15.

Emerson, E. (2004) Poverty and children with intellectual disabilities in the world's richer countries. *Journal of Intellectual and Developmental Disability* 29(4): 319–338.

Fisher, K.R. and Li, J. (2008) Chinese disability independent living policy. *Disability & Society* 23(2): 171–185.

Fisher, K.R, Shang, X. and Blaxland, M. (2011). Review Article: Human rights based social policies – challenges for China, *Social Policy & Society* 10(1): 71–78.

Fisher, K.R., Shang, X. and Li, Z. (2011) The absent role of the state: analysis of social support to older people with disability in rural China. *Social Policy and Administration* 45(6): 633–648.

Hernandez, V.T. (2008) Making good on the promise of international law: the Convention on the Rights of Persons with Disability and Inclusive Education in China and India. *Pacific Rim Law and Policy Journal* 17(2): 497–527.

Holroyd, E. (2003) Chinese cultural influences on parental caregiving obligations toward children with disabilities. *Qualitative Health Research* 13(4): 4–19.

Huang, Y.T., Fried, J.H. and Hsu, T.H. (2009) Taiwanese mothers' attitude change toward individuals with disabilities. *Journal of Social Work in Disability and Rehabilitation* 8: 82–94.

Jenks, E.B. (2005) Explaining disability: parents' stories of raising children with visual impairments in a sighted world. *Journal of Contemporary Ethnography* 34(2): 143–169.

Kayess, R. and French, P. (2008) Out of darkness into light? Introducing the Convention on the Rights of Persons with Disabilities. *Human Rights Law Review* 8(1): 1–34.

Kohrman, M. (2005) *Bodies of Difference: Experiences of Disability and Institutional Advocacy in the Making of Modern China*, Berkeley: University of California Press.

Law on the Protection of Persons with Disabilities (2008) China Disabled Persons Federation   www.cdpf.org.cn/english/laws1documents/200804/t20080410_267460. html [2 May 2015].

Ma, H.L. (ed.) (2002) *Social Welfare for China's Disabled Persons*, Beijing: China Social Press.

McCabe, H. (2008b) Two decades of serving children with autism in the People's Republic of China: achievements and challenges of a state-run mental health center. *Disability & Society* 23(3): 271–282.

McCabe, H. (2010) Employment experiences, perspectives, and wishes of mothers of children with autism in the People's Republic of China. *Journal of Applied Research in Intellectual Disabilities* 23(2): 122–131.

McLoughlin, C.S., Zhou, Z. and Clark, E. (2005) Reflections on the development and status of contemporary special education services in China. *Psychology in Schools* 42(3): 273–283.

Meekosha, H. (2004) Drifting down the gulf stream: navigating the cultures of disability studies. *Disability & Society* 19(7): 721–723.

Muir, K. and Goldblatt, B. (2011) Complementing or conflicting human rights conventions? Realising an inclusive approach to families with a young person with disabilities and challenging behaviour. *Disability & Society* 26(5): 629–642.

Rajivan, A. and UNDP Team (2010) *Power, Voice and Rights: A Turning Point for Gender Equality in Asia and the Pacific*. New Delhi: Macmillan Publishers India Ltd.

SEU, Social Exclusion Unit (2001) *Preventing social exclusion*, Report by the Social Exclusion Unit to the UK Cabinet Office, March, London.

Shang, X. (2008) *The System of Social Protection for Vulnerable Children in China*, Beijing: Social Sciences Academic Press.

Shang, X. (2012) Looking for best practice in caring for disabled children: a case of socialized foster care in China. *Asia Pacific Journal of Social Work and Development* 22(1–2): 127–138.

Shang, X. and Fisher, K.R. (2013) *Caring for Orphaned Children in China*, Lanham: Lexington Books.

Shang, X. and Wu, X. (2004) Changing approaches of social protection: social assistance reform in urban China. *Journal of Social Policy and Society* 33: 259–271.

Shang, X., Wu, X. and Li, H. (2005) Social policy, gender and child abandonment in China. *Youth Studies* 4: 1–5.

Shang, X., Wu, X. and Wu, Y. (2005) Welfare provision to vulnerable children: the missing role of the state. *The China Quarterly* 18(1): 122–136.

UNCRC, United Nations Committee on the Rights of the Child (2006b) *General comment no. 9, The rights of children with disabilities*, Forty-third session, Geneva, 11–29 September.

WHO, World Health Organisation (2011) *World Report on Disability 2011*. WHO Press, Geneva whqlibdoc.who.int/publications/2011/9789240685215_eng.pdf [2 May 2015].

3 Profile of children with disabilities and families in China

This chapter is a profile of children with disabilities and their families in China. It describes differences in the incidence of child disability, as context for the investigation of their rights in the rest of the book. The analysis profiles the distribution of children with disabilities and variation by age, sex, urban and rural location and family structure. The data used in this chapter are from the Second China National Sample Survey on Disability (SCNSSD 2006; CDPF 2007, 2008), described in Chapter 1.

Geographical distribution of children with disabilities

An advantage of the national dataset is that information is available about differences in the experience of disability between urban and rural areas and across provinces. A higher proportion of children in rural areas had disabilities (1.77 per cent) than in urban areas (1.24 per cent; Table 3.1). More boys than girls had disabilities in both rural and urban areas (rural ratio 1.19; urban ratio 1.40), which was also higher than the ratio of boys to girls in both areas. At the time of the survey, more people lived in rural areas in China than in urban areas (that changed by 2011; China News Agency 2012), including children.

Table 3.1 Rural, urban distribution of children with disabilities aged under 18 years by sex

		All	*Boys*	*Girls*	*Boy/girl ratio*
Rural	Children	44,741	24,055	20,686	1.16
	Per cent with disabilities	1.77	1.91	1.61	1.19
Urban	Children	16,814	8,972	7,842	1.14
	Per cent with disabilities	1.24	1.43	1.02	1.40
All	Children	61,555	33,027	28,528	1.16
	Per cent with disabilities	1.63	1.78	1.45	1.23
Rural/urban ratio children with disabilities		1.43	1.34	1.58	

Source: Second China National Sample Survey on Disability (SCNSSD 2006) 10 per cent sample

Table 3.2 and Figure 3.1 show the regional distribution of children with disabilities. In general, the proportion of children with disabilities was higher in the poorer and inland regions, such as Tibet, Xinjiang and Hebei. Just under half the provinces (14/31) had a higher proportion of children with disabilities than the national average.

Table 3.2 Regional distribution of children with disabilities aged under 18 years by location in China

Province[1]	All children	Children with disabilities	Children with disabilities as a per cent of children in province
Tibet	776	30	3.87
Xinjiang	1,506	47	3.12
Hebei	2,335	48	2.06
Hubei	2,480	49	1.98
Fujian	1,839	36	1.96
Gansu	1,771	33	1.86
Yunnan	2,437	45	1.85
Shaanxi	1,892	34	1.80
Guizhou	2,456	44	1.79
Sichuan	3,236	57	1.76
Hainan	1,264	22	1.74
Chongqing	1,977	34	1.72
Guangdong	3,743	64	1.71
Guangxi	2,345	39	1.66
Jiangxi	2,560	40	1.56
Ningxia	1,481	23	1.55
Anhui	2,860	43	1.50
Shandong	2,752	41	1.49
Hunan	2,468	36	1.46
Henan	3,609	52	1.44
Shanxi	1,983	28	1.41
Jiangsu	2,185	30	1.37
Jilin	1,460	19	1.30
Qinghai	806	10	1.24
Liaoning	1,531	19	1.24
Heilongjiang	1,357	16	1.18
Tianjin	1,226	14	1.14
Inner Mongolia	1,345	15	1.12
Zhejiang	1,938	19	0.98
Beijing	1,106	9	0.81
Shanghai	831	6	0.72
Total	61,555	1,002	1.63

Source: Second China National Sample Survey on Disability (SCNSSD 2006) 10 per cent sample
Note: 1. Province includes City Municipalities and Autonomous Regions

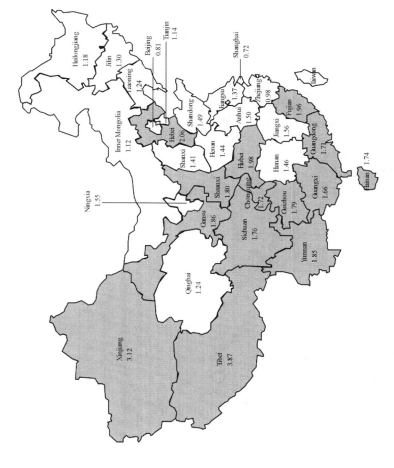

Figure 3.1 Proportion of children with disabilities aged under 18 years by location in China

Source: Second China National Sample Survey on Disability (SCNSSD 2006) 10 per cent sample

Note: Shaded provinces have a higher proportion of children with disabilities than the national average (1.63) and non-shaded have a rate lower than the national average (Table 3.2). Province includes City Municipalities and Autonomous Regions

Demographic characteristics of children with disabilities

The incidence of disability by children's age groups differed (Table 3.3), but the differences were not significant and were not as wide as the variation by location and sex (Table 3.1).

Young people aged fifteen to seventeen years were less than a quarter of children with disabilities (23.15 per cent). Irrespective of disability, almost no young people had married – only one rural woman with disabilities and 68 young people without disabilities, mainly women and mainly in rural areas (less than one per cent) had married. The differences are too small to draw conclusions about the impact of disability on marriage.

For the purpose of the survey, disability was categorized by type (SCNSSD 2006; for a critique see Kohrman 2005). The most common disability types were intellectual, multiple and physical (Table 3.4). The most common incidence of disability types for children differed from adults in the survey (physical, hearing, multiple and vision). The difference probably reflects life stage; recent changes in health care and support; and contemporary understandings about disability.

Disability type also differed by children's age group – the proportion of children with intellectual disability and speech disabilities was higher for younger children (Table 3.4). Again, this probably reflects life stage, support and diagnosis.

Table 3.3 Age of children with disabilities by sex and location, per cent of all children

Age	Number	Sex	Rural	Urban	Total
0–5 years	273	All	1.77	1.34	1.66
		Boys	1.86	1.51	1.77
		Girls	1.66	1.14	1.52
6–14 years	497	All	1.74	1.19	1.59
		Boys	1.92	1.30	1.75
		Girls	1.54	1.06	1.41
15–17 years	232	All	1.85	1.24	1.69
		Boys	1.95	1.64	1.87
		Girls	1.74	0.79	1.48
Total	1002	All	1.77	1.24	1.63
		Boys	1.91	1.43	1.78
		Girls	1.61	1.02	1.45

Source: Second China National Sample Survey on Disability (SCNSSD 2006) 10 per cent sample

Note: Significant p<0.01 sex and location, but not by age groups

Table 3.4 Disability type by children's age compared to all people with disabilities

	Intellectual	Multiple	Physical	Speech	Vision	Hearing	Mental	Number
Number children with disabilities	324	281	185	80	51	51	30	1002
Per cent by age								
0–5 years	44.69	28.94	8.42	9.89	4.40	1.47	2.20	273
6–14 years	29.38	28.17	19.72	8.45	4.83	7.04	2.41	497
15–17 years	24.14	26.72	27.59	4.74	6.47	5.17	5.17	232
All children with disabilities	32.34	28.04	18.46	7.98	5.09	5.09	2.99	1002
Number people with disabilities*	10,844	26,080	48,045	2,510	23,840	38,370	11,790	161,479
Per cent	6.72	16.15	29.75	1.55	14.76	23.76	7.3	

Source: Second China National Sample Survey on Disability (SCNSSD 2006) 10 per cent sample

Note: *Full SCNSSD sample. Significant: P<0.001

Household status of children with disabilities

Household sizes

The number of members in a household can positively and negatively affect the availability of care and support for children, in dimensions such as economic security, time and people who provide care or need care. Households varied in size by location in urban or rural areas and by age groups of children (Table 3.5). Households were smaller in urban areas and with younger children. Most children of all age groups, with or without disabilities, lived in three to five person families.

Table 3.5 Household size by age of children, disability and location, per cent within age group

		Number of household registered members									
	Age	*1*	*2*	*3*	*4*	*5*	*6*	*7*	*8*	*9*	*Total*
All children (n=45,061)											
Rural	0–5	0.04	1.93	19.94	29.69	23.14	15.28	6.24	3.35	0.40	100
	6–14	0.24	2.90	19.93	35.53	21.94	12.12	4.55	2.46	0.33	100
	15–17	0.36	3.31	21.21	39.04	19.97	9.90	3.97	2.02	0.21	100
	Total	0.21	2.73	20.22	34.74	21.82	12.48	4.88	2.60	0.32	100
Urban	0–5	–	1.61	41.36	24.33	19.10	8.39	3.09	1.94	0.18	100
	6–14	0.05	3.97	43.88	28.57	13.85	6.18	2.12	1.23	0.14	100
	15–17	0.32	6.62	44.30	29.99	11.24	4.63	1.83	1.02	0.05	100
	Total	0.10	3.95	43.32	27.79	14.63	6.41	2.31	1.37	0.13	100
Children without disabilities (n=44,332)											
Rural	0–5	0.04	1.93	19.93	29.70	23.06	15.29	6.28	3.37	0.40	100
	6–14	0.23	2.89	19.99	35.61	21.86	12.08	4.53	2.45	0.33	100
	15–17	0.37	3.30	21.35	39.05	19.95	9.86	3.93	1.99	0.21	100
	Total	0.21	2.72	20.28	34.78	21.76	12.45	4.87	2.60	0.33	100
Urban	0–5	–	1.63	41.52	24.31	19.01	8.34	3.04	1.96	0.19	100
	6–14	0.05	3.96	44.07	28.50	13.82	6.16	2.09	1.20	0.14	100
	15–17	0.33	6.62	44.61	29.93	11.00	4.63	1.85	0.98	0.05	100
	Total	0.10	3.95	43.53	27.74	14.54	6.38	2.28	1.35	0.13	100
Children with disabilities (n=729)											
Rural	0–5	–	1.40	20.47	29.30	27.44	14.88	3.72	2.33	0.47	100
	6–14	0.25	3.31	16.54	31.04	25.95	13.99	5.85	2.80	0.25	100
	15–17	–	4.30	13.44	38.71	21.51	12.37	5.91	3.76	–	100
	Total	0.13	3.02	16.88	32.37	25.31	13.85	5.29	2.90	0.25	100
Urban	0–5	–	–	29.31	25.86	25.86	12.07	6.90	–	–	100
	6–14	–	4.81	27.88	34.62	16.35	7.69	4.81	3.85	–	100
	15–17	–	6.52	19.57	34.78	30.43	4.35	–	4.35	–	100
	Total	–	3.85	26.44	32.21	22.12	8.17	4.33	2.88	–	100

Source: Second China National Sample Survey on Disability (SCNSSD 2006) 10 per cent sample

Note: Significant (p<0.001) urban, rural and age groups. Significant (p<0.01) disability for urban and children 6–17 years only.

In rural areas, four person families were the largest proportion (34.74 per cent) of the households with children; compared to three person urban families (43.32 per cent). Single parent households (two person families) and large households were rare.

Children with disabilities were also most likely to live in four person families in both rural (32.37 per cent) and urban areas (32.21 per cent). The household size varied by disability in the urban area only and for older children with or without disabilities – that is younger urban children with disabilities were more likely to live in three person households. Older urban children with disabilities were more likely to live in four person households, unlike their peers without disabilities.

People with disabilities within a household with children

The number of people with disabilities in the household can affect the availability of care and other care needed in the family. Most of the households with children in the survey did not have another member with disabilities (82.98 per cent households without; 17.02 per cent households with members with disabilities; Table 3.6). Rural families with children were more likely than urban families to include one or more members with disabilities.

In households with members with disabilities, whether the children had disabilities was also related to the number of people with disabilities in the household (Table 3.7). In most households with children and people with disabilities, only one member of the family had a disability (86.71 per cent). That was the same if the child had a disability, but the likelihood of at least one other member of the household also having disabilities was higher in their households.

Table 3.6 Households with children by number of people with disabilities, per cent

| | *Household members with disabilities* | | | | | |
	0	*1*	*2*	*3*	*4*	*Children in survey*
Rural	81.19	16.30	2.24	0.23	0.03	44,741
Urban	87.72	10.65	1.47	0.15	0.01	16,814
Total	82.98	14.76	2.03	0.20	0.03	61,555

Source: Second China National Sample Survey on Disability (SCNSSD 2006) 10 per cent sample
Note: Significant p<0.0001

Table 3.7 Households with children and people with disabilities by child disability and number of members with disabilities, per cent

| | *Household members with disabilities* | | | | |
	1	*2*	*3*	*4*	*Children in survey*
Child without disability	88.17	10.94	0.81	0.07	9,477
Child with disabilities	72.85	21.36	4.89	0.90	1,002
Total	86.71	11.94	1.20	0.15	10,479

Source: Second China National Sample Survey on Disability (SCNSSD 2006) 10 per cent sample
Note: Significant p<0.001

Summary of the profile of children with disabilities in China

The profile of children with disabilities and their families in China shows that they were unevenly distributed around China. They were more likely to live in poorer and inland areas. A higher proportion of boys and children in rural areas had disabilities.

The most common disability types were intellectual, multiple and physical, although a higher proportion of younger children had speech disabilities. Adults in the survey were more likely to report physical, hearing, multiple and vision disabilities. The differences probably reflect life stage; more recent access to diagnosis, health care and support; and contemporary understandings about disabilities. Age and sex affected disability incidence and impact as discussed in later chapters.

Most children with disabilities lived in small households (three to four people) although some older children and those in rural areas lived in larger families. This was the same for children without disabilities. Children with disabilities were more likely than their peers to live in a household with other people with disabilities. Almost no children lived alone or with only one other family member.

These results are a preliminary profile of the experiences of children and their families with disabilities. The rest of the book examines the profile further by addressing the questions that are raised about the extent and reasons for these negative experiences of their rights and the implications for policy. It does so by situating the profile in the larger Chinese social policy context and considering the detailed personal experiences of children with disabilities in the research locations in relation to each set of rights.

References

CDPF, China Disabled Persons' Federation (2007) *Handbook of Main Data from the Second National Sampling Survey on Disability (2006-2007).* Office of the Second China National Sample Survey on Disability, Beijing: Huaxia Press.

CDPF, China Disabled Persons' Federation (2008) *Data Analysis of the Second China National Sample Survey on Disability.* Office of the Second China National Sample Survey on Disability and the Institute of Population Studies (IPS) Peking University, Beijing: Huaxia Press.

China News Agency (2012) *Statistics given by the Statistical Bureau show that more people lived in rural areas in China that in urban areas in China,* http://finance. chinanews.com/cj/2012/01-17/3610120.shtml [11 July 2014].

Kohrman M. (2005) *Bodies of Difference: Experiences of Disability and Institutional Advocacy in the Making of Modern China,* Berkeley: University of California Press.

SCNSSD, Second China National Sample Survey on Disability (2006) see CDPF (2007, 2008).

4 Welfare provision of children with disabilities

The Chinese experience of disability is highly diverse, and families' contact with social support varies from the developed city municipalities in the east to the remote poorer areas in the centre and west. Central policy responsibility for children with disabilities is shared between the Chinese Disabled Persons Federation (CDPF, a quasi-government organization) and the Ministry of Civil Affairs (MCA; Kohrman 2005; Chung, Packer and Yau 2011). Implementation and service provision is managed by the lower four levels of provincial and local government of these two bodies and numerous other agencies, described in this chapter.

Like other social policy in China, child disability policy is subject to change, generally progressive, due to China's status as a developing, transition country, now ranked as a middle income country (Shang and Wang 2012; Wang, Wang and Wang 2012). Important aspects of this transition affect children's access to support. Social values are changing as the Chinese population has urbanized and relies on employment as its largest income source (more than half the population now lives in an urban environment; National Bureau of Statistics 2011). One effect of these changes is that less informal care is now available for dependent family members (Shang and Wu 2011). While government systems of support for some citizens resemble those of developed countries in the largest cities (such as Beijing, Guangzhou, Shanghai, Shenzhen and Tianjin) and other wealthier areas in the eastern provinces that can afford to supplement central government financial allocations, very few such services are available elsewhere (Shang and Wang 2012).

This chapter complements the introductory chapters as an overview of the formal system of welfare provision to children with disabilities in China. The system that supports children with disabilities developed before China's transition to a market economy in the 1990s, and remains based on the premise that the primary source of protection for children with disabilities is the family (Law on the Protection of Persons with Disabilities 1990, 2008). But the large social, economic and demographic changes are having significant impacts on all aspects of childhood, including the values and material circumstances of children, and on the informal system of social support for children. This has severely reduced the capacity of family and kinship networks to support children with disabilities, who are most affected by these changes (Johnson, Huang and Wang 1998).

Moreover, China's social welfare provision for families of children with disabilities is developing more slowly than the socioeconomic changes. The coverage of public health does not extend to all families of children with disabilities, and local schools do not receive enough resources for additional support needs (McLoughlin, Zhou and Clark 2005). This chapter introduces the welfare system as the context for the critical analysis of family experiences of the rights of their children with disabilities in the remaining chapters of the book.

Chinese welfare system

The People's Republic of China was established in 1949 and is the world's third largest country by land area. The Chinese civilization is one of the earliest in the world. For more than 4,000 years, China's political system was based on monarchies, known as dynasties. Most Chinese are of Han ethnic background, with approximately 8 per cent from other ethnic groups (National Bureau of Statistics 2011).

Economic development and revenue

From 1949, China had a centralized plan economy. In 1978, China started implementing economic reforms and opening to the world, introducing a market-based economy. It then became the world's fastest growing major economy over the next three decades. Accelerated economic development and industrialization in the 1990s reduced its poverty rate dramatically. In 2012, the estimated per capita GDP was US$7945 (2005 PPP), ranked 90 among 192 countries in the world (UNDP 2013).

As China experienced economic development, government revenue increased even faster. In 2012, GDP increased 7.7 per cent, central government revenue increased 12.8 per cent and expenditure increased 15.1 per cent (Ministry of Finance 2012). As financial revenue has continued to increase in the past decade, the government has more financial resources to spend on child welfare. This is especially the case for the central government, although the resources vary greatly between provinces (Table 4.1).

Demographic changes

Although China has one of the largest populations in the world, 1.3 billion people in 2011, its demographic structure is ageing fast. The median age continued to increase from 30.8 years in 2000 to 34 years in 2010, as the proportion of children in the total population decreased. In 2010, the population that was aged 0–14 years old was 220 million, 16.6 per cent of the total population (6.29 per cent less than in 2000; National Bureau of Statistics 2011). The proportion of children varied by province (Table 4.2).

The ageing population decreased the ratio of the working population to dependent population and the ratio between the working population and minors decreased between 2002 and 2011, indicating that the Chinese working population will support

Table 4.1 Provincial and regional financial revenue and expenditure, 2011

Province	Regional financial revenue (100 million yuan)	Increase rate %	Financial revenue per capita yuan	Financial expenditure (100 million yuan)	Increase rate %	Financial expenditure per capita yuan
Guangdong	5514.8	22.1	5285.35	6712.4	24.04	6438.24
Jiangsu	5148.9	26.2	6544.42	6221.7	18.9	7769.29
Shandong	3455.9	25.7	3607.48	5002.1	20.7	5220.86
Shanghai	3429.8	19.4	14899.74	3914.9	18.5	17007.11
Zhejiang	3150.8	20.8	5789.05	3842.6	19.8	7060.30
Beijing	3006.3	27.7	15328.59	3245.2	21.1	15111.38
Liaoning	2643.2	31.7	6035.94	3902.1	22.1	8919.84
Sichuan	2044.8	30.9	2542.23	485.1	9.8*	5811.92
Hebei	1737.8	30.4	2417.95	3537.4	24.4	4884.33
Henan	1722.0	24.6	1831.33	4248.8	–	4515.58
Hubei	1526.9	45.4	2568.41	3214.7	26.3	5520.48
Hunan	1517.1	34.6	2216.26	3520.8	28.2	5275.13
Fujian	1501.5	30.4	4068.93	2198.2	29.6	5953.78
Shaanxi	1500.2	56.5	4016.09	341.3	32.0	7846.52
Chongqing	1488.3	46.2	5159.09	224.6	45.5	8921.46
Anhui	1463.6	27.3	2459.48	3303.0	27.8	5555.75
Tianjin	1455.1	36.1	11244.57	1796.3	28.2	13570.92
Neimenggu	1356.6	27.0	5500.22	2989.2	31.5	12100.16
Shanxi	1213.4	25.1	3397.17	2363.9	22.7	6633.33
Yunnan	1111.1	27.5	2416.53	282.1	28.2	6373.30
Jiangxi	1053.4	35.4	2363.59	2534.6	31.5	5675.62
Heilongjiang	997.6	32.5	4229.00	2794.0	26.3	8868.82
Guangxi	947.7	22.7	2058.94	322.1	26.8	5586.68
Jilin	850.1	41.1	3096.59	2201.7	23.2	8019.94
Guizhou	773.1	44.9	2225.13	307.2	37.6	6458.69
Xinjiang	720.4	44.0	3304.48	245.4	34.4	10460.30
Gansu	450.1	27.4	1761.08	174.9	21.9	6999.73
Hainan	340.1	25.5	3922.05	82.0	34.1	8988.08
Ningxia	220.0	43.2	3491.32	52.0	27.9	11284.88
Qinghai	151.8	37.7	2697.84	65.4	30.1	17192.96
Tibet	54.8	30.0	1822.02	95.9	40.1	24981.97

Source: Summarized by provincial financial accounts implementation (2011) and financial budget implementation draft report (2012)

Note: The financial revenue in this table refers to general budget revenue, excluding other revenues, e.g. central allocation of income, and so as the expenditure. *Earthquake

Table 4.2 Provincial population structure of China

Region	Total population '0000	Population by age groups – '0000			Per cent of total population		
		0–14 years	15–64 years	65+ years	0–14 years	15–64 years	65+ years
Nation	134091	22259	99938	11894	16.60	74.53	8.87
Guangdong	10441	1762	7965	704	16.89	76.36	6.75
Shandong	9588	1507	7129	943	15.74	74.42	9.84
Henan	9405	1975	6642	786	21.00	70.64	8.36
Sichuan	8045	1364	5797	881	16.97	72.08	10.95
Jiangsu	7869	1023	5986	857	13.01	76.10	10.89
Hebei	7194	1209	5384	592	16.83	74.93	8.24
Hunan	6570	1157	4769	642	17.62	72.60	9.78
Anhui	5957	1070	4275	606	17.98	71.84	10.18
Hubei	5728	796	4407	520	13.91	77.00	9.09
Zhejiang	5447	719	4216	508	13.21	77.45	9.34
Guangxi	4610	999	3178	425	21.71	69.05	9.24
Yunnan	4602	953	3293	351	20.73	71.64	7.63
Jiangxi	4462	975	3143	339	21.88	70.52	7.60
Liaoning	4375	500	3424	451	11.42	78.27	10.31
Heilongjiang	3833	458	3054	319	11.96	79.72	8.32
Shaanxi	3735	549	2865	318	14.71	76.76	8.53
Fujian	3693	571	2828	291	15.46	76.65	7.89
Shanxi	3574	611	2690	271	17.10	75.33	7.58
Guizhou	3479	876	2300	298	25.22	66.21	8.57
Chongqing	2885	490	2061	333	16.98	71.46	11.56
Jilin	2747	329	2187	230	11.99	79.63	8.38
Gansu	2560	464	1883	211	18.16	73.61	8.23
Neimenggu	2472	348	1936	187	14.10	78.34	7.56
Shanghai	2303	199	1870	233	8.63	81.25	10.12
Xinjiang	2185	453	1593	135	20.77	73.04	6.19
Beijing	1962	169	1622	171	8.61	82.68	8.71
Tianjin	1299	127	1057	110	9.80	81.68	8.52
Hainan	869	173	626	68	20.00	72.20	7.80
Ningxia	633	135	454	40	21.48	72.11	6.41
Qinghai	563	118	409	35	20.92	72.78	6.30
Tibet	301	73	212	15	24.37	70.53	5.09

Source: Summarized according to the 2010 national census Sixth BASIC consolidate (National Bureau of Statistics 2011)

more old people in the future (Table 4.3). The national dependency ratio continued to decline until 2013, when the general dependency ratio increased. The low ratio meant the country had a large working population that supported a relatively small dependent population. The declining child dependency ratio means that the country will have a lower proportion of working population in the future to support the dependent population. China's dependency ratio is predicted for the near future to continue to be lower than its peak in the past (Xinhua News 2010).

Table 4.3 National child and total dependency ratio

Province	Dependency ratio – per cent		Province	Dependency ratio – per cent	
	Child	Total		Child	Total
Nation	22.13	34.40	Sichuan	22.57	39.34
Shanghai	9.88	19.27	Guangdong	22.61	32.21
Beijing	10.62	21.31	Gansu	22.74	32.74
Tianjin	13.39	25.66	Hebei	23.72	34.32
Liaoning	14.59	28.42	Hunan	24.99	39.63
Heilongjiang	14.62	24.58	Anhui	25.20	39.85
Zhejiang	16.00	26.87	Yunnan	26.91	37.47
Jilin	16.19	27.27	Xinjiang	27.16	36.15
Jiangsu	17.05	31.24	Hainan	27.21	36.61
Neimenggu	17.22	25.89	Qinghai	27.98	36.04
Hubei	18.93	32.30	Ningxia	28.43	35.87
Shaanxi	19.64	30.74	Henan	29.43	41.91
Fujian	20.58	30.60	Jiangxi	30.28	41.03
Shandong	21.06	35.65	Tibet	32.00	38.70
Shanxi	21.24	31.45	Guangxi	32.07	45.99
Chongqing	22.42	39.78	Guizhou	36.21	49.85

Source: Calculated from National Bureau of Statistics 2011

Note: Child dependency ratio is the proportion of the population aged 0–14 years to 15–64 years. Total dependency ratio is the proportion of population aged 0–14 years plus 65 years and above and 15–64 years.

Role of the family in child disability support

The main characteristics of child welfare, including child disability welfare, is that child welfare is regarded as a family responsibility, unless the child has no family, when the state takes responsibility. This assumption underlines the policy of family planning in China. Individuals and families have to obtain permission for any new birth. Parents who have new births without permission must pay a heavy penalty called a social support fee, which is as high as 60–80 per cent of three to six years' total income of both parents, depending on the situation (such as birth before marriage, more than one child outside the regulations), or between three and ten times the local average annual residents' income. Third children without permission can incur a penalty as high as 20 times the local average annual residents' income, or parents' income, whichever is higher (Beijing Family Planning Committee 2012). The one child family policy has many exceptions related to the characteristics of the family, such as where they live, their ethnicity, whether the parents are from one-child families and if the first child has a disability.

Families also bear the financial and care responsibilities of supporting children with disabilities, including economic support, care, health care and therapy. Maintaining the capacity of the family to support members with disabilities is encouraged through the policy that parents whose first child has disabilities has permission to have a second child (see discussion in McCabe and Barnes 2012). The cost of supporting children with disabilities can be very high, especially the costs of health care and therapy. This is beyond the capacity of most Chinese families, and is discussed further in Chapter 8.

In most parts of China, the state only provides support to children with disabilities whose parents are dead or cannot be found. Children in the care of the state receive full support from the government. Because of this, some parents may abandon their children with disabilities to the local urban State Children Welfare Institution with the hope that the state will provide their children with the medical and therapy services they need to survive. In China, there are about 20 million families of people with disabilities (Chapter 3). Of the five million children with disabilities, only about 100,000 are the responsibility of State Child Welfare Institutions. All the other children with disabilities rely on family support (MCA 2011). The number of children with disabilities cared for by NGOs is very small.

Laws, regulations and policies of welfare provision to children with disabilities

The National People's Representative Congress has the power to make laws and monitor their implementation. The Internal and Judicial Committee is responsible for laws about the interests of women, children and people with disabilities. It has a specific working team and full-time staff for these responsibilities. The Social and Law Committee in the Chinese People's Political Consultative Conference also has the responsibility to supervise the implementation of laws and regulations about the welfare and interests of women, children and people with disabilities and to make proposals to the government about how to improve these policies.

In 1992, the UN Convention on the Rights of the Child (CRC) formally came into effect in China. China developed country-specific programmes, including the National Programme of Action for Child Development in China (1992–99, 2001–10, 2011–20). The Programme sets objectives and strategies to be fulfilled for the survival, protection and development of Chinese children, including children with disabilities. China was also one of the first signatories to the UN Convention of the Rights of Persons with Disabilities (CRPD) in 2007. New policies and implementation to respond to the government obligations under CRPD are the responsibility of CDPF.

Chinese laws, regulations and policies to protect children with disabilities stem from the Constitution. Relevant Articles in the Constitution are:

> The state promotes the all-round moral, intellectual and physical development of children and young people (Article 46); The state and society help make arrangements for the work, livelihood and education of the blind, deaf and other handicapped citizens (Article 45); Marriage, the family, and mother and child are protected by the state. Parents have the duty to rear and educate their

minor children, and children who have come of age have the duty to support and assist their parents. Maltreatment of old people, women and children is prohibited (Article 49).

With the Constitution as the core, other provisions include the Law on the Protection of Disabled People, the Criminal Law, the General Principles of Civil Law, the Marriage Law, the Education Law, the Compulsory Education Law, the Law on the Protection of Minors, the Law on the Protection of Women's Rights and Interests, the Law on Maternal and Infant Health Care, the Law on the Prevention and Control of Infectious Diseases, and the Law on Adoption.

In addition, government departments have regulations on child welfare, such as the Regulation for Education for Disabled People; the Interim Measures for the Administration of Social Welfare Institutions, the Protocol for Child Welfare Institutions, the Notice on Further Developing Welfare for Orphans and Disabled Children, and the Opinions on Accelerating Socialization of Social Welfare.

In 2006, MCA and 14 other government organizations jointly issued the document, *Opinions on Strengthening the Work of Orphan Assistance*, which provides comprehensive income protection and support to orphans in China (MCA 2006). Most orphans in state care are abandoned children with disabilities, who become state wards unless they are adopted. The other important document about orphans and children with disabilities is the State Council's *Opinions on Strengthening the Work of Protection Orphans* (2010). It states that all Chinese orphans are eligible for orphan allowance or other benefits from 2010. Children with disabilities who are state wards have a standard allowance 80 per cent higher than other beneficiaries. Welfare policy for all people with disabilities was also developed although not widely implemented (State Council 2008).

Government child disability support structure

China is run by the Communist Party of China (CPC), which is guaranteed power by the Constitution. The political system is highly centralized with limited democratic processes internal to the party and at local levels. The other political parties are referred to as democratic parties, which participate in the People's Political Consultative Conference and the National People's Congress.

China has jurisdiction over 23 provinces (including Taiwan), five autonomous regions, four directly administered municipalities (Beijing, Tianjin, Shanghai and Chongqing), and two highly autonomous special administrative regions (SARs; Hong Kong and Macau). The capital is Beijing. The administrative structure of China is in five levels (Table 4.4). Subsidiary levels of government are allocated central government funds to implement child disability policy, but their capacity to supplement these funds to the full cost of care varies considerably.

Child disability welfare agencies

Social support for children with disabilities is a large part of child welfare in China. Protection of the rights of children with disabilities is the responsibility of

Table 4.4 Administrative structure in China

Level	Name	Definition	Number
One	Province	Provinces, Autonomous regions, Municipalities, Special administrative regions	34
Two	Prefecture	Prefectures, Autonomous prefectures, Prefecture level cities, Leagues	333
Three	County	Counties, Autonomous counties, County-level cities, Districts, Banners, Autonomous banners, Forestry areas, Special districts	2,852
Four	Township	Townships, Ethnic townships, Towns, Subdistricts, District public offices, Sumu, Ethnic sumu	40,446
Five	Village	Neighbourhood committees, Neighbourhoods or communities, Village committees, Village groups, Administrative villages, Natural villages	680,000

Source: MCA 2013b

Chinese legislative and judicial organizations, government departments and government organized social organizations (Table 4.5). In addition to the general responsibility of all government organizations towards children with disabilities, the main organizations responsible for the welfare policy of children with disabilities include the Ministry of Civil Affairs, Ministry of Judicial, National Health and Family Planning Commission, and Ministry of Education. They each make relevant institutional arrangements for the rights and welfare of children with disabilities, including monitoring, implementation and service provision.

China Disabled Persons' Federation

The main organization responsible for implementing child disability policy is the CDPF. Established in 1988, the CDPF is a unified organization of and for all people categorized as having disabilities in China (CDPF 2013). It has a national network of offices at the five levels of government, with about 80,000 full-time workers. It is notionally a non-government organization, but it functions similarly to government in the absence of a government agency with responsibility for disability policy formation and implementation. CDPF is officially committed to the promotion of: humanitarianism; the human rights of people with disabilities; and the integration of people with disabilities in all aspects, social participation and sharing the benefits of development in China.

CDPF's major functions are representation, service and administration of disability policy implementation. Their responsibilities are to represent the common interests of people with disabilities and safeguard their legal rights and interests; to develop support and activities to serve people with disabilities directly; to take charge of partial administrative functions with the authority to develop and manage the government affairs of people with disabilities (CDPF 2013; for a critical review, see Kohrman 2005).

Table 4.5 Functions of government organized child welfare organizations relevant to disability

Government	
Ministry of Human Resources and Social Security Department of Employment Promotion Department of Health Insurance Department of Labor Relations	To ensure the implementation of laws, regulations and policies on labour protection for female workers; prohibit the use of child labour; organize vocational technical training for special social groups, and create more job opportunities for women, young people with or without disabilities; and establish and improve the maternity insurance and medical insurance.
Ministry of Civil Affairs Bureau of Social Welfare and Charity Promotion Bureau of Social Assistance Department of Civil Society Organization Administration China Charity Federation China Centre for Child Welfare and Adoption	Responsible for the administrative management of the protection of the rights and interests of people with special needs such as older people, orphans, and households enjoying 'five guarantees', providing guidance for the protection of the rights and interests of people with disabilities, and formulating related guidelines, policies, regulations and rules; developing strategic plans of social welfare services and standards of various social welfare facilities; developing standards for the identification of social welfare enterprises and policies for supporting and protecting these enterprises; and stipulating guidelines and policies on adopting children.
National Health and Family Planning Commission Department of Policies and Laws Department of Maternal and Child Health Care Department of Health Law Enforcement and Supervision Department of Family Planning and Development	To formulate plans and policies on women's health and maternal and child health care; guide the implementation of primary health programmes and technical protocols on maternal and child health care; publicize scientific health knowledge such as maternal and child health care, disease prevention and reproductive health; improve and standardize maternal and child health care services; raise the quality of newly born babies; and reduce infant mortality, under–five child mortality and maternal mortality to protect the right of women and children to survival and health.
Ministry of Education Department of Basic Education One Department of Basic Education Two	To popularize nine-year compulsory education, guarantee the enrolment of children of school age and reduce the number of children of school age leaving school; develop pre-school education and increase the proportion of children receiving pre-school education; and develop special education for children with disabilities.

Table 4.5 continued

Government organized non-government organizations (GONGO)

China Disabled Persons' Federation (CDPF) Special Associations	The State Council National Coordination Committee on Disability is a national organization for persons with disabilities. CDPF is composed of people with disabilities, their families/relatives and social workers and fulfils three functions: representing their interests and protecting their rights; uniting, educating and serving them; and supervising their affairs.
All China Women's Federation (ACWF) NWCCW Office Children's Department Rights and Interests Department	ACWF includes local branches and group members, aims to safeguard the legal rights and interests of women and children (under fourteen years old) and participates in the development and improvement of laws, regulations and policies on protection.
Communist Youth League of China Young Workers, Young Farmers School Department, Young Department China Youth Social Service Center Community and Youth Rights and Interests Department	The CYL is a mass organization of advanced youth led by the CPC, a school for the broad masses of youth to study communism in practice and an assistant and reserve of the CPC. The CYL is responsible for strengthening moral education among children and youth, leading Young Pioneers and giving full play to the role of Young Pioneers in uniting, guiding and educating children and youth, and safeguarding legal rights and interests of children and youth according to law.
China National Committee for the Wellbeing of Youth	Established in 1990, mainly organized by retired officials and experts, providing educational and special services to children and young people to promote the interests of youths in the communist party and the government, organizing activities suitable for health development of children and young people. It's the only organization in China with staff at the local level to provide services to children and young people nationwide.
National Minors Protection Committee (NMPC)	NMPC was established in 2003 by the All China Lawyers Association (ACLA), a unit directly under the Ministry of Justice. NMPC is responsible for disseminating laws and regulations on protection of minors and supervising their implementation; coordinating education and protection of minors among relevant departments; taking in complaints and accusations concerning violations against legal rights and interests of minors, submitting such cases to relevant departments for investigation and prosecution and providing legal assistance for victims; recommending appropriate bodies to apply administrative sanctions or impose criminal liability.

Local DPFs are responsible for assessing and issuing a certificate of disability. With this certificate people with disabilities can enjoy preferential policies and disability services, but obtaining a certificate is difficult for most children, (discussed further in Chapter 8). Without a certificate, children are not eligible for most assistance and can struggle for economic participation when they enter the labour market as young adults (Kohrman 2005).

As the local government organization officially responsible to the State Council, the DPF has stable funds from public finances and receives the revenue from the tax penalty to businesses that do not employ the required proportion of people with disabilities (1.5 to 2 per cent of employees). This resource base contrasts with that of informal groups. The DPF is also potentially a channel for enabling people with disabilities to participate in government decision-making, as well as having responsibility for administering policies relating to people with disabilities (including disability NGOs) on behalf of the government (CDPF 2013). Chapter 12 discusses a case study of the strengths and limitations of these types of interest representation.

Government child disability support services

Services for children with disabilities play a key role in children's wellbeing. Information about disability and support services is lacking in most of China (Lim *et al.* 2013). Services are starting to be available for children in large cities and rich areas, but are rarely available elsewhere (Fisher and Li 2008). Apart from services from government, some non-government child welfare organizations also provide services for a fee or are subsidized.

Social support to children with disabilities in China is mainly embedded in general welfare schemes. Children may benefit from general welfare provision, such as income support, education, health care, and disability services. Welfare services specified for children are in the process of developing. The state role in welfare provision is mainly residual. Social welfare provision in general, and welfare provision to children with disabilities in particular, are characterized by decentralization and the differentiation between the systems of rural and urban areas, and between high and lower income areas. The state bears different responsibilities for children with disabilities depending on whether they have rural or urban resident registration.

Some cities, especially Beijing, Shanghai, Shenzhen and Guangdong, have some welfare provisions for children with disabilities with local resident registration (Shang and Wu 2011). In most rural areas and poor areas, parents and the family networks are almost the only support to children with disabilities. With economic growth and the increase in state revenue, more state welfare services are now intended to cover children, such as partially free health insurance for all residents, and free nine-year education for all children.

Where disability services are available, costs are covered by families, the state and charity, but parents bear most costs. Government funding is through three channels: first, routinely provided funding, including reimbursing therapy costs through the three medical insurance programmes and funding for State Welfare Children's Institutions for orphans; second, through specified rehabilitation funds, such as the 6,915 rehabilitation service centres or stations in China (CDPF 2015); and third, funding provided by earmarked programmes run by the DPF.

The first channel of routine funds is the most reliable. Many disability services are not, however, covered by medical insurance. The second channel of specialist funds is also reliable, but it is only available in the most developed areas of China. Apart from rehabilitation centres, state-owned hospitals are the main providers of therapy services. Most services provided are not free to children, except in the wealthier provinces. Parents pay a fee at the market price. They often express dissatisfaction at the quality of the support because it is not specific to their children's needs or the staff are not sufficiently trained (e.g. Lim *et al*. 2013). The third channel of CDPF-funded support is only piecemeal and it is difficult for parents to get information about support (e.g. Lim *et al*. 2013). Funding from charities is a very limited resource unavailable to most families.

Non-government sector

In addition to government support, the non-government sector increasingly provides services to families of children with disabilities. A consequence of China's 30-year social and economic reforms is the emergence of civil society organizations (White, Howell and Shang 1996; Howell 2009; Fisher, Shang and Li 2015). Before the reforms starting in 1978, about 6,000 social organizations operated in China. By 2011, registered NGOs reached 445,000 and many unregistered grassroots organizations are also operating (Lu 2009). NGOs are subject to a government system of social organization management (Unger 2008; Kang and Feng 2014). The system was established in 1990 following the Tiananmen Event to control social organizations and prevent potential organized responses to social unrest (Shang and Wang 2012). Because of this history, NGO regulation is a highly politicized system and it is difficult for NGOs without government backing to gain registration.

Child welfare NGOs must have approval from three government agencies to obtain NGO registration if they serve orphans or abandoned children. For these reasons, many child welfare and disability NGOs do not register at all or register as for-profit companies. Some child welfare and disability NGOs have operated for decades without becoming legal entities, but local governments neither ban them nor encourage them to register (Shang, Wu and Wu 2005). As a result, the government often does not monitor or support the activities of child welfare NGOs and commonly does not enforce the accountability requirements of registered NGOs (Fisher, Li and Fan 2011; Edele 2005; Lu 2009). The consequences for some children supported by unregulated NGOs can be extreme. For example, even when some child welfare NGOs have operated for more than three decades, their practices are so lax that some children reach adulthood without formal education, or a legal status, because the NGO failed to register their birth (Shang, Wu and Wu 2005).

Child welfare and disability NGOs developed in the 1990s in response to the shortcomings of state and market provision of support to children and their families, especially orphans and children with disabilities (Shang, Wu and Wu 2005). Four types of registered NGOs operate in China. They are registered NGOs, non-registered, registered as a profit-making firm, and NGOs attached to another registered social organization. Among all the NGOs providing services to children with disabilities, a large proportion are user-initiated NGOs, which are started by families and communities to develop services for their own children because they cannot find existing services to support their children (Shang and Wang 2012; Cotton *et al.* 2007). Some employ workers and others rely on volunteers. In addition, child disability welfare is also provided by other NGOs (e.g. international, charity and religious), government agencies and private organizations (Shang and Wang 2012). The quantity and quality of government support can be poor; and services provided by commercial providers can be expensive and low quality (Shang and Wang 2012).

The third sector is now attracting more policy attention. In 2013, the government announced that 200 million yuan would be spent on purchasing services from social service NGOs (State Council 2013). This can be regarded as a turning point of policy change. The government is also reforming the process of NGO registration to simplify the steps (Kang and Feng 2014). At the same time, the Chinese government adopts a very cautious policy towards NGOs – for example, it is trying to limit the development of NGOs that care for orphans and abandoned children, reinstitutionalizing children to State Child Welfare Institutions (Shang and Fisher 2013).

Social security provision to children with disabilities

The main social welfare provision in China is social security, which includes social assistance (the most common for families of children with disabilities) and social insurance. The types of social security are described below. Apart from the national social security programmes, in some areas, families of children with disabilities receive income support from local or municipal government, such as in Shanghai. The Twelfth Five-Year Programme for the Development of the China Disabled Persons, which started in 2011, aimed to complement the coverage of the social security system for all people with disabilities, giving people with disabilities special assistance, basic living, care, social insurance subsidies (CDPF 2006). However, these policies are not specific for children with disabilities, and have only been achieved in wealthier areas.

Social assistance provision

Apart from a programme for orphans and HIV/Aids-affected children, China does not have a formal social assistance system that is specifically for children with or without disabilities. The largest welfare programme in China is social security, which includes social insurance and social assistance. Social insurance schemes include insurance of retirement, health, work-related injury and diseases, maternity and unemployment, which focus mainly on the urban workforce, rather than children.

The social assistance programmes are targeted programmes. The primary target groups of these schemes are households in poverty, including their children. All the social assistance programmes are residual in nature. People have to rely on their family and extended family first. They are only eligible for help from the state when all the other channels fail.

The available programmes include the minimum living security for urban residents (*dibao*, or MLS) with 23.15 million beneficiaries, for rural residents (with 52.14 million beneficiaries), five guarantees programme (*wubao*, FG) with 5.56 million beneficiaries, the rural assistance for the extreme poor programme (*tekun*, RAEP), with 0.59 million beneficiaries in 2010. *Wubao, tekun* and other social assistance programmes are gradually being replaced by the minimum living security (MLS) for urban and rural residents (MCA 2011).

Minimum living security (MLS) for urban and rural residents

The Minimum Living Security (MLS) for Urban Residents was first established in 1993 in Shanghai. The coverage of the programme has expanded to the whole urban population since 2003 and has more than 22 million beneficiaries (Shang and Wu 2003). Only urban residents are entitled to MLS benefits and eligibilities are subject to means-tested results. Only urban residents whose household income is below the local poverty line are eligible to the benefits. Most urban orphans who are not in the care of the state receive the MLS benefits. The programme is expanding gradually to rural areas to replace other social assistance programmes.

Five guarantees programme (wubao) in rural areas

The *wubao* programme provides five guaranteed provisions (clothes, food, fuel and education/funeral services) to the most disadvantaged people in rural areas. In 1978, *wubao* households were legally defined as 'older people, people with disabilities or children who are unable to look after themselves, have no income and nobody legally responsible for their wellbeing'. In general, children with disabilities are not covered by the project because they have families to support them. The financial base of the *wubao* programme used to be the rural collective economy. After the dismantling of the people's communes in rural China in the 1980s, the *wubao* programme was based partly on the income from cultivating land owned by *wubao* households, and partly from levies from villagers. In 2006, the financial base of *wubao* shifted from community levies to public finance. The government formally provides financial support to the *wubao* programme from local government budgets.

Social relief for the extreme rural poor and temporary social relief

The policy of providing social relief for the extreme rural poor (*tekun*) originated in the 1950s. It is generally *ad hoc* payments from the local government, such as at festival times. However, the arrangement is gradually being institutionalized. There are big gaps among regions in terms of whether or not the policy has been carried out, how to check the eligibility of *tekun* households and the standard of benefits. Some families of children with disabilities receive support under this programme.

Temporary relief targets rural households whose income is above the poverty line and whose living standard is also slightly higher than the *wubao* or *tekun* households. However, the capability of these households to take risks is usually weak and they could fall into poverty when they encounter disasters, accidents or illness. When these events happen, some governments provide temporary relief to these households, which takes the form of small lump sum benefits in cash or in kind, before Chinese New Year. The local government usually only provide very limited financial resources to the programme in their regular budgets. Local civil affairs officials often have to use money or goods meant for disaster relief to provide temporary relief. Many of them are families of children with disabilities. The level of temporary relief is too low to be very helpful.

Basic Living Protection Allowance for Orphans

Opinions on Strengthening the Work of Protection Orphans (State Council 2010) states that all Chinese orphans are eligible for orphan allowance or other benefits from January 2010. At the end of 2010, 250,000 orphans in China received the payment of basic living protection allowance. The project focuses on orphaned children, not children with disabilities. However, most of them are children with disabilities, and as children cared for by the state, their living standards greatly increased after the new policy was implemented.

Other social assistance

Government social assistance requires a means test based on household income. It usually fails to provide adequate protection to children with disabilities cared for by their parents or kin. Apart from the social assistance programmes, the existing rural land system guarantees almost all rural households have a piece of land among their assets. The land system plays an important role in protecting children with disabilities in rural areas. Combined with the labour from extended families, children usually receive some benefit (mainly food) from the land that belongs to their family; or the land can be rented out for a little income.

Most extended families usually provide children with basic living support. In traditional Chinese society, extended families were obliged to care for children with disabilities so these children had social rights in their extended families. However, children with disabilities are gradually losing their rights as the result of social change loosening the connections among extended families and the commercialization of social relations in rural society. The MCA is considering how to provide social assistance to children with disabilities because of the urgency for new social support to them.

Care and protection for orphaned children with disabilities

When children's parents have died or cannot be found, the state takes guardianship responsibility for their care and protection (state wards in alternative care) (Shang and Fisher 2013). Government funded and provided services are mainly provided to abandoned children with disabilities and without parents. Local State Child Welfare Institutions, which are managed by the local level of Civil Affairs, are only responsible for orphans, mainly children with disabilities. Some Institutions are now supporting children with disabilities within their families to try to prevent abandonment, discussed in Chapter 7. The State Child Welfare Institutions are fully funded by the state, and only take on a guardianship responsibility for children without parents in urban areas, who are mainly children with disabilities. Rural children with disabilities are sometimes abandoned in cities for this reason.

About 100,000 children, most with disabilities, are cared for by 335 State Children's Welfare Institutions nationwide (MCA 2011). The government provides both financial support and care services to these children. The first priority for the government is to place them with permanent homes through adoption. However, it is difficult to find adoptive families for most state wards with disabilities and they often remain in state care until adulthood.

Before 2003, the main approach of alternative care for the children cared for by the state in China was institutional care. Partly because of financial pressures on the State Child Welfare Institutions, after 2003 foster care was accepted as one of the main approaches of alternative care for children with disabilities cared for in State Child Welfare Institutions (Shang and Wu 2003). About 60 per cent of children in the care of the state were placed with foster families in eight State Child Welfare Institutions in 2001 (Shang 2001b). Three models of foster care in China have developed since 2003: urban family foster care (Shanghai), urban community based foster care (children are fostered with families within selected urban communities) and rural community based foster care (children are fostered with families within selected rural communities; Shang 2008). In 2003, the MCA made the first regulation for foster care: *Temporary Methods for Managing Foster Care (Jiating Jiyang Guanli Zanxing Banfa)*. There were no official statistics for children cared for in institutions in 2011. But at least 50 per cent of all children in care are cared for in families because the State Child Welfare Institutions have only 50,000 beds for more than 100,000 children nationwide (MCA 2011). An example of specialized foster care for children with disabilities is discussed in Chapter 7.

The institutions provide care, therapy, education and other services to orphaned children. The MCA raised 600 million yuan from 2005 to 2007 to cover the costs of surgery for children in the care of the state who were waiting for operations because the costs of therapy and surgery for these children are not included in routine budgets of State Child Welfare Institutions. The project was called 'Planning for Tomorrow: Operational Rehabilitation for Orphans with Disabilities', with 50 per cent of funds paid by the money raised by national lotteries, and 50 per cent of fund raised by provincial governments (Shang and Wang 2012). After the project, because the number of children who were waiting for operations reduced, many SWCIs have been able to pay the costs of such operations with the money from their routine budget, donations, and extra money applied from the centre and provincial government.

Since 2005, the government has increased its investment to State Child Welfare Institutions. Large amounts of newly increased funds were used, however, to build more institutions, provide better facilities or more rooms in existing State Child Welfare Institutions (Interview with MCA officials). There is increased government pressure on State Child Welfare Institutions to re-institutionalize children cared for in families. The main argument behind the trend of re-institutionalization is that it is difficult to meet the needs of children with disabilities for therapy in communities, and State Child Welfare Institutions have better facilities and trained staff for meeting the therapy needs of children with disabilities. The policy debate means that there is a challenge ahead on how to promote good practice in child care and protection, especially for children with disabilities in China.

In 2013, the MCA started a pilot reform to establish a universal child welfare system in China. The pilot requires all State Child Welfare Institutions to establish a Baby Safety Haven to accept abandoned children, most of whom are children with disabilities (MCA 2013a). With new approaches in caring for children with disabilities, one approach has been to transform the existing State Child Welfare Institutions into new shelter and resource centres, which could provide services to children with disabilities and children with special needs in communities. Trials for this goal started in 2013 and are underway in six Provinces (Shang and Wang 2013).

Conclusions about child disability welfare policy

This chapter has described the formal family and child welfare system relevant to disability support in China, including organizations, laws, regulations, policies and implementation. In the formal system children with disabilities rely on their families. The state provides only limited welfare services to these families. In the past 30 to 40 years, the size and capacity of Chinese families has greatly reduced in terms of providing support to children with disabilities. China is gradually developing a comprehensive welfare system, including income security, health care, education, care and disability services, to support these families and children. The institutional gaps are large in all the aspects of welfare, as discussed in the following chapters.

Given this background, it is understandable that most families of children with disabilities face many difficulties, such as poverty and responsibility for care, and their children's needs for education, health care and disability services cannot be met. However, welfare services continue to change. Whether families of children with disabilities are experiencing the increased government commitment to responsibility for welfare provision and whether it is sufficient to meet children's rights compared to their peers is explored in the rest of the book.

References

Beijing Family Planning Committee (2012) *Methods of Collection and Management of Social Support Fee in Beijing*, www.bjfc.gov.cn/web/static/articles/catalog_ff8080813678bee3013678cd20c70015/article_ff80808136880dd601368b020e7a0050/ff80808136880dd601368b020e7a0050.html [21 May 2012].

CDPF, China Disabled Persons' Federation (2006) *A Notice of Issuing the Speech of Senior Officials in the Workshop of Rehabilitation work for Children with Disabilities*, www.cdpf.org.cn/2008old/kangf/content/2006-10/27/content_75604.htm [10 September 2011].

CDPF, China Disabled Persons' Federation (2013) www.cdpf.org.cn/english/aboutus/aboutus.htm [3 December 2013].

CDPF, China Disabled Persons' Federation (2015) *Statistical Communique on the Development of the Work for Persons with Disabilities in 2014*, www.cdpf.org.cn/zcwj/zxwj/201503/t20150331_444108.shtml [3 May 2015].

Chung, E.Y.-H., Packer, T. and Yau, M. (2011) When East meets West: community-based rehabilitation in Chinese communities. *Disability & Rehabilitation* 33(8): 697–705.

Cotton, J., Edwards, C., Zhao, W. and Gelabert, J. (2007) Nurturing care for China's orphaned children. *Young Children* 62: 58–63.

CRPD, United Nations Convention on the Rights of Persons with Disabilities (2006) www.un.org/disabilities/default.asp?id=150 [1 February 2012].

Edele, A. (2005) Non-governmental organizations in China. *CASIN Report*. Geneva: Programme on NGOs and Civil Society and Centre for Applied Studies in International Negotiations.

Fisher, K.R. and Li, J. (2008) Chinese disability independent living policy. *Disability & Society* 23(2): 171–185.

Fisher, K.R., Li, J. and Fan, L. (2011) Barriers to the supply of nongovernment disability services in China. *Journal of Social Policy* 41(1): 161–182.

Fisher, K.R., Shang, X. and Li, J. (2015) Accountability of children's services organizations in China. *Asian Social Work and Policy Review* 9: 94–107.

Howell, J. (2009) Government-organised nongovernment organisations. In: Pong Dea (ed.) *Encyclopedia of Modern China*. Detroit: Gale.

Johnson, K., Huang, B. and Wang, L. (1998) Infant abandonment and adoption in China. *Population and Development Review* 24(3): 469–510.

Kang, X. and Feng, L. (2014) *Observation Report on the Third Sector of China*. Beijing: Social Sciences Academy Press.

Kohrman, M. (2005) *Bodies of Difference: Experiences of Disability and Institutional Advocacy in the Making of Modern China*, Berkeley: University of California Press.

Law on the Protection of Persons with Disabilities (2008) China Disabled Persons Federation, www.cdpf.org.cn/english/laws1documents/200804/t20080410_267460.html [2 May 2015].

Lim, F., Downs, J., Li, J., Bao, X.-H. and Leonard, H. (2013) Caring for a child with severe intellectual disability in China: the example of Rett syndrome. *Disability and Rehabilitation* 35: 343–351.

Lu, Y.Y. (2009) NGO-state relations in contemporary China: the rise of dependent autonomy. *Development Issues* 11: 23–25.

MCA, Ministry of Civil Affairs (2003) *Temporary Methods for Managing Foster Care*, www.mca.gov.cn/article/zwgk/tzl/200711/20071100004024.shtml [3 May 2015].

MCA, Ministry of Civil Affairs (and 14 government organizations) (2006) *Opinions on Strengthening the Work of Orphan Assistance*, www.china. com.cn/chinese/PI-c/1183979.htm [11 February 2013].

MCA, Ministry of Civil Affairs (2011) *Social Service Development Statistical Report 2010*, www.mca.gov.cn/article/zwgk/mzyw/201106/20110600161364.shtml [1 January 2012].

MCA, Ministry of Civil Affairs (2013a) *Notice of Improving Works about Abandoned Babies*, www.mca.gov.cn/article/zwgk/fvfg/shflhshsw/201305/20130500460312.shtml [4 November 2013].

MCA, Ministry of Civil Affairs (2013b) *Statistical Report of the Development of Social Services in China, Ministry of Civil Affairs, China 2013*, www.mca.gov.cn/article/zwgk/mzyw/201306/20130600474640.shtml [3 May 2015].

McCabe, H. and Barnes, R.E. (2012) Autism in a family in China: an investigation and ethical consideration of sibling issues. *International Journal of Disability, Development and Education* 59: 197–207.

McLoughlin, C.S., Zhou, Z. and Clark, E. (2005) Reflections on the development and status of contemporary special education services in China. *Psychology in Schools* 42(3): 273–283.

Ministry of Finance (2012) *Report of Revenue and Expenditure*, http://gks.mof.gov.cn/zhengfuxinxi/tongjishuju/201301/t20130122_729462.html [2 May 2015].

National Bureau of Statistics (2011) Communiqué of the Sixth National Census Data in 2010 No. 1. 2011, www.stats.gov.cn/tjfx/jdfx/t20110428_402722253.htm [10 July 2012].

Shang, X. (2001b) *Orphans and Disabled Children in China and Alternative Care*, Report to the Ministry of Civil Affairs and UNICEF, Beijing: UNICEF.

Shang, X. (2008) *The System of Social Protection for Vulnerable Children in China*, Beijing: Social Sciences Academic Press.

Shang, X. and Fisher, K.R. (2013) *Caring for Orphaned Children in China*, Lanham: Lexington Books.

Shang, X. and Wang, X. (2012) *Discovery Report: Emerging Issues and Findings for Child Welfare and Protection in China (2011)*, Beijing: Social Sciences Academic Press.

Shang, X. and Wang, X. (2013) *Leading Research on Child Welfare and Protection in China: 2013*, Beijing: Social Sciences Academic Press.

Shang, X. and Wu, X. (2003) Protecting children under financial constraints: the case of Datong. *Journal of Social Policy* 32: 549–570.

Shang, X. and Wu, X. (2011) Care regime in China. *Journal of Comparative Social Welfare* 27(2): 123–131.

Shang, X., Wu, X. and Li, H. (2005) Social policy, gender and child abandonment in China. *Youth Studies* 4: 1–5.

Shang, X., Wu, X. and Wu, Y. (2005) Welfare provision to vulnerable children: the missing role of the state. *The China Quarterly* 18(1): 122–136.

State Council (2008) *Opinions on the development of welfare for persons with disabilities*, www.gov.cn/jrzg/2008-04/23/content_952483.htm [28 January 2012].

State Council (2010) *Opinions on Strengthening the Work of Protection Orphans* www. gov.cn/ zwgk/2010-11/18/content_1748012.htm [14 May 2012].

State Council (2013) *Opinions of the Office of the State Council on the government purchasing services from social forces*, www.mca.gov.cn/article/zwgk/fvfg/ mjzzgl/201310/20131000525921.shtml [4 December 2013].

UNDP, United Nations Development Programme (2013) *2013 Human Development Report: The Rise of the South: Human Progress in a Diverse World*, New York: UNDP.

Unger, J. (2008) *Associations and the Chinese State: Contested Spaces*, Armonk: M. E. Sharpe.

Wang, X., Wang, L. and Wang, Y. (2012) *The Quality of Growth and Poverty Reduction in China*, Beijing: Social Sciences Academic Press.

White, G., Howell, J. and Shang, X. (1996) *In Search of Civil Society: Market Reform and Social Change in Contemporary China*, Oxford: Clarendons Press.

Xinhua News (2010) 2013 dependency ratio of population in China is at the turning point, still has 25 year dividend, http://news.xinhuanet.com/politics/2010-05/18/c_12115988. htm [3 May 2015].

5 Right to life and protection

The first set of rights of children with disabilities is about the right to life and protection. Changes to Chinese social policy that support parents in caring for their children is vital to address the urgent social problem of children with disabilities being abandoned. One type of abandonment results when parents intentionally make the decision to leave their child, or cease medical intervention, knowing the child is likely to die, or even kill their child. Focusing on these limits to the protection of the right to life of these children (Art. 10, 16 CRPD) is an extreme case that helps us to understand the effectiveness of Chinese child disability policy. Analysing these uncomfortable circumstances can inform directions of change needed to prevent such threats to children and young people and to support them within their families.

This chapter examines five case studies where parents decided whether to abandon their child. It analyses whether current Chinese child protection mechanisms actually protect the right to life of children born with disabilities and whether the right to life of these children is unconditional; the role of social services in decisions about the children's right to life; and why parents decide to abandon their children. This analysis is important for exploring the interaction between formal social service mechanisms to protect the right to life of children with disabilities and parents' social expectations. Unless Chinese parents are convinced that their children's needs will be addressed through social support, reduced discrimination and shared financial costs, they may continue to rationalize that life is not in their children's best interests.

Children born with disabilities

China has a high rate of children born with disabilities. Up to 1.2 million children with disabilities are born every year (between 4 and 6 per cent of births), including 200,000 to 300,000 babies born with disabilities obvious at birth. The remainder are children where the disabilities become apparent in the months or years after birth (Ministry of Health 2002).

The most recent estimate of children with disabilities (over five million children, from the 2006 survey, is lower than the 1986 estimate of 8 to 9 million (Shang 2008). The difference might be explained by improvements in medical services during prenatal and postnatal care. However, the reduction could also be explained by practices such as abandoning babies with disabilities, including ceasing medical treatment, and the failure to register the birth of babies with disabilities. Tens of thousands of children with disabilities, mainly very young babies, are recorded as abandoned by their parents every year (CDPF 2007). Some of them become the responsibility of the state and an unknown number of others die from a lack of care and protection (Shang and Fisher 2013).

Internationally, the rights of children with disabilities were restated most recently in the United Nations Convention on the Rights of Persons with Disabilities (CRPD 2006). Watson and Griffiths (2009) also examined the long history of the concepts of the right to life of children with disabilities, including devaluing and denying the right, such as in eugenics policies. They conceptualize the recognition of seven rights to life: i) to be conceived; ii) to be born; iii) to not have one's life terminated at birth because of social devaluation; iv) to be nurtured and provided with the elements to sustain life to its fullest; v) to safety and security of one's life; vi) to continue life through appropriate medical treatment and support; and vii) to choose life.

Both the law and practice in China encourage pre-marriage and prenatal tests and abortion. People who have serious genetic conditions or mental illness are by law prohibited from giving birth (Marriage Law and the Law of Maternal and Child Health; Kohrman 2005), denying the first two rights to life. This chapter analyses further rights iii–vii, which are protected by law but are often denied in social policy and practice. These breaches occur despite China ratifying the CRPD, which obliges China to comply with the principles on the rights to life (Petersen 2010; Stein 2010).

Parents' decisions about abandoning their children are made in the context of their limited access to an equitable social welfare system in China (Fisher and Shang 2013). Most families bear the cost of medical care, disability support and specialist education for their family members during childhood and adulthood (Fisher, Shang and Xie 2011; Fisher and Li 2008). State Child Welfare Institutions, which arrange adoptions, foster and institutional care, receive many children who are abandoned because of their disabilities. Many of these disabilities are temporary if the children receive minor, but costly surgery, such as for a cleft lip or palate. Other bodily differences have no functional impact, such as a six-fingered hand or face pigmentation, which reflects parents deciding to abandon the child for reasons other than cost (Shang 2008).

Disability and child welfare policies are gradually improving in the richer eastern provinces through access to income support and free or subsidized health and welfare services (Fisher, Shang and Blaxland 2011; Fisher, Shang and Guo 2014). Other policy improvements that affect children with disabilities are changing nationally; for example, responsibility for health costs is moving from individuals and families towards the state, driven by major public health crises during the SARS epidemics in China in 2004. In 2008, the central government announced two policy goals for people with disabilities: full health insurance coverage and free rehabilitation (State Council 2008). Some local governments, in the most developed areas in China, provide free or subsidized services for children, such as autism support, although the availability and quality of services varies (Shang, Saldov and Fisher 2011).

In the context of these broader policy improvements, the basic rights to life and protection of children with disabilities in China have not received sufficient attention. Most existing research on child abandonment in China has focused on the prevalence and patterns of child abandonment (Shang and Fisher 2013; Shang, Wu and Li 2005; Johnson, Huang and Wang 1998; Johnson 1996). However, research about the child protection system itself and protecting the right to life of children with disabilities is weak (Research Team of Anti-Infant Abandonment, Nankai University 2006a, 2006b).

Research about Chinese child protection has found that basic elements of a child protection system are missing in China, including mechanisms to report child neglect or abuse, or a lead government agency for child protection (Katz, Shang and Zhang 2011; Qiao and Chan 2005). This chapter identifies another fundamental gap in the child protection system by analysing how the right to life is protected or breached for children born with disabilities.

Cases to analyse the right to life

The cases are drawn from the larger research project on the experiences of families of children with disabilities in China in this book and elsewhere in our research (Fisher and Shang 2014). In the larger project, 52 families of children with disabilities in 15 Chinese provinces and large cities (Figure 1.1) participated in semi-structured interviews in 2009–11. Parents frequently said that they considered abandoning their children while they were raising them, because they did not have support from government or elsewhere. The national analysis for this larger project also showed that most children in state care are children with disabilities (Shang and Fisher 2013).

The five case study children were selected as an analytical qualitative sample to conduct in-depth analysis of the decision making in the families (Table 5.1). The analysis is not about whether the parents made the right decisions, but rather about the functioning of the child protection system as reflected in these cases to reveal limitations in the protection of the right to life of children with disabilities.

Table 5.1 Case studies for right to life analysis

Child	Sex	Age (years)	Parent		Place
Niuniu	Girl	2	Zhou	Father	Beijing city
Xing*	Boy	15	Wang*	Mother	Fujian province, rural
Hope*	Girl	New born	Li*	Parents	Tianjin city
Heng and He*	Boys	13	Han	Mother	Guangdong province
Gao	Girl	3	Liu	Mother	Jinmen city

Note: *Alias

Detailed data through the primary and secondary sources about the cases was sufficient for this purpose. The situations of the families, why each case was selected, and the methods of data collection and analysis are described below.

In the first case study, a girl named Niuniu, was born in Beijing in 1990. Her parents had higher education qualifications. She was blind from multiple retinoblastoma, which threatened her life. The doctor recommended surgical treatment, but because she would be blind and had a 50 per cent chance of the cancer recurring before she was aged 30 years, the parents decided not to proceed with the treatment. She died aged nineteen months.

This case was selected because detailed information about her life from the parents' perspective was available in a book by her father, Zhou Guoping, a well-known Chinese philosopher (Zhou 2000). The book provides rare information to address the research question, with detailed reflections about how the parents gave up their daughter's life for fear of her disability, including their reasoning at the time and the regret they felt later. The secondary data for the analysis are from the book and community reaction publicly available from print and social media.

The second case is a boy named Xing (alias), born in 1995 in Fujian. He lived with his parents in an urban area. His mother, Wang, was a temporary teacher in a rural school and then worked at a hotel. His father was a farmer and then worked in the same town. Xing had multiple disabilities including intellectual disability, speech and vision disabilities and a cleft lip and palate. Informed of the boy's disabilities, the members of Xing's father's extended family, especially his grandmother, wanted to abandon him. Despite the pressure from her husband's extended family, Xing's mother took responsibility to support him. She was able to save his life and provided him with care, medical treatment, therapy and education at a local primary school. At the time of the fieldwork, he was aged fifteen. This case was selected because the researchers had contemporary primary data from fieldwork in the larger project. It is a case that illustrates the role of family members and absence of intervention from community and government.

The third case is a girl called Hope (alias) who was born in 2010 in Tianjin. Her parents have higher education qualifications. She had a congenital health condition, which the doctor advised could be addressed with surgery, but she would still have disabilities. Her parents decided against surgery and sent her to a hospice. Volunteers from Children's Hope, a nongovernment (NGO) charity, tried to save her life by removing her from the hospice, taking her to a hospital and offering to pay for the treatment. However, their efforts failed because her parents would not consent or transfer guardianship to the NGO. When the child was on the verge of death, the NGO leader asked Dr Shang for advice about the law on child protection. After consulting a judge from the Chinese Supreme People's Court, the leader concluded that, within the current legal system, no one was permitted to provide lifesaving treatment for the child without the consent of her parents. The secondary data about the case are from internet research and participatory observation data from the involvement of Dr Shang during the NGO contact.

The case was selected because, in 2010, her situation aroused nationwide internet discussion. As a result, information about protection of the right to life of children with disabilities and how the event developed were available publicly. In addition, it led the public to reflect on and discuss the principles and procedures for protecting the right to life of children with disabilities. The case caused strong responses, with opposing opinions about the rights of children with disabilities.

The last two cases were chosen because the mothers ended the lives of children by direct killing, which differs from the more indirect question of whether to intervene with life saving medical care in the other cases. Legally both cases can be defined as infanticide although both mothers killed their children while under great pressure (Rao *et al.* 2011). Both cases caused widespread public debate and sympathy for the children and mothers.

The fourth case is 13-year-old twins, Heng and He, who had cerebral palsy in Guangdong. In 2011, their mother, Han, killed them and attempted suicide. She was sentenced to five years imprisonment. The case induced public debate in traditional and social media on how to protect the right to life of children with disabilities, and caused public pressure on the government to provide more support to families of children with disabilities in Guangdong (Zhang, Rao and Wei 2011; Rao and Liu 2011; Liu 2011; Liu and Zhao 2011).

The fifth case is a three-year-old daughter Gao, of Liu Qin, a teacher in Jinmen city. The daughter was born with a heart condition and the family was struggling to save money for the operation. When she was aged three years, Gao fell on a shopping centre elevator, breaking her right hand. Immediately after the surgery, the doctor told Liu that her daughter's hand could not be reconnected and she would be permanently disabled. Her mother left the hospital, purchased a knife and stabbed her daughter to death. She attempted suicide, leaving a suicide note on her mobile phone. In an interview, Liu said that she did it in the interests of her child – as a teacher, she knew about the life of children with disabilities in school and she did not want her child to face such a life. The court sentenced her to ten years imprisonment (Liu 2010a, b).

The detailed primary and secondary data from the five cases were qualitatively analysed against a coding framework based on the research question. The limitations of the methods are that the five cases are opportunistically selected and are not representative of the current status of children with disabilities in China. Some of the case studies analyse data from public media, which adds strength to the case where the opinions are from a wide range of citizens. But it also means the researchers could not intentionally collect data that were comparable between the case studies. Only the boy, Xing, survived, which is consistent with patterns for abandoning children in rural China, but the sample is too small to draw conclusions about sex. Future research could enlarge the sample to extend the implications. The cases occurred over fifteen years, when great social and economic changes occurred, including the policy changes described above. Throughout this time, however, no in-depth analysis of experiences of the right to life of children with disabilities has been conducted and the policies and public perceptions about the questions do not appear to have changed. Therefore, the problems revealed through these cases continue to have relevance to current social service research. To address the limitations, in addition to these five cases, the chapter also refers to the larger research project and work from the Research Team on Anti-Infant Abandonment.

Deciding to abandon the life of a child with disabilities

The first part of the question considers whether the right to life of the children is conditional or absolute. Most children are born into a community that recognizes their right to life. Their parents, other family members and the public, safeguard their lives. In China, however, children born with disabilities or illnesses that may lead to disabilities may encounter life-or-death dilemmas from the first moments of life and through their childhood because their parents or extended family members may decide whether or not to support the children's survival.

The five cases have factors in common in relation to the children's right to life. All the children were born with health or disability conditions that required medical intervention or would have benefited from disability therapy. In the first three cases their lives could have been saved if medical treatment had been available to the families, and the children would have lived with disabilities. In the last two cases, the quality of life of the children and families would have benefited from disability therapy, which might have prevented their mothers' desperation. In each case, the parents and extended family members considered whether to abandon the child's life; that is, whether to save the life with the necessary medical treatment; to let the child die by denying any medical treatment; to abandon the child to the state; or in the extreme last two cases, kill the children. These parents made their decisions more or less alone and none of them was forced to do so. Their decisions contrast with some other parents who leave their children to the care of State Child Welfare Institutions because, among other reasons, they are unable to afford the medical costs and decide that the only chance to save the child is to hope the government will take responsibility for the orphan.

In Niuniu's case, her parents continued to care for her, but decided against the medical treatment that would save her life, with the predicted result that she died before she was two years old. In Xing's case, the father's extended family wanted to abandon him. Xing was very weak at birth and frequently hospitalized. At about the age of one year, he was diagnosed with physical and intellectual disabilities. His grandmother was determined from the time of his birth not to provide support or medical treatment. Other relatives from the father's side, with the same attitude, believed that the child was born as a burden for them, and they blamed the mother for giving birth to the boy. However, because his mother held strong opinions against abandoning him, she supported him and paid for his treatment. Hope's parents had planned to have a child for five years before her birth. After a discussion with the doctor when she was born, they carefully considered whether to deny medical treatment and at a meeting of more than 30 members of the extended family, decided to send her to a hospice instead.

In the last two cases, the families believed when the children were born (twins Heng and He with cerebral palsy and Gao with a heart condition) that with adequate intervention the children could live a good life. Heng and He's mother

Han believed if she found proper therapy her children would walk and live like other children. She gave up her good job to care for them full time. The family resources were exhausted and they incurred high debt buying therapy. When Han realised the children's condition was actually deteriorating rather than improving when they were thirteen, she drowned them. Similarly, Liu hoped to save sufficient funds to pay for her daughter's heart operation, but when the emergency hand surgery added to her disabilities, she killed Gao and tried to kill herself.

In the five cases, from the time the children were born and through their childhood, their right to life was questioned and was far from unconditional. The decisions to continue or end the children's lives were completely the responsibility of their parents, who made the arrangements they believed were best for the child.

Decision processes about the children's lives

The second part of the question concerns the decision-making process about the child's right to life, including the role of the parents and social services. In all five cases, the decisions were made through similar procedures. The process was informal; there was no state intervention or participation of professionals; and the parents and other family members made their decisions based on considerations such as their assessment of the interests of the child and whether the families could afford disability support.

The first step was the realization that their children were born with health problems or disabilities. Second, they sought advice from doctors about the medical treatment options, rather than whether or not to treat. The third step was the parents' choice to treat or abandon. Without professional help, the parents turned to their relatives. In rural areas, these relatives, especially those on the paternal side, have an important role in family decision making (Shang 2008). The analysis revealed varied participation in the decision by parents, extended family members, children, community members, professionals and government, discussed below.

Parents

In the five cases, the parents had the decision-making power, which was consistent with their guardianship and financial responsibilities for the children. Chinese law recognizes the rights, duties and responsibilities of parents (Marriage Law 1980, 2001) and in practice parents are responsible for the costs of disability of their children. The cases of Heng, He and Gao differed when their mothers made the desperate decision to kill the children and themselves.

While other members of the extended family offered their opinions, the parents made the final decision. In the case of Xing, the family could not abandon him despite their preference to do so, because of his mother's opposition. After withstanding the extended family's preference to abandon his life, his mother had to manage all the financial and care-giving responsibilities alone. In the case of Hope, community members intervened, offering to support the surgery and promising financial support, but the father rejected the temporary guardianship transfer, and the NGO could not force an alternative decision.

The role of each parent varied between the cases. Niuniu's mother and father both considered the doctor's treatment suggestion and jointly decided to abandon their daughter's life. Hope's mother at first did not know about the father's decision to give up treatment, because of her own poor health, but was informed later. She then expressed her wish to hide from the public, together with her daughter (Tan 2010). Xing's mother protected his right to life and her husband supported her wishes. The position of the fathers and extended families in Heng, He and Gao's cases are unknown, although they supported their wives during the plea for light sentences.

Extended families

The extended families were also involved in all the cases, but to different degrees. Niuniu's grandmother told the parents that there would be lots of trouble if Niuniu survived the operation, but she was not active in the decision. For Hope, the parents' decision to abandon her life was made with the extended family. The decision about Xing was made by his father's extended family, who informed his mother, but she rejected their decision. These cases illustrate the powerful role of the extended family in influencing decision-making about right to life, yet in Xing's case it was not powerful enough to override the mother's decision.

In practice then, the extended families provided their opinions, but the decisions were made by the parents. In the last 20 years, the role of extended family members in decisions about the life of a child and financial support for parents and children with disabilities has weakened, in part because younger generations have greater independent earning capacity. Xing's grandparents insisted on their right to make the decision because they had financial responsibility to support the young couple, as is common in rural families, and after Xing's mother refused to abandon Xing, they stopped their support.

Children

The children were the subjects of the life-or-death question, but their voice or a voice on their behalf was negligible in the absence of a child advocate. The interests of Heng, He and Gao were absent from the court proceedings, except that the judges found the mothers guilty of infanticide and argued for the supremacy of a right to life of children with disabilities. Niuniu's parents reflected on how their opinion about understanding their child's interests changed later in her life,

> [earlier] It is commonly said that a healthy body is the only thing parents can give their child. But we cannot even do this, and she will complain about it when she has grown up.

[later] She wouldn't forgive our abandoning her life if she could now understand what is happening.

(Zhou 2000)

Xing was also too young to have a voice in the decisions about him. But his mother safeguarded his right to life. At the time of our fieldwork Xing was aged fifteen years. He had experienced discrimination and marginalization, but also happiness and love. The interviewer recorded,

> Xing likes his school where he has fun watching so many children playing, even if he cannot join them. Having a younger sister added a lot of fun to his life. His mother is the one he most loves and relies on. Xing is very courteous and modest. When his mother buys new clothes as Spring Festival gifts, he always allows his sister to get hers first... Xing is very polite to his teacher... and any visitors to his home.

Like other people with disabilities, Xing was also discriminated against by some and he tried to avoid these people. The interviewer noted, 'He fights the discrimination by running away. He has two sharply contrasted colours in his world – love and discrimination, and he cherishes the love.'

Community members

Information put on the internet by a member of Hope's extended family to help their decision sparked widespread internet discussion about what was in her best interest. A young girl questioned the decision by Hope's father,

> I am a child, and ... as I know, you, as a father, are deciding by considering your daughter's future. But, have you ever considered this: ... How can she have her future if you don't give her the opportunity to survive now? In fact, she doesn't want to leave this world ... even if she has to face suffering in her future life. ... She wishes to call you mummy and daddy, wishes to stay at a kindergarten listening to her teacher, just like other children. ... but, you don't give her the opportunity to survive.

(Tianya Milk Powder 2010)

Other people supported the family's decision, imagining the child questioning her parents' decision if she grew up, 'If I were the child, I'd rather die when I was a naïve child' (Mop 2010). Another person wrote,

> Just imagine that the girl survived after multiple painful surgeries and other treatments, but she had to live on with her life-time disabilities and care from others. And after growing up, she might be incapable of normal work, marriage and pregnancy, or she might suffer from all kinds of discrimination and frustration ... 'Why did you give me this life, why didn't you let me die,

and why did you let me suffer so much?' How ashamed would her parents and other relatives feel?

(Mop 2010)

Some community members also acted on behalf of Hope, when it became clear to them that the state would remain silent and inactive in this case, despite the internet attention. Volunteers from an NGO wanted to intervene when they read on the internet that Hope had been left to die in a hospice. They illegally took her from the hospice, but had to return her because they could not obtain guardianship to authorize treatment. While the NGO was able to advocate for her interests, they were unable to reverse the parents' decision, because the state would not intervene on her behalf to force a change to the guardianship or treatment.

Other community members contributed to the public debate to try to understand the position of the parents making the decisions, considering the implications for the child and parents. For example, a mother sympathized with Han killing her twins and attempting suicide, 'I was a mother with a child with cerebral palsy; my experience was that to live with a child with cerebral palsy is a life time sentence' (Liu and Zhao 2011). International research has similarly found public understanding for parents when they kill a child with disabilities (e.g. Mackay and Covell 2013; Porter and Gavin 2010).

In all the heated public debate about the cases of Heng, He and Gao discussed below, their voice and the voice of people with disabilities was drowned out. The overwhelming opinion was support and sympathy for the mothers (Table 5.2). The negative impact of the cases on protecting the lives of children with disabilities was ignored. One person with disabilities from Dongwan posted on social media an opinion about the consequences of no legal punishment for the behaviours of ending the life of children with disabilities,

> Mother Han murdered her twin sons, both her husband and villagers pleaded the court gives her light sentence. However, we all understand, people with cerebral palsy are not brain dead. Nobody has the right to kill them. If the court gave the mother light sentence, it is the society and the parents killed the twins together. In that case, we are no different from Nazis … In the future, we may see more people with disabilities, including older people with disabilities, being murdered. (In the history) Nazis killed people belonging to so called 'inferior races'; Is our law also going to kill 'inferior races'?

Following the media reporting of the court cases, both mothers Han and Liu, received a large amount of social support and sympathy from local communities, mothers with children with disabilities, internet users, and NGOs for women and children (Rao *et al.* 2011). Most people expressed sympathy for Han's thirteen years' care and support for her children. The main discussion point was that she had paid enough by caring for her children. Mother Liu also received social support, and the main discussion point emphasized that her motivation was to help her daughter to avoid future suffering in her life with disabilities (Liu 2010b).

Table 5.2 Internet survey – what is your opinion of the case of Mother Han?

Opinion	Per cent (n=3666)
Harsh situation for the mother due to the absence of the state and social assistance	61
Understanding the mother's situation, agree to give light sentence	31
Cannot avoid death penalty (sharenchangming)	3
Other	6
	100

Source: Sina internet survey, Rao *et al.* 2011

Community members were not directly involved in the other cases. When Niuniu's father published the book about their decision, the public discussion was at first focused only on the philosophical questions about the meaning of life and the father's love and bravery. The media discussion ignored the question of the right to life of the child, until a fifteen-year-old boy with cancer (who died a year later) questioned the common opinion, and declared that he found the discrimination against people with disabilities in Zhou's philosophy offensive (Ziyou 2005).

Professionals

Professionals' involvement in the cases comprised advice about the options to address the medical problems through treatment and other therapy. The doctors advised the parents that treatment was available that would save the children's lives and that they would continue to live with disabilities. Xing, Heng and He's mothers opted for medical treatment and therapy, and, in the case of the twins, the cost of the therapy left the family financially destitute. In Gao's case, the doctor advised that medical treatment for her fractured hand had resulted in further permanent disability, even before her family could afford the heart treatment she needed. In the internet discussions about Hope, both sides justified their opinions by referring to the doctors' advice. The doctors did not advise whether or not the children's lives should be saved.

Government

Despite the extensive public debate about the cases of Niuniu and Hope the government was silent about the parents' decisions and did not comment on the subsequent public discussions. It appears from this absence that in China the government views the protection of the lives of children with disabilities through the withholding of treatment as a private responsibility, outside the realm of public authorities. This was different for the mothers of Heng, He and Gao, where the act of intentionally killing was recognized as criminal (discussed below).

The government position of no intervention in the first two cases contrasts with public opinion about the role of government articulated in the internet discussions about the cases. This public opinion is consistent with the results of a survey conducted by a research team from Nankai University in 2006, about how the responsibility for protecting abandoned children should to be divided among the parents, the state and civil society (Table 5.3). It indicates that citizens expect the state to take a shared responsibility in child protection. In general, policy reform is moving slowly towards this expectation, for example through increased government resources for disability policy implementation (State Council 2008); and ratification of the CRPD.

A positive impact of the publicity about Heng and He's death was the public attention to families of children with disabilities, and they successfully lobbied the government to take more action to support them. The Guangdong Disabled Persons Federation and the City government both announced more support and services to families (Liu and Zhao 2011).

In the cases of Heng, He and Gao, their mothers' acts were recognized by the state as infanticide. The court cases were followed by the public as described above. In the face of overwhelming public opinion for Han, the judge emphasized that it was a case of intentional murder but only sentenced her to five years imprisonment. In China, this was a very light sentence, contrasting for example with another case in 2011, where a young man was sentenced to immediate death after he killed a rural woman in a road accident in Shanxi (Western Net 2011). Even so, Han's relatives thought the sentence too harsh as they had expected less than three years sentence plus probation. The judge emphasized that the right to life is a basic human right for everyone and no one, including parents, has the right to end the lives of others. He said that children with cerebral palsy have the right to life; they should be protected by the state and parents. He said she was given a lighter sentence because her motivation was not to rid herself of the responsibility of supporting her children, but instead that she could not see any future hope for their improvement. In a desperate mood, she killed her sons and attempted suicide to relieve her family and sons from a life not worth living. The court also found she was in deep depression and she was regarded as a person of limited criminal responsibility (Tang, Zhou and Huang 2011). Liu was sentenced to ten years imprisonment. Public opinion exerted huge pressure on judges in both cases (Tang, Zhou and Huang 2011).

Table 5.3 Citizens' opinions about how to solve child abandonment

	Per cent (n=1217)
Rely on the whole society	40.18
Solve it by a state agency specializing in abandoned children	34.95
It is a private issue and the family solve it within itself	18.73
Other ways	6.16
	100.00

Source: Research Team on Anti-Infant Abandonment (2006a)

Summary of participation in the decision to end a child's life

In summary, the five cases show how parents, extended families and community members expressed their perceptions of the interests of the children. They sometimes took opposite positions about what was in the children's best interests, including ending the child's life. No government intervention was available to protect the interests of the children, reconcile conflicting opinions or separate the interests of the parents and child in decisions about life. The state intervened after three of the children were killed, when the cases became criminal matters.

The absence of government or professionals advocating for the child's rights in the decision making had the effect of breaching the right to life of the child in several ways. First, the decision did not necessarily prioritize the child's rights. Public opinion also focused on the parents' interests rather than the children. The voice of people with disabilities is drowned out. Second, the decision to abandon their lives was affected by the preferences of the family, their perceptions about living with disabilities and their financial responsibilities, rather than the rights of the child or the availability of therapeutic interventions. Third, the parents and relatives were solely responsible for the consequences of the decision. As a result, for example, before his daughter's death, Niuniu's father felt deep regret about their earlier decision. In a positive turn, the most recent cases (Heng, He and Gao) resulted in public pressure on government to better support families so that parents are not placed in this difficult situation.

Reasons parents decide to abandon their children's lives

The final part of the question is the parents' considerations when deciding whether to abandon their child's life. Deciding to abandon the life of their child was a painful process for the parents. In all five cases, the parents expressed love for their children and believed they made the decision in the best interests of their children. The two themes that emerged in the parents' deliberations about abandoning their children were the future interests of the child and financial responsibility for the cost of disability.

Interest of the child not to live with disabilities?

The families who decided to abandon the life of a child considered that it would be worse for their children to live with disabilities than to die. The parents said that because the children would have disabilities even after medical intervention or therapy, it was better to abandon their lives. Medical costs were not the most important consideration for Niuniu and Hope's families since both the families were in a relatively good financial position. Hope's father said, 'It is not that we are unable to afford the medical cost but that we are afraid she would have a miserable life.' Both sets of parents agreed that a life with disabilities was not worth living and decided to let their daughters die. In contrast, Xing's family was in the poorest financial condition and his mother was not as well educated. In more desperate decision making, Heng, He and Gao's mothers were driven the kill their children and themselves when they felt lives with disabilities would be unbearable for their children.

Yet after having made the decision to abandon her after Niuniu's birth and continuing to live with her for the remaining months, her father changed his mind after it was too late to intervene. He wrote,

> At that time (when we decided to give up Niuniu's life), I did not really realize that a life with disability could be so beautiful and with such rich content. It was Niuniu's blindness that opened my eyes to see how superficial and conceited I was before and to see such a world of people with disabilities that is defective but still nice and dynamic. She would have grown up to be an outstanding girl in this world, but I pushed her out of this world.
>
> (Zhou 2000)

While Niuniu's parents revised their initial value judgement about their daughter's interests after caring for her, such prejudice is rooted in Chinese society. This was illustrated in the internet discussions about Hope's life. For example, someone criticized the volunteers who were ready to rescue Hope,

> I don't think we should neglect her future reality just for a slogan of 'Respect for Life.' Loving mothers, do you really need to save a life that is destined to be miserable forever, merely for the slogan? Do you feel satisfied and comfortable only when she is alive (living with life-time misery and grief, and bringing the same grief to the family), just because you think you have safeguarded the life?
>
> (Mop 2010)

Many people with disabilities experience difficulties, including discrimination. For example, as Xing grew up, his mother said she had to fight discrimination against him and herself. Some people who witness this discrimination fear a life with disabilities to the extent that they say they would rather die than survive. A discussion between Niuniu's parents (Zhou 2000), illustrates how afraid they were for the future life of their child if she had disabilities,

> It's hard to decide, since all options are the worst. Maybe we can choose the surgery. I'll be staying with her for my lifetime and taking good care of her. I care nothing but her living on. We will find happy things for sure.
>
> No. A blind girl would not be our daughter any longer.
>
> We will give her the best love and make her a blind but happy girl.
>
> It sounds like other children are calling her a 'little blind'. I really can't stand to see her being humiliated. How terrible it is if she would be raped by someone she could not identify with eyes, as I saw in a movie.
>
> We can't worry about so many things. Some raped girls are not blind.

They conflated the likelihood of discrimination with extreme events, such as rape, and concluded that death by denying access to medical treatment was a better outcome. Similarly, in an internet discussion about whether Hope's life should be rescued, two young people said death was better than a life with disabilities,

> The girl [Hope] would hate those who had rescued her if she would grow up with all the diseases, when it could be hard for her either to get married or find a job, and when she would be suffering from all kinds of miseries. Would you feel comfortable if you were in such an ugly shape in your golden twenties? If I were so, I'd rather die when I was a naïve child.
>
> Even if she could be cured, she could never become as healthy as others. And, even if she could become as healthy, she would be in poverty for most part of her life. The girl wouldn't feel grateful to anyone for saving her life. Therefore, I believe that her parents did the right thing.
>
> (Mop 2010)

The mothers of Heng, He and Gao felt strongly at the time of their deaths that their lives were no longer worth living. Both mothers believed that they made the best choice for their children. They had both cared for their children up to that point. The public opinion about the cases sympathized with the mothers' position. The judges disagreed, emphasizing that the right to life of children with disabilities was inalienable. In the public discussions, most people supported the mothers' opinions, although some blamed them. Many comments were to blame the state for failing to provide support to mothers of children with disabilities (Rao *et al.* 2011; Tengxun Forum 2010).

Financial responsibility for the costs of disability?

Responsibility for the high costs of disability was one of the main reasons that some people supported abandoning children with disabilities, although this was not the case for Niuniu and Hope's families since they were financially secure. For other families of children with disabilities, consideration about responsibility for the cost of disability was critical to determining the children's right to life. Heng, He and Gao's families had reasonable household resources when the children were born, but had become poor through the process of buying therapy for Heng and He or saving for the surgery for Gao. Concern about the high costs of disability was common in public discussions about abandoning children with disabilities.

Medical treatment, therapy and other support can address the needs of many children with disabilities, yet in most parts of China parents are responsible for the cost of this support and some parents feel they must abandon their child's life because the cost is unaffordable. Consideration of the cost of disability therefore has three parts: the additional items that contribute to the costs of disability; the responsibility to pay for them; and how to protect the child's life if parents cannot afford the costs.

Costs of disability in China are dominated by medical expenses for which the family is usually responsible, although some employment insurance covers most of the medical costs of employees' children. In all five cases, medical treatment was necessary to save the child's life. In the case of Hope, the medical cost was estimated as RMB500,000 (£45,000), without any complications. In addition, there would have been other ongoing disability support costs. However, her father did not agree to treatment even after the NGO offered to pay the medical expenses to save her life. The internet discussion repeatedly referred to the expenses subsequent to the initial treatment, arguing that the family would face a greater financial burden and worse poverty if the girl's life were saved,

> Just imagine standing in the family's shoes: When volunteers leave after the girl is rescued, what can her parents do? For her health conditions, lots of money will be needed, far beyond their affordability. Then she will die sooner or later.
>
> If you have real loving hearts … you need a perfect plan – you should not only send the child to a hospital for surgery but also think of the future. Otherwise, what will happen to the child? And, how can the family live with a child with disabilities without any more money for further medical treatment?
>
> (Mop 2010)

In the case of Xing, after the cost of the initial treatment, there were other expenses for subsequent therapy and treatment, extra support and education costs. Indirectly, the parents also influenced the cost of caring for their son, reducing his job opportunities and depriving him of extended family support. Moreover, the grandmother punished them economically by reallocating Xing's land entitlement of a preferential share of hillside field to an uncle. The father's siblings also forced Xing's parents to pay back the money that they had borrowed for their wedding. His mother paid for his medical treatment and therapy with her meagre earnings as a rural primary-school teacher, then as a hotel worker. They lived between his maternal grandmother's home and at a hospital for four years and received financial support from his mother's two brothers.

The cost of disability depended on the child's condition and how much the parents could invest in intervention and therapy. For Heng and He, the cost included medical procedures and therapy, paid carers, extra living and travel costs to attend therapy, their mother's job and career, and other living costs. Financial pressure, after 13 years of the financial costs of support as a full-time carer, was one of the main factors that drove Han to her desperate decision. After the deaths, she told her sister, 'How can I survive in the future, I have lost everything – my house, my savings, my children and my job and career' (Zhang *et al.* 2011) Similarly, Liu was already feeling the financial pressure of saving for the live-saving heart surgery before her daughter fractured her hand.

The financial precariousness of the families was worsened when parents had to give up their jobs or take lower paid job opportunities to fit with their care responsibilities, including Han's to care for her twins and Wang's to move with Xing to somewhere she could get treatment for him. In none of these cases were the parents offered financial or other assistance from the state. Hope's family were offered NGO support due to the publicity about the case. Secure access to state or NGO support could have alleviated their immediate and future financial considerations when deciding whether the child should live.

These cases demonstrate that parents consider the future quality of life of their children, discrimination in the community and responsibility for the costs of disability. In the face of making these decisions alone and unable to share responsibility for the life-long support of their children, they inevitably question whether it is better for the child to live or die.

Conclusion about right to life

This chapter analysed whether Chinese child protection mechanisms protect the right to life of children with disabilities (Art. 10, 16 CRPD) and in what circumstances parents decide to abandon their children. The families' decision making in these five cases showed that as soon as the children with disabilities were born and throughout their childhood, their right to life was questioned. Whether to allow their children to die was a private decision, informed by the opinions of extended family members. The state did not intervene and the role of the professionals was about medical treatment rather than whether the child should live. The state only intervened after the deaths of the two direct cases of infanticide of older children. For the parents who decided to abandon the lives of their children, their main consideration was not the right to life, but the problems their children would face if they were to live, including discrimination and costs of disability support. In such a context, the right to life of children with disabilities was not fully protected.

Although the decisions remain a private responsibility, the case studies demonstrate that protecting the lives of children with disabilities is also becoming a public concern, as community members have an interest in and the means to express their opinions to a wide audience through internet discussion and NGO activity. Their expectation of state intervention contrasts with the lack of state involvement, even at the level of contributing or reacting to public discussion. The state was forced into reacting in the more recent and extreme cases of infanticide, announcing better support for families and children.

The policy implications are that China has not yet established an effective system to protect the lives of young children with disabilities. First, China needs to establish a system to protect children with disabilities who are abandoned, neglected or abused by their parents. Decisions about the life or death of a child should not be a private family one. It implies a need for government intervention. Until government accepts guardianship responsibility to intervene in situations where parents choose not to protect the right to life of their child, all other family and community members or professionals who advocate on behalf of the child remain powerless to protect the child's life.

Formal mechanisms to protect the right to life of children with disabilities are unlikely to be enough. Only attitudinal change about the rights of children and adults with disabilities will address the larger social and cultural considerations of parents (see, for example, Dauncey 2007, 2012). The government has a responsibility to support parents of children with disabilities, and to create an inclusive social environment for children with disabilities. Some of the disadvantages faced by children with disabilities and their families can be addressed by policy, thereby gradually challenging private and public perceptions about quality of life of people with disabilities (e.g. Lin *et al.* 2014 in Taiwan). Government policy and resources to implement policy nationwide for affordable health and disability support services, income support, inclusive education and employment opportunities would be positive steps towards empowering families and children to confront the discrimination they experience in their communities. These themes are discussed further in later chapters in this book.

References

CDPF, China Disabled Persons' Federation (2007) *Handbook of Main Data from the Second National Sampling Survey on Disability (2006-2007)*. Office of the Second China National Sample Survey on Disability, Beijing: Huaxia Press.

CRPD, United Nations Convention on the Rights of Persons with Disabilities (2006) www.un.org/disabilities/default.asp?id=150 [1 February 2012].

Dauncey, S. (2007) Screening disability in the PRC: the politics of looking good. *China Information* 21: 481–506.

Dauncey, S. (2012) Three days to walk: a personal story of life writing and disability consciousness in China. *Disability & Society* 27: 311–323.

Fisher, K.R. and Li, J. (2008) Chinese disability independent living policy. *Disability & Society* 23(2): 171–185.

Fisher KR and Shang X. (2013) Access to health and therapy services for families of children with disabilities in China. *Disability & Rehabilitation* 35(25): 2157–2163.

Fisher, K.R. and Shang, X. (2014) Protecting the right to life of children with disabilities in China. *Journal of Social Service Research* 10.1080/01488376.2014.922521.

Fisher, K.R., Shang, X. and Blaxland, M. (2011) Review Article: Human rights based social policies – challenges for China, *Social Policy & Society* 10(1): 71–78.

Fisher, K.R., Shang, X. and Guo, P. (2012) Gender, social policy and older women with disabilities in rural China. In Sung, S. and Pascall, G. (eds) *Gender in East Asian Welfare States: Confucianism or Gender Equality*, Basingstoke: Palgrave MacMillan.

Fisher, K.R., Shang, X. and Guo, P. (2014) Gender, social policy and older women with disabilities in rural China', in Sung, S. and Pascall, G. *Gender and Welfare State in East Asia: Confucianism or gender equality?* Basingstoke: Palgrave, Chapter 5: 141–170.

Fisher, K.R., Shang, X. and Xie, J. (2011) Support for social participation of children and young people with disability in China, in Carrillo, B. and Duckett, J. (eds) *China's Changing Welfare Mix: Local perspectives*, London and New York: Routledge.

Johnson, K. (1996) The politics of the revival of infant abandonment in China, with special reference to Hunan. *Population and Development Review* 22(1): 77–98.

Johnson, K., Huang, B. and Wang, L. (1998) Infant abandonment and adoption in China. *Population and Development Review* 24(3): 469–510.

Katz, I., Shang, X. and Zhang, Y. (2011) Missing elements of a child protection system in China: the case of LX. *Social Policy & Society* 10(1): 93–102.

Kohrman, M. (2005) *Bodies of Difference: Experiences of Disability and Institutional Advocacy in the Making of Modern China*, Berkeley: University of California Press.

Lin, H.-C., Knox, M. and Barr, J. (2014) A grounded theory of living a life with a physical disability in Taiwan. *Disability and Society* 29: 968–979.

Liu, F. (2010a) A girl breaking her palm in a lift, her mother killed her and committed suicide, but was rescued, http://news.sina.com.cn/s/2010-05-11/043120243838.shtml [25 July 2012].

Liu, F. (2010b) Jinmen woman killed a 3 years sick daughter and facing homicide prosecution, http://news.qq.com/a/20100721/000142.htm [25 July 2012].

Liu, G. (2011) Caring for twin children with cerebral palsy for thirteen years, a desperate suicided mother who drowned two sons was rescued, http://dg.oeeee.com/a/20110516/991351.html [25 July 2012].

Liu, G. and Zhao, Q. (2011) The court open day decided, thousands of mothers pleading for her, http://dg.oeeee.com/a/20110531/994990.html [25 July 2012].

MacKay, M.E. and Covell, K. (2013) What about the rights of the infant with disabilities? Responses to infanticide as function of infant health status. *Canadian Journal of Disability Studies* 2(2): 35–57.

Marriage Law of People's Republic of China (1980, 2001) www.npc.gov.cn/englishnpc/Law/2007-12/13/content_1384064.htm [2 May 2015].

Maternal and Child Health Law of People's Republic of China (2005) www.gov.cn/banshi/2005-08/01/content_18943.htm [31 January 2012].

Ministry of Health (2002) *Notice on Printing and Distributing China Action Plan of Promoting the Quality of Newborn Population and Reducing Birth Deficiencies and Disabilities (2002-2010)*, www.cjr.org.cn/zcfg/GuoJiaFaGui/24216.html [6 July 2010].

Mop (mop.com) (2010) *Discussion on the Baby with Aproctia in Tianjin*, http://dzh.mop.com/default.jsp?url=http://dzh.mop.com/topic/readSub_10931212_0_0.html [6 July 2010].

Petersen, C. (2010) Population policy and eugenic theory: implications of China's ratification of the United Nations Convention on the Rights of Persons with Disabilities. *China: An International Journal* 8(1): 85–109.

Porter, T. and Gavin, H. (2010) Infanticide and neonaticide: a review of 40 years of research literature on incidence and causes. *Trauma, Violence, and Abuse* 11(3): 99–112.

Qiao, D.P. and Chan, Y.C. (2005) Child abuse in China: a yet-to-be-acknowledged 'social problem' in the Chinese mainland. *Child and Family Social Work* 10(1): 21–27.

Rao, D. and Liu, Z. (2011) Families with children with cerebral palsy urge the government to build additional rehabilitation agencies, http://dg.oeeee.com/a/20110519/992292.html [25 July 2012].

Rao, D., Wei, W., Li, M. and Chen, Y. (2011) The case of Han Qunfeng: most net users pleading for leniency, http://dg.oeeee.com/a/20110603/995895.html [25 July 2012].

Research Team of Anti-Infant Abandonment, Nankai University (2006a) *Survey of Public Opinion on Child Abandonment*, Beijing: UNICEF.

Research Team of Anti-Infant Abandonment, Nankai University (2006b) *Survey and Policy Suggestions of Families with Children with Disabilities*, Beijing: UNICEF.

Shang, X. (2008) *The System of Social Protection for Vulnerable Children in China*, Beijing: Social Sciences Academic Press.

Shang, X. and Fisher, K.R. (2013) *Caring for Orphaned Children in China*, Lanham: Lexington Books.

Shang, X., Saldov, M. and Fisher, K.R. (2011) Informal kinship care of orphans in rural China. *Social Policy & Society* 10(1): 103–116.

Shang, X., Wu, X. and Li, H. (2005) Social policy, gender and child abandonment in China. *Youth Studies* 4: 1–5.

State Council (2008) *Opinions on the development of welfare for persons with disabilities*, www.gov.cn/jrzg/2008-04/23/content_952483.htm [28 January 2012].

Stein, M.A. (2010) China and disability rights. *Loyola of Los Angeles International and Comparative Law Review* 33(7): 7–26.

Tan, Y. (2010) *'Hope' event fading out: mother wishes not to be disturbed*, http://news.enorth.com.cn/system/2010/02/11/004494951.shtml [6 July 2010].

Tang, H., Zhou, R. and Huang, J. (2011) *Court announcement of the case of 'Mother who drowned her twin children with cerebral palsy', husband said the punishment was too heavy*, http://baobao.sohu.com/20110629/n311982183.shtml [25 July 2012].

Tengxun Forum (2010) *Young mother killed 3 year old sick daughter, claimed to alleviate suffering of the child*, http://comment5.news.qq.com/comment.htm?site=news andid=24931015 [25 July 2012].

Tianya Laiba Milk Powder (2010) *Story about a baby girl with aproctia in Tianjin*, http://laiba.tianya.cn/laiba/CommMsgs?cmm=43194andtid=2718017910248651052 [2 July 2010].

Tianya Laiba Women (2010) *Follow-up story about the baby with aproctia*, http://laiba.tianya.cn/laiba/CommMsgs?cmm=876andtid=2717672208334590140 [6 July 2010].

Watson, S. and Griffiths, D. (2009) Right to life, in Owen, F. and Griffiths, D. *Challenges to the Human Rights of People with Intellectual Disabilities*, London: Jessica Kingsley Publishers.

Western Net (2011) *The court announcement of the case of Yao Jiaxin: Yao was sentenced to death*, http://news.163.com/11/0422/11/7286SHQR00011229.html [25 July 2012].

Zhang, X., Rao, D. and Wei, X. (2011) *The track of the thirteen years of a mother who drowned her twin children with cerebral palsy*, http://dg.oeeee.com/a/20110517/991813.html [25 July 2012].

Zhou, G. (2000). *Niuniu: The Notes by a Father*, Guilin: Publishing House of Guangxi Normal University.

Ziyou (2005) *Whose Youth Is As Mad As Mine?* Shanghai: Children's Publishing House.

6 Right to care and protection
Support for mothers

The second aspect of the right to care and protection is that of support for mothers so that it becomes feasible for children with disabilities to remain with their families. This chapter analyses mothers' gendered experiences of caring for children with disabilities in their families (Art. 23 CRPD). Now that China is a middle income country, with a developing social welfare system, do mothers continue to take a disproportionate responsibility for the needs of their children with disabilities? Some mothers do not have support to meet their children's needs, including their daily care, financial security and child development. Their experience of social support to share these responsibilities with other community members or the government is affected by the specific needs and capacities of the children, mothers and other family members. These struggles are similar to mothers of children with disabilities in other countries (Goodley and Runswick-Cole 2011).

This chapter analyses the experiences of six case study children in rural and urban China, their mothers and other family and community members. It examines whether the Chinese social welfare system has responded to the rights of children with disabilities and their families, and whether social services have improved mothers' experiences of sharing responsibility within their communities.

As background to the empirical data about mothers' experiences in China, the chapter introduces the relevant literature that theorizes parents' responsibilities for children with disabilities; disability, children's and women's rights; and child disability in China. It highlights the need to understand the experience of mothers of children with disabilities to inform the development of social services and income support in China.

Parenting responsibilities for children with disabilities

Internationally, social approaches to disability theorize that the difficulties faced by children with disabilities and their families are due to social barriers, where social relations fail to adjust to children's disabilities, needs and differences (Oliver 1996) and their mothers experience the related stigma and discrimination (Ryan and Runswick-Cole 2008; Chiu et al. 2013). In the social policy context, these adverse social factors include, for example, insufficient financial support, protection, care and development services for children with disabilities and their families, including protection against social discrimination.

Current social constructions of childhood, parenting and disability can disadvantage children with disabilities and their mothers. Mothers of children with disabilities are positioned as unsuccessful if judged against norms such as childhood being a time of investment for the child's future potential; parents being responsible for managing that investment process; the mother and child having capacity to achieve that future potential; and policy being neutral on the gendered role of parenting responsibility, particularly for children with disabilities (Lister 2006; Goodley and Runswick-Cole 2011).

An alternative construction is to recognize the parenting experience of mothers of children with disabilities in terms of capacities developed to acquire resources and overcome social discrimination for the benefit of the child and mother (Ryan and Runswick-Cole 2008). The failure of social policy to recognize and provide support to overcome these discriminatory social constructions and recognize their capacities, excludes children and mothers from the opportunities of their peers without disabilities (Shakespeare 2006). Similar research about fathers of children with disabilities in Taiwan emphasizes the importance of the cultural context of the role of each parent within the family unit and in finding quality support (Huang, Chen and Tsai 2012).

Applying these social policy theories about rights of children with disabilities and their mothers, the chapter analyses mothers' experiences in China. The social context in China is similar to international experience, where mothers take the primary parenting responsibilities for children with disabilities. In the Chinese context, the impact on mothers is accentuated by the local cultural conceptions of disability and responsibilities (Huang, Fried and Hsu 2009). The impact of these attitudes is likely to affect negatively not only the rights of children with disabilities, but also the rights of their mothers. Their rights are likely to be compromised where there is a social expectation that mothers are solely responsible, resulting in poor support from family, community and the state for both children with disabilities and their mothers.

The chapter poses two questions. In China, what are mothers' responsibilities for children with disabilities and how are the responsibilities shared? What is the impact of parenting responsibilities on the rights of children with disabilities and their mothers? It draws conclusions for social policy interventions to support children and mothers in the context of emerging social welfare systems.

Family case studies

Qualitative data were collected in rural and urban communities to address these questions. Life histories of six children with disabilities were collected using semi-structured in-depth interviews and observation with the children's main carers and other family and local community members. The six cases were chosen from the total sample of 52 (Table 1.1), as cases in which mothers were the main carers of their children as the study subjects for this chapter (Shang and Fisher

2014). They were selected across the three different family structures: single parent, nuclear family and multiple generational households (Table 6.1).

Preference was given to households with older children so that changes during childhood and over a number of years could be analysed. The interviews were conducted with the main carer in each family. In the six cases selected for this chapter, mothers were the main carers. In four of the six cases, other adults in the family or neighbours joined the discussion after the formal interview. In addition, to address limitations of this sub-sample, some data from the other cases were analysed to further investigate the question.

The data from the various sources were analysed to address the research questions about who took responsibility, what the responsibilities were, how the responsibilities were shared, the extent of community and government support, and the impact of social care arrangements on the child and mother. This analytical framework adopts the approach of Ryan and Runswick-Cole (2008) that mothers are active agents in the construction of disability in the mothering of their children with disabilities.

Limitations to the methods are that the number of case studies is small, which could limit the validity of general conclusions drawn from these cases; and second, the cases are about older children, so the social context might now be different in these communities for families of children born today. The risk of this limitation is most likely for children in the richer eastern coastal locations because of the more significant policy improvement during their lifetimes. The limitations are addressed by including data from the larger sample when relevant.

The chapter includes a description of the case studies; an explanation about who takes responsibility for care, financial security and child development; and an examination of how the responsibilities are shared between the mother, her social networks and support services. The discussion explains this distribution of the rights of the children and their mothers in relation to Chinese context. It draws implications for social welfare system change.

Table 6.1 Sample case studies of mothers of children with disabilities

Child*	Sex	Age	Disability	Location	Household
Xiaojie	Boy	8	Physical	Xinjiang, rural	Single mother
Xinxin	Boy	9	Physical	Hunan, urban	3-generation family
Qianqian	Girl	14	Physical and intellectual	Hunan, urban	Mother remarried
Xiaoxing	Girl	15	Multiple	Fujian, rural	3-generation family
Anqi	Girl	16	Vision and physical	Beijing, urban	Nuclear family
Xiaoyan	Girl	16	Physical	Xinjiang, urban but registered as rural	Single mother

Note: *Alias

Children with disabilities and their families

The circumstances of each of the cases are described first to understand the context of the analysis. The children with disabilities were aged eight to sixteen. They all had disabilities that required considerable additional support from their families. The disabilities included vision, hearing, physical and intellectual, each affecting their support needs. They came from a wide variety of social backgrounds. They all lived with their mothers, in households that were nuclear families or extended families with three generations, single mothers and remarried mothers. The mothers were aged 35–45 years and included a range of education, socio-economic class, rural and urban locations, and women with disabilities themselves. All names are aliases.

Xiaojie was an eight-year-old boy with cerebral palsy. He lived with his mother and older sister in a village on the outskirts of Urumqi, the capital of Xinjiang, a predominantly Muslim autonomous region. He was cared for by his mother. His grandmother and aunt who lived nearby also cared for him. His father refused to live with him because of his disability, which was the main reason why his parents separated. The family relied financially on the mother's farming work.

Xinxin was a nine-year-old boy with cerebral palsy, which affected his ability to walk and see. He was in his third year of primary school. He lived with his parents, younger brother and grandmother in a city in Hunan province. His aunt also occasionally stayed with his family.

Qianqian was a fourteen-year-old girl with physical and intellectual disabilities. She was independent in basic daily living activities, following extensive therapy, and could write simple words and calculate simple numbers. Her mother had remarried after her parents divorced. Qianqian lived with her mother, stepfather and younger sister. They lived in a city in Hunan province. When she was young, her family did not receive any government support, so her mother spent all their savings on her medical treatment and therapy. The family's financial conditions had improved at the time of the research because the government had begun providing the minimum living security (MLS, *dibao*), low-rent housing and medical insurance.

Xiaoxing was a fifteen-year-old girl with multiple disabilities (intellectual, speech, vision and a cleft lip and palate remedied with surgery). Her mother moved with Xiaoxing and her younger sister into a rented home (120 yuan (£11) per month, near the railway station), so that the sisters could attend a school in the county, in the coastal province of Fujian. Her mother worked at a hotel (650 yuan (£59) per month). Xiaoxing was a pupil in the special education class at a primary school in the county, and her sister attended a grade 3 class at the same school. Her father and grandfather remained in the family home in the rural area, earning money from growing crops, other farm work and odd jobs.

Anqi was a twelve-year-old girl, with total blindness and physical disabilities affecting her arm and leg. She lived with her parents and three-year-old brother in Beijing. Her father was a worker in a company, usually at work on weekdays and at home on weekends. Her mother was a primary school teacher. During the week,

Anqi was a boarding school student. Her parents drove her between home and school each Monday and Friday. The above average monthly household income over 4,000 yuan (£364) was enough for the family's needs. Her mother took responsibility for making major family decisions.

Xiaoyan was a sixteen-year-old girl with physical disabilities. She lived with her mother in a rented two-room home in Urumqi, the capital of Xinjiang, although they were both registered as rural residents. Her mother also had physical disabilities. Xiaoyan's father died when she was less than two years old. Her mother worked as a farmer in a rural area to support the family. They moved to the city because of their poor financial situation and the lack of medical services in the rural area. The mother's small retail business was their only source of income.

Analysis about how the mothers and communities met their responsibilities towards these six children are presented below.

Mothers' responsibilities to children with disabilities

The mothers spoke about how they met three sets of responsibilities towards their children – daily care, financial security and child development – and the impact of the responsibilities on the lives of their children and themselves. The complementary conceptualization of these responsibilities is the rights of these children to care, security and development relative to other children, irrespective of their disabilities. The mothers all spoke of their love towards their children and commitment to taking responsibility for their children in their daily life. Analysis of each of these three rights is presented below.

Daily care

The impact of disability on parental care for their children differed to the extent of the children's additional support needs, affecting the physical, emotional and time responsibilities and the longevity of the support. The families thought that the greatest impact was the care responsibilities, which usually fell to the women in the family and especially the mothers.

Some of the children needed high levels of personal care for daily needs, such as washing, eating, mobility and communication, causing distress to the child and family. Xiaojie's aunt said,

> When he was six years old, he cried all day … We guessed that he had a pain somewhere he could not tell us … He crawled on the floor until he was seven years old, and therefore his clothes wore out very fast. One third of the time every day is used for the boy. When he is outside, we rush to get him back because we are afraid of traffic accidents.

The mothers emphasized the additional time commitment to meet the children's needs. A mother said,

He is completely dependent in daily life. He needs somebody to be with him at almost all the time – about ten hours every day, or he would always cry if left alone … I use most of the day for him … Even at night he must sleep with me. Because he is skinny due to muscle atrophy, he cannot sleep for long without moving or he would feel pain. He has to ask me for help since he cannot move his body.

The mothers also supported their children outside their home, for example to get to and from places such as school or hospital. The cost of travel meant that the mothers usually travelled alone. For example, Xinxin's mother, who took him for medical treatments, said,

A railway ticket is so expensive, and we cannot afford more than one … When we came back from the hospital … the Zhengzhou train railway station is so big, I was walking in it with my son on my back, with bags in my hand, and with a trunk behind me, and so I attracted many eyes.

Some of the parents sent their children to school, so that they could have a break, rather than because they valued the education. However, the schools often asked mothers to take care of their children while they were at school. Xinxin's mother supported him at school,

He … needs to go to the washroom after the second class. He can walk by pushing his hands against the wall … but the teachers and other children do not help much … I need to be at the school four or five times every day, which is really a hard job.

Financial security

The second responsibility was financial. Most of the families had to solve their financial needs alone. The mothers said financial responsibility for their child with disabilities caused great pressure. They sought to earn sufficient money to support their families and to pay for the costs of disability support, including medical treatment, therapy and education. It was common for husbands to seek a divorce because of their child's disability and to refuse to support the family. In these cases, the mother both cared for the child and financially supported the family.

The mothers spoke about three problems fulfilling their financial responsibilities: some could not do any paid work because of their caring responsibility, which put extreme financial pressure on the family; some took responsibility for both work and care, which reduced their income capacity and, for most families, the extra costs of disability, such as medical treatment, therapy and school, necessitated borrowing and repaying money.

The financial responsibility was particularly heavy for single mothers, mothers whose husbands refused to financially support their families, and mothers who themselves had disabilities. Some mothers took whatever job they could to earn income, resulting in insecure jobs with flexible timing, low income and poor stability. Xiaoyan's single mother said,

> Now I feel great financial pressure on me because I have to take care of my daughter and cannot go out for work. I have been with her all the time since she was very young and I can never meet the hours of a normal job.

The minimum living security (MLS, discussed below) was not available to her or her daughter because they were registered as rural residents (MLS was an urban social security programme only at the time of this research). Without work, she operated a small retail shop at home to earn a limited amount of money. However the shop was on the brink of closing, because she did not have enough capital, cared for her daughter and could not open the shop regularly. Observing the financial difficulties, her daughter offered to go begging as the only thing she can do to help her mother. Her mother said,

> This shop generates very limited profit, only enough for the cost of electricity and house rent ... And the shelves are nearly empty because I cannot leave the child alone and go out to get more things. We often cope by borrowing. It's really hard ... I have not paid the house rent for a few months. The landlord keeps asking me for the rent every day, and says that I must move out if I cannot manage it.

In another case, Qianqian's parents divorced, and her father did not financially contribute to the mother and daughter. The mother quit her well-paid job in the wealthy city of Shenzhen to take Qianqian around China for medical treatment which used up all their savings. When they came back to their hometown, they had no income or housing, and had to live with the mother's sister, which caused frequent quarrels between the sister and her husband. The mother quickly married a farmer to address their financial strife. At the time of the research, the mother was working as a bookkeeper in the county town for a monthly pay of 300–400 yuan (£26–37; average national monthly income at the time was 2000 yuan – £181). Qianqian's stepfather worked with crops on the farm most of the time and came home to his wife and the child in the county town only when he was not busy.

In addition to living expenses, families spent large amounts of money for medical treatment, therapy and education to support their children with disabilities. Mostly, it was the mother of the child who was responsible for raising such money through borrowing, because they did not have sufficient income. Borrowing money and repaying debts usually lasted for years, adding to the heavy financial responsibility on the mothers. According to Anqi's mother, the surgery for her daughter cost hundreds of thousands of yuan, which she had to borrow and had been repaying the debt for seven years.

In another case, to meet the cost of family living and the cost of education and medical treatment for her child, a mother changed to a job to earn a higher salary rather than stay in the one for which she was qualified. She said, 'To repay the money I borrowed from my friends for a major surgery of my child, I had to change from teaching to selling insurance, which is much harder but more profitable than a teacher.'

Other mothers of children with disabilities had similar experiences of debts. Xinxin's mother said, 'Having such a child, you'll turn your wealth to nothing if you started with such wealth.' Similarly, Xiaoxing's mother took care of her daughter and at the same time worked hard for money to support the family and to repay her debt.

Child development

The third set of responsibilities was towards their children's development. Due to their support needs, the children needed more medical and therapy services, had difficulties accessing education, and were likely to require support when they were adults. Their mothers invested heavily in these immediate needs to improve the future prospects for their children.

In most parts of China, children with cerebral palsy did not receive therapy, either because it was too expensive or it was not available. Qianqian's mother took her daughter wherever therapy was available or where they heard of a famous doctor. They came home when they ran out money and continued the therapy at home. Her mother would help her,

> Every day whenever I was not at work, I helped her to walk. When she fell down, neither I nor others would help her to stand up, and I let her do it herself as an extra exercise. Later, she succeeded with her first steps, and then it was much easier.

After daily exercises with her mother's help, Qianqian learned to walk slowly by supporting herself with a walking stick or against the wall, and could help herself with most daily living activities. Her mother also taught her to speak and write because schools would not enrol her. Her mother said,

> At that time, I made myself as a child. I imitated the teacher in children's TV programmes in all ways including voices, facial expressions and gestures. I taught her with pronunciation, speaking and children's songs ... At the beginning, she wrote very big characters because she could not control her fingers. Then, I helped her by holding her hand. Now she can write beautiful characters.

Similarly, Xiaoxing's mother was completely focused on her daughter's support and future life prospects. The mother and daughter spent most of their time at hospitals until she was five years old. She had her cleft lip and palate repaired, so that she could eat well and improve her physical health. Because she needed support for daily living activities, her mother stayed with her most of the time and spoke with her as much as possible to help her progress. Her mother taught her by holding her hand in her own until she could write simple Chinese characters.

The mothers also took responsibility for the emotional resilience of their children, as they were likely to encounter discrimination. Anqi's mother taught her daughter to have an open mind, to use her imagination, and to be positive. She said, 'My daughter is an excellent girl. I believe she is a winner in life, not a loser, absolutely not. And I'm proud of her.'

Four of the six mothers also had a younger child (Qianqian, Anqi, Xiaoxing and Xinxin), with the expectation that the second child would support the child with disabilities after their parents died. McCabe and Barnes (2012) has a detailed discussion of this sibling relationship. Family planning rules in most locations allow a second child if the first child has disabilities. Anqi's mother said, 'I want my son to develop very well, so that his sister [Anqi] can get help from him in the future.' Xinxin's mother said that she had the second son, 'because Xinxin is very alone.' She said, 'The children can play together … and in the future when they grow up and we parents are no longer in this world, the brothers can support each other. At least Xinxin will not feel alone in this world.'

The mothers felt empathy with their children facing discrimination. Most of the mothers struggled for the rights of their children, including within the extended family, in the community and in institutions intended to provide support, such as schools, government agencies and the DPF. Sometimes they succeeded in gaining the services that should be unconditionally available according to the children's lawful rights but more often they failed to do so. Nevertheless, without the persistent struggle by their mothers, these children would not have received the support. The effort of Xinxin's mother was typical of the other mothers. Even when it was first clear that he had a disability, she had to fight with the other members of the family to obtain and pay for medical treatment. As she said, 'Without my strong demands, they would have given up [abandoned] the child very soon.'

In summary, the mothers took primary responsibility for meeting their children's rights to care, financial security and development, as they did with their other children. The rights of the children and mothers were compromised because the mothers were not able to share the responsibilities adequately through support from other family, community members or government services, as discussed later.

Shared responsibility in the community

The second aspect of the analysis is how the responsibilities were shared between the mother, other people and formal support services. The UN Conventions articulate the rights of children with disabilities and their mothers and place the responsibility on government to implement policies that construct a cultural, social and economic context to enable the fulfilment of these rights. The findings in this section reveal the degree to which the Chinese children and mothers experience a local context which supports that fulfilment.

Gendered role of sharing care

Most responsibilities fell on the mothers. A mother said, 'Since this is my own child, what else can I do?' If they had female relatives, they were sometimes able to share that responsibility. Single mothers without extended family members experienced the most difficulty. Xiaoyan's aunt said,

> Since the child's father died early when the child was less than two years old, the care responsibility has been completely put on her mother. When the child's grandmother was alive, she shared the care work, enabling the child's mother to work outside to support the family.

Sometimes, help from other relatives was needed, as the aunt said,

> Since the child needed care, her mother could not do anything else. When her mother fell ill, her grandmother would take over the care job. However, her grandmother got old and was in poor health, and therefore the responsibility moved onto us uncles and aunts.

She added, 'After the girl's grandmother passed way, her mother had to bear the complete care responsibility.'

The gendered responsibility for caring for children with disabilities was reflected in the mothers' experience of discrimination. When Xiaoxing was rejected by all of her father's family, including her grandparents and other relatives, they claimed her disability was her mother's fault, believing that their whole family was doomed by marriage to such a woman. Similarly, when Qianqian's mother and stepfather returned to the stepfather's hometown, a relative laughed at the mother and asked, 'How come you delivered a daughter who cannot walk? And, as an urban woman, how come you married a country guy?' She replied, 'God asked my daughter not to walk, so that I could tell good people from bad ones.'

While mothers were determined to fight the social discrimination against their children and themselves, such a responsibility took a heavy emotional toll on them. Once when Xiaoxing's mother could not endure the taunts of her sister-in-law any longer, she hid in her room with Xiaoxing, sobbing for three days without eating. When Qianqian and her mother were in Beijing for medical treatment, her mother fell down, injured her leg and she could not stand the pain. However, she dared not weep in front of others, but hid in a washroom and cried. These experiences reflect Chiu *et al.*'s (2013) analysis of affiliate stigma.

The consequences of not being able to share the responsibility fell on the mothers and the children. The fieldworker who interviewed Anqi's mother recorded,

> She bears all pressures from outside, including pressure from her family, negative attitude from others and discrimination. She never transfers her depression and resentment to her daughter, but does her best to provide the

love and education that the child needs. This is good for the child, but it puts the mother on the verge of a mental breakdown.

Qianqian's mother experienced emotional pressure caring for her daughter, even greater than the financial pressure. She said,

> At that time, I often cried at night, feeling out of breath, like there was a heavy stone on my chest … I dared not to think about her future, or I would break down … Sometimes I felt that I simply could not stand it anymore. I suffered from severe insomnia, and it was very hard, so I bought sleeping pills. I even thought that it would be good if I ate the pills and never woke up.

Anqi's mother minimized the expenses for herself so that she had the time and money to support her daughter. She said,

> Since Anqi was found with the disability, I have never had a single day for myself. This year, for example, I have never had any day off, except half a day of rest because of my cervical problem. I have devoted all my time to the girl.

The pressure on the mothers also affected the children. A fieldworker recorded that Xinxin's mother kept speaking about the great pressure on her from caring for two children and managing paid employment. She said sometimes she was tired from caring for the children, and was rude to them when they did not behave well.

Social support for the mothers

The social networks of the mothers were largely constrained. Qianqian's mother sighed, 'Speaking of friends, you know who your true friends are when you have real difficulties.' She said that many of her former classmates and good friends did not keep in touch with her any more. They were even reluctant to give any words of courtesy such as 'please drop in'. This was because they were afraid she would visit their homes and bring them trouble. They were especially afraid she would borrow money from them. Another mother said,

> Because of my daughter's conditions, I usually do not visit any of my friends together with her, except for really intimate friends. And I do not invite any friends to my home either … This is because I wouldn't like my blind daughter known to any more people, otherwise it seems that I'm asking for help from others. I don't think it is necessary to embarrass anyone in this way. This more or less alienates me from some of my friends.

Instead, their circles of relatives and friends were small, restricted to people who understood, respected and supported them. Qianqian's mother said she would feel shame if she spoke with others to relieve the pressure on her and she did not think it would help to improve their life. Another mother said, 'Those truly kind-hearted are my friends, and I'll always remember them … and those who mistreat people with disabilities are simply not human.' Parents in McCabe's (2008a) short-term intervention programme emphasized that the most important support in the programme was from each other.

Income and social service support

In addition to sharing responsibilities with extended family and friends, some mothers were able to access government income and social service support. Financial responsibility was alleviated for families who lived in locations with government support. The major government income support programme relevant to families of children with disabilities was the minimum living security (MLS). The MLS coverage was limited to the most poverty-stricken families and the payment was very low (Shang and Wu 2004). Of the 52 families of children with disabilities in the full research study, those living in Beijing had slightly better financial conditions than those in other areas, and they received more support from the state. In other areas, social security was improving for families of children with disabilities, but in general, state subsidies were only available to a small proportion of families of children with disabilities in China.

In Hunan province, Qianqian's mother received the MLS, which met their basic financial needs. In locations without social security support, mothers' financial situation could be desperate, especially when a father did not contribute. Qianqian's mother for example said they only used a very low-wattage bulb in their room and only turned it on when it was very dark, because they could not afford the electricity.

Government support services for mothers or children with disabilities also remained scarce in most locations. Even central policies intended for these children, such as inclusive education in mainstream schools, were only available if their mothers persistently argued their case. The exception was in some big cities, such as Beijing. For example, Anqi received special school education that was almost free. After her mother repaid the debt for her medical treatment, her family's financial status was stable and at a living standard similar to families without children with disabilities.

Apart from Anqi, all the other children had experienced many barriers before they could attend school. When Xinxin reached school age the school refused to enrol him and his mother had to fight for him to attend. His mother had to negotiate with the headmaster of the school indirectly, through a connection in the local education bureau. Xinxin's enrolment was granted with many conditions, including that his mother had to sign an agreement to exempt the school from liability for any accident, and that he would not take the school examinations (so as not to lower the school average). She said,

> I agreed to the conditions because I wished he could be educated, could learn about some common knowledge on life and the society … and there is

something like interpersonal communication that cannot be learned at home. This is a design for his future.

Then at school, Xinxin encountered discrimination in the classroom – without consideration of his poor eyesight, the teacher insisted that he sit at the back of the class, furthest from the blackboard, arguing that he would be in the way of others if he sat in the front. Xinxin's mother repeatedly asked the teacher to move the boy forward, but the teacher refused.

Other mothers of children with disabilities encountered similar treatment. Xiaoxing was regarded as a burden by all family members except her mother; and only after her mother's persistent effort did she receive medical treatment and education. In contrast, Xiaoyan's mother did not try to enrol her daughter at school because she knew she did not have sufficient influence to win the arguments.

In summary, although most mothers sought assistance from others to meet the rights of their children, they were stymied by unsupportive attitudes from family, friends and community members. They also encountered discrimination when seeking access to formal services to which other children were entitled, such as education. Limited government support was common for all families, such as having to pay fees for medical and therapy and no income support in rural areas. The difference for children with disabilities however, was that they were more likely to need this formal support to meet their basic rights.

Conclusion about support for mothers

The case studies of families of children with disabilities around China showed that these mothers took primary responsibility for their children's rights to care, financial security and development. They felt an emotional cost for these responsibilities because they often had no choice to share them. Some mothers had no support within their nuclear families if the father had abandoned the family due to the child's disabilities. These fathers did not contribute socially or financially to the child or mother's needs.

Some mothers were able to call upon their extended family members, particularly other women, for support. Other mothers, however, experienced condemnation from the extended family for having children with disabilities. Equally, they described rejection by friends, who were fearful of the mothers calling upon them to provide financial and emotional support to care for their children. For these social reasons, many of the mothers were protective of their emotional vulnerability and did not seek help from friends or people in the community (also Wang *et al.* 2011). For a similar finding about support for Chinese parents in the US, see Lo (2008). Unfortunately, only mothers who were urban residents in large developed cities were able to access government financial or social service support. Even then, they had to argue to protect their children's right to free services such as primary school education.

Clearly the rights of these children and mothers to be cared for within their family (Art. 23 CRPD) were compromised by these circumstances. In the Chinese context, the impact of few options for mothers to share their responsibilities was accentuated by the local cultural conceptions of disability and mothering responsibilities. These attitudes negatively affected not only the rights of children with disabilities, but also the rights of their mothers. Their rights were compromised by the social expectation of mothers' isolated responsibility, resulting from poor support from the fathers' extended family, former friends and the state. Negative factors included social discrimination against mothers and children with disabilities, insufficient social support to families of children with disabilities, and failure to allocate resources and implement policies at a local level.

The social discrimination and indifference to families of children with disabilities were not alleviated by support from the government agencies that were expected to provide services for families of children with disabilities according to central government policy. In regions where adequate support was available from the government and the service agencies were responsible, such as Beijing, the mothers experienced much less pressure.

These findings are not dissimilar to the experiences of mothers of children with disabilities in other countries (Ryan and Runswick 2008), although perhaps more stark. An interesting aspect of the analysis is the contrasting experience of the mothers in Beijing and other large cities, which were not as dire but still illustrated the emotional isolation of the mothers. This contrasting experience parallels the differential economic development, where eastern municipal governments have the financial resources to implement the aspirational national policies to meet the rights of people with disabilities, such as income support, social services and inclusive education. Further research comparing the experiences of mothers and fathers in the areas of China that are in the process of economic change could alter the social service implications of these findings. Related research about fathers' support and interactions with social services emphasizes the need for service providers to communicate with parents to support maintenance of strength within the family (Huang, Chen and Tsai 2012).

This economic development interpretation of the families' experiences avoids the need to resort to cultural and historical generalizations about Chinese attitudes to disability and mothering, referred to in the background literature to this chapter (Ma 2002; Huang, Fried and Hsu 2009). Similar historical norms were evident in European disability experience, where mothers and their children with disabilities continue to experience discrimination (Goodley and Runswick-Cole 2011), but these attitudes are no longer tolerated in legal, policy and social standards. Economic development and redistribution through social policy would seem to be the key to addressing the right of children with disabilities to live in their families and to supporting mothers to sustain that right.

References

Chiu, M.Y.L., Yang, X., Wong, F.H.T., Li, J.H. and Li, J. (2013) Caregiving of children with intellectual disabilities in China – an examination of affiliate stigma and the cultural thesis. *Journal of Intellectual Disability Research* 57: 1117–1129.

CRPD, United Nations Convention on the Rights of Persons with Disabilities (2006). www.un.org/disabilities/default.asp?id=150 [1 February 2012].

Goodley, D. and Runswick-Cole, K. (2011) Problematising policy: conceptions of 'child', 'disabled' and 'parents' in social policy in England. *International Journal of Inclusive Education* 15(1): 71–85.

Huang, Y.-P., Chen, S.-L. and Tsai, S.-W. (2012) Father's experiences of involvement in the daily care of their child with developmental disability in a Chinese context. *Journal of Clinical Nursing* 21: 3287–3296.

Huang, Y.T., Fried, J.H. and Hsu, T.H. (2009) Taiwanese mothers' attitude change toward individuals with disabilities. *Journal of Social Work in Disability and Rehabilitation* 8: 82–94.

Lister, R. (2006) Children (but not women) first: New Labour, child welfare and gender. *Critical Social Policy* 26, 315–335.

Lo, L. (2008) Perceived benefits experienced in support groups for Chinese families of children with disabilities. *Early Child Development and Care* 180: 405–415.

Ma, H.L. (ed.) (2002) *Social Welfare for China's Disabled Persons*, Beijing: China Social Press.

McCabe, H. (2008a) The importance of parent-to-parent support among families of children with autism in the People's Republic of China. *International Journal of Disability, Development and Education* 55: 303–314.

McCabe, H. and Barnes, R.E. (2012) Autism in a family in China: an investigation and ethical consideration of sibling issues. *International Journal of Disability, Development and Education* 59: 197–207.

Oliver, M. (1996) *Understanding disability: from theory to practice*, Hampshire: Palgrave.

Ryan, S. and Runswick-Cole, K. (2008) Repositioning mothers: mothers, disabled children and disability studies. *Disability & Society* 23(3): 199–210.

Shakespeare, T. (2006) *Disability Rights and Wrongs*, New York: Routledge.

Shang, X. and Fisher, K.R. (2014) Social support for mothers of children with disabilities in China. *Journal of Social Service Research* 10.1080/01488376.2014.896849.

Shang, X. and Wu, X. (2004) Changing approaches of social protection: social assistance reform in urban China. *Journal of Social Policy and Society* 33: 259–271.

Wang, P., Michaels, C.A. and Day, M.S. (2011) Stresses and coping strategies of Chinese families with children with autism and other developmental disabilities. *Journal of Autism and Developmental Disorders* 41(6): 783–795.

7 Right to care and protection
Alternative family care

Not all children with disabilities have the option to remain living with their families (Art. 18, 23 CRPD). Children without parents who are in the guardianship of the state are the responsibility of a local State Child Welfare Institution, as introduced in Chapter 4. This chapter focuses on the growing practice of some institutions that arrange foster care for children with disabilities. It considers how some children are placed with foster families and receive therapy services in that community. In a pilot project in Greentown (name changed), the State Child Welfare Institution trained foster parents in home-based therapy and provided professional services to children with disabilities living with foster families in selected rural villages. The practice has operated for more than a decade, where more than 600 children with disabilities have grown up in alternative family care in these communities. The chapter explores whether specialized foster care could be an option at all State Child Welfare Institutions in China, where most of the orphaned children who still live in institutions have disabilities.

Greentown State Child Welfare Institution foster care project

Greentown State Child Welfare Institution arranges care for about 700 children in foster care and in the institution. The Institution's policy is to arrange permanent family placement for children, so it prioritizes adoption, consistent with the UN Guidelines on Alternative Child Care (UNGACC 2009). From 2000 to 2010, 474 children were adopted, leading to a higher proportion of children with disabilities remaining in the institution. Children with disabilities for whom the Institution was responsible reached 90 per cent (Table 7.1) at the end of 2010. The reasons for this change included the fact that fewer children without disabilities came into state care and when they did, it was easier for the Institution to find adoptive families for them (Shang and Fisher 2013).

The Greentown State Child Welfare Institution began foster care in 2000. Now their main care model is foster care in rural villages and only a small proportion of children (14 per cent) live in the institution. New children receive temporary institutional care for observation, treatment or while waiting for adoption. The children living permanently in the Institution all have additional care needs, such

Table 7.1 Children with disabilities in the guardianship of the Greentown State Child Welfare Institution

| | | Per cent of children with | |
	No disability	Mild/moderate disability	Severe disability
2000	62	38	0
2001	36	31	32
2002	30	22	47
2003	24	39	36
2004	24	31	45
2005	25	29	46
2006	16	48	35
2007	13	46	41
2008	12	44	44
2009	10	17	73
2010	9	17	74

Source: Greentown State Child Welfare Institution n=approximately 700 children per year

Note: By 2010 most children lived in foster care (86 per cent), and the remainder lived in the Institution

as severe disabilities, congenital heart conditions and infectious diseases which, by central policy, means they are ineligible for adoption or foster care.

The high proportion of children with disabilities for whom the Institution has guardianship poses extra responsibilities. As these children have no known parents or extended family, the care provided to them must not only create stable foster family attachment, it must also provide disability support and professional intervention specific to the child's needs. The challenge facing the Greentown Institution is how to provide community-based foster care and therapy services to the children. This has become a major policy issue facing most State Child Welfare Institutions in China.

The Greentown response was to develop a new specialized type of foster care programme, so that the children could both live in a family and receive the disability support they needed. The approach has the following features: specialized foster care therapy centres established in local communities; foster parents trained with skills for therapy; family homes adapted for simple therapy facilities according to the needs of the children; doctors and professionals from the State Child Welfare Institution working in the foster villages; and children supported with an individual development plan and receiving support, training and supervision from their trained parents. This chapter examines the effectiveness of this design.

Research methods

The research examined the specialized foster care practices with the following question: are the children's needs for quality family-based care; health and therapy services; and social inclusion met through the foster care? In this book, we refer to therapy and therapist, rather than rehabilitation, to be consistent with a social understanding of disability, except in proper nouns. The analytical framework was child rights, outlined in Chapter 2. Participatory methods were used; that is, the children and families actively participated in the research collection and the child welfare providers (including managers and staff of the child welfare institution) participated in all research stages, including the analysis. The staff used the research process to strengthen its institutional capacity building and develop human resources for family foster caring. The Institution director asked Dr Shang to conduct the research because she had conducted earlier research at the same site when the programme first began, so had the benefit of observing change (Shang 2002, 2012).

Methods included questionnaires, in-depth interviews and seminars to collect data about the programme. Respondents included staff at the Institution, foster parents and children aged seven and older. Questionnaires were specific to each group but common to the analytical framework to enable triangulation between the results. Interviews were conducted with the participation of Greentown State Child Welfare Institution staff. Three foster care villages were sampled. The face-to-face questionnaire survey was conducted with all eligible parents and children in these communities. A total of 100 pairs of questionnaires were distributed to parents and children in the group (99 questionnaires were completed by parents and 100 by the children). Thirty questionnaires were distributed to Greentown State Child Welfare Institution staff. Foster families were also selected for semi-structured in-depth interviews based on the age, sex, disability status and other characteristics of the children in the household. The interviews were conducted in the families' homes to obtain observation data. The research team organized two focus groups with children and parents, and two focus groups with managers and professional staff. The research team also conducted field observations in the foster care villages to observe the conditions of foster families, the therapy approaches used by the foster parents, the daily life of the fostered children and therapy training. In addition, the child records at the Institution were reviewed, and typical cases over the past ten years were selected for follow-up to conduct comparative research in terms of time sequence and cross-sectional situations. The Institution appointed another team to conduct anthropological research about the impact of the foster care project on the rural communities, which was not available to this research team, although the two teams met during the research to discuss preliminary findings.

The limitations to the methods were that although the research was initiated by the Institution, the staff were unfamiliar with participatory research approaches and were wary about the risks of scrutiny. The opportunities for self-reflection by the staff were therefore limited during most of the research. The visits to the foster families were arranged by the Institution staff so were probably biased towards good examples. In addition, the researchers were unable to meet young people with disabilities who had left the programme to ask their opinions because, in this city, young adult orphans with disability were the responsibility of another part of the government. These limits were mitigated by the use of mixed methods, observation and critical analysis of the data.

Management of the foster care programme

A foster care programme needs arrangements to ensure the safety and wellbeing of children placed in family-based care. This programme focused on establishing quality family-based care, professional therapy services and a means to integrate the children into the community. The policies they developed to meet these three goals are described below.

Foster carer recruitment, training and supervision

The main determinant of quality in foster care is the relationship with the foster care family. The programme established procedures for foster carer recruitment, training and supervision. The methods used by the Greentown State Child Welfare Institution included: setting high criteria for selecting foster families (at least two adults in the household, experience raising their own children, quality housing including number of rooms and internal sanitation; helping families to prepare for fostering children; and providing pre-fostering parent training, including procedures for application, making an agreement, rights and duties of foster families, children and the Institution, and expectations of the parents. The training also covered technical issues, such as physical and psychological characteristics of orphans and children with disabilities, scientific child-rearing and safety.

After being trained, interested families could apply to become foster families by completing an assessment form. Staff from the Institution and village leaders visited the applicant's home to assess sanitation, housing and living conditions. These reports were the foundation for matching children and foster families. After all these procedures, a child was placed with the family that was regarded as the most suitable for his or her development. The parents received ongoing training specific to the needs of the child, as described below.

Foster supervision was highly regulated and well resourced in comparison to international norms. The Institution supervised the foster families with regular and random visits to protect the rights and interests of the children and promoted the sustainable development of foster arrangements. It operated a three-tiered supervision network from the township, village committee and villagers' team, leveraging the structured roles of each in the Chinese local governance system. The procedures included home visits by staff, performance assessments of foster families, reports of emergencies via telephone and follow-up reports from the responsible people. This supervision system provided a powerful organizational structure for foster care. The foster care office was responsible for the planning, coordination and implementation of the supervision. The townships, village committees and villagers' teams were responsible for contacting and coordinating villagers. This close co-operation enabled all-round supervision and monitoring of the care given to fostered children and helped integrate the fostered children into the community.

The foster care office also organized weekly home visits from therapy, care, education and medical professionals. During home visits, professionals provided guidance for foster families based on the families' reports and their own observations of changes in the children. Together with the foster parents, they developed individual plans and guidance on diet and nutrition for different ages of fostered children. This follow-up mechanism ensured the participation of professionals in family fostering.

The Institution supervised all aspects of the children's lives and provided support and training for foster parents, including guidance and supervision of family diet, skill training and evaluations every three months. For children younger than six, growth and development measurements were conducted every one or two months. If children failed to meet growth and development indicators an examination was conducted to identify possible causes and recommendations for improvement or, if necessary, punishment measures were then made to the foster family. The families were accountable to the point of surveillance, all in the interests of protecting the children. Although the families did not voice their dissatisfaction, local researchers commented on the intrusive level of supervision.

Over the last ten years, the Institution had developed a system to assess the quality of foster care. It consisted of a hundred-score assessment and management. This system combined fund management and project management ensuring the quality of fostering through the linkage of the hundred-score assessment with fund management. Staff responsible for the management of foster families provided guidance during weekly home visits. Monthly wrap-up meetings were organized for foster families to identify and address existing problems. Annual summary meetings were also held to summarize and evaluate the performance of foster families, and to select families with excellent performance and present them with awards.

Financial management

Adequate financial support for children with disabilities and their foster parents was essential for successful foster care. The Institution implemented unified, strict and standard procedures for supervising and managing foster funds as well as for monitoring the quality of foster care, including process controls, result assessments, and disciplinary measures based on performance auditing. When the families first applied to be foster carers, the Institution also provided financial assistance to modify their homes to meet sanitary and safety requirements. The Institution provided a living allowance for the children and a care payment for parents, and tried to increase the payments regularly to match increases in average wages. Between 2000 and 2010, the monthly payment for each child increased from 100 to 1000 yuan (£9 to £91). On average, the annual increase rate reached 126 per cent, which was greater than the increase in GDP or the residents' average income.

The Institution developed rules about allowable expenditure items to supervise the use of the children's living allowances. It encouraged foster parents to participate in the management of the programme to enhance quality of life for the children and ensured their access to better services. It tied the care payment increases to new standards for quality of care each time. It also paid more to parents caring for children with severe disabilities, as they provided more therapy services to these children.

Given the diverse characteristics of fostered children, foster families could make reasonable adjustments to the use of foster fees, as long as they adhered to the principle of fully protecting the rights and interests of the children and meeting their nutritional needs, daily necessities, medical treatment, therapy, education and care. Once these needs were covered, the remaining portion could be used at the discretion of the foster families, to achieve optimal benefits. The parents said they were satisfied with the level and timing of the living expenses for the foster children in the focus groups. The positive contribution to household financial security is discussed further in the next section.

The Institution organized pooled purchase of the commodities most needed by children, such as milk powder and clothes to ensure that the children had access to quality commodities. This helped foster parents to buy high-quality commodities and avoid inferior or fake products that might negatively affect the children's health.

Family-based care

The research examined whether the children's needs for quality family-based care were met. Principles of good quality alternative care included stable family-based care, permanency, culture and identity, and participation (UNGACC 2009). The Institution made a great effort to instil good practice and ensure children's needs for quality care were met. As described above, this included choosing the right foster families, training and supervising them and providing adequate professional and financial support. Research observations about the practices developed to support quality family-based care are described below.

The most important factor in meeting the need for quality family care was the foster parents: did they have the capacity and intention to provide quality care for the children? The findings in this section are from the questionnaires and interviews. The relationships between the children and parents appeared close and natural, especially for young children, who were obviously very attached to their foster parents. The children were asked, in the absence of their parents, 'Who do you prefer to stay with when you're ill?' Most children said their foster member, and others said other extended family members including their father, mother, grandfather, grandmother or sister. Others selected a schoolmate or a friend. When asked, 'What would you buy if you had one yuan?', a few choose to buy a gift or food for their foster family members (mother, brothers or others), while most selected stationery. These answers seem typical of family relationships.

Most of the foster parents were forty to fifty years old. It was an appropriate age for fostering children with disabilities support needs because they were still physically capable and were experienced in raising children and taking on responsibilities. Most families the researchers visited had three generations living together, typical of village households. The families included up to four foster children, the foster parents' own children (and sometimes the adult children's children), the foster parents and grandparents. The foster children in each family were placed to be diverse in age and sex, forming a similar structure to other families.

Most of these parents had some school education – 44 per cent primary school, 48 per cent junior high school, 5 per cent high school (including technical and vocational high schools). Only 3 per cent had no education. The foster parents had multiple motivations for fostering a child (Table 7.2).

The families seemed financially secure. Most foster parents did fostering full time, with no other job (80 per cent). They told us how beneficial it was to the household that the family members no longer needed to do low-paid, sometimes dangerous, migrant work in the city. The income from the foster care was sufficient that they could stay home and support the child and other family carers instead. A large proportion of the villages were foster care households so this had increased the number of adults staying in the villages. The younger generation of adults with their own young children now also wanted to become foster carers. Other villagers who were not currently fostering children told the researchers they would like to become foster parents.

The Institution records on foster care household conditions demonstrated above average conditions in the villages, reinforced by the family questionnaire results and observations in ten households. Average net family annual income was 10,000 yuan (£909). The houses were at least 120 m², and more than half were double that size (200–300 m²). A requirement of the programme was that they had clean drinking water and sanitary bathrooms; electrical appliances, including television, telephones, refrigerators and electric ovens; and toys and books for the children. The quantity and quality of their food and drink was similar to those of other villagers.

The foster parents said they were satisfied with their relations with their children, their payment and the support from the Greentown State Child Welfare Institution. Nearly 93 per cent of the foster parents said they had a sense of pride and honour in their work, which contrasts with most State Child Welfare Institution nurses, who complained about their pay and career opportunities. This parental pride benefited the children, who were fostered by people who cared for them full time, felt proud of their work, and were satisfied with their pay.

Table 7.2 Motivations for fostering a child

	Per cent
Income from foster care fees	95
Help children in need	79
Like children	71
Own children are adults or do not have children	51
Companion for own children	39

Source: Parent questionnaire n=99

The Institution provided emotional support to families because of the additional demands of foster care for children with disabilities. The therapy that they required the parents to conduct required long-term commitment to be sustainable and beneficial for the children. On festival days, Institution staff brought foster families and their foster children gifts, to demonstrate the care and respect from the public for their work. Every year, outstanding foster families were identified and commended to encourage their enthusiasm and sense of responsibility towards the child foster work.

Health and therapy

The next question was whether the children's health and disability therapy needs were also met. The State Child Welfare Institution invested considerably in this aspect of the support to families and children, particularly related to additional disability support to achieve child development goals. The foster parents need professional and emotional support to care for and support children with disabilities. When a new child joins a foster family, the Institution begins continuous follow-up support to the family. Professional rehabilitators devise individual therapy plans for the children and their foster families. The families are given therapy training and information on how to take care of foster children in different age groups. Medical workers visit each foster site every month for vaccinations and periodic physical examinations of foster children in different age groups. Institution staff follow-up observations of the therapy of 125 family fostered children with disabilities show that most children improved on most measures (Table 7.3).

The Institution's approach to sustainable therapy was to build a therapy and special education centre in the largest foster village, train the families in home-based therapy and support them with regular visits from professionals for ongoing professional and emotional support. The centre supports therapy and special education for more than 140 children with disabilities fostered in the village. After the success of the first centre in a village, the Institution built similar centres of various sizes and facilities in the other villages, with the assistance of NGOs and active support of foster families.

Table 7.3 Children's measures of development from Institution staff observations

	Per cent of children improved		
	Total	Some improvement	Great improvement
Emotional development	97	–	–
Sense of family	95	–	–
Physical health	90	46	44
Personality	88	43	45
Sociability	86	61	25
Living skills	82	–	–
Language development	–	–	50
Learning ability	61	–	–

Source: Institution records of children's follow up observations n=125. – indicates missing data

Table 7.4 Type of support foster families said they needed

	Per cent
Technical therapy support	95
Emotional support	75
Social connection support	65
Financial support	59

Source: Parent questionnaire n=99

The key to the quality of the approach was the professionals who visit the village and each family to design and support the implementation of an individual therapy plan for each child. Their professional support reinforced the commitment from the parents to provide therapy to each child every day. This approach makes the therapy model sustainable and addresses the shortage and cost of therapists in welfare institutions. In addition, the critical role of the foster parents in the therapy of the children with disabilities was reflected in the research meeting with 30 foster parents. Asked how confident they were helping in the therapy, most parents smiled and raised their hands, showing that they were very confident. This was due to the sustained encouragement and training from the professionals, the peer support training they receive from each other and the visible change in the children.

The training of parents to support the development and therapy include basic child care training before they are accepted into the foster care project and specific individual and group courses designed to improve the quality of care. The topics included education for healthy foster children; training in parenting infants and mother–child education; and therapy for children with disabilities. Many of the children had cerebral palsy so the family- and group-based activities encouraged physical therapy to maximize mobility. Most foster families said they needed all the types of support offered, particularly technical support for caring for a child with disabilities (95 per cent; Table 7.4). Interestingly, most families also recognized that they needed emotional support for the demanding role they played (75 per cent), demonstrating the need for ongoing professional support.

Social inclusion and education

The last question was whether the children's needs for social inclusion and education were met. As described above, the households generally included three generations and appeared relaxed with each other and with the foster children. Foster children were playing with siblings and other children in the streets, community hall and houses during the research visits. The children appeared well loved and the young ones seemed happy, animated and settled in their relationships. Some children proudly showed the researchers their house and bedroom and introduced their siblings and friends.

The villages are in rural areas with convenient transportation and communication. The physical setting of the villages are pleasant, having recovered from a past history of mining. The children are growing up in a healthy environment with fresh air, clean water, and safe open spaces for playing. The region where the foster care villages are has a drug use problem, but it was not evident in the villages or the foster families.

The Institution was concerned to achieve community inclusion for the children so that they could develop social networks to sustain them into adulthood. It had coordinated local resources to create child friendly communities, such as an accessible community hall. It negotiated with local authorities to have all the local schools accept the children with disabilities. Most school age children were enrolled in local schools, with more children in foster care at a local school (92.2 per cent) than children who lived in the Institution (61.5 per cent).

Some children could not enter either local or special schools because of inaccessibility for their physical disabilities, wheelchairs or special care that local schools did not provide. For example, a few children with disabilities were denied enrolment at local schools because the schools did not have accessible classrooms or toilets and the teachers were not trained to support the children. Such circumstances are common in China, especially in rural areas (Chapter 10 and Chapter 1). The Institution was negotiating with local schools to try to address the problems.

Some of the children were frustrated that they could not attend school due to inaccessibility. Some of the teenagers seemed less satisfied than the younger children, as reported by staff and observed by the researchers. They had become more aware of the implications for their family relationship of the foster arrangements and their post-school options were limited due to their disabilities and living in a rural village. Between middle school age (fifteen years) and adulthood (eighteen years) there is a gap in welfare services for these children, helping them to manage the transition to adulthood and employment services. This has serious consequences for the young adults because the project is designed and implemented by the State Child Welfare Institution. When they turn eighteen, they are no longer the responsibility of the child welfare system. If at eighteen they do not have a job or means to live independently, they are once again institutionalized in aged care institutions or adult disability institutions. Some young women have managed to marry within the village to avoid this. Young people with high disability support needs are the most disadvantaged, because they have no capacity for independent income and the families can no longer afford to care for them without the financial support from the Child Welfare Institute.

Another social risk arises because these villages were selected and created as 'foster mother villages', and for the efficiency of the Institution, large numbers of foster children now live in them. It is likely that these villages are labelled, or even discriminated against, in the wider community. It also makes the villages economically and socially vulnerable to policy change in the Institution or central government.

From the perspective of child social inclusion, the project was very successful. The strictly applied supervision and management rules may not, however, consider the rights of the foster parents. For example, to guarantee the quality of purchased milk powder, the parents have to purchase the milk powder recommended by the Institution, and provide the Institution with empty bags as evidence; to check the quality of every day meals provided to the children, the responsible staff have the right to enter any foster family at dinner time without an appointment. All of these arrangements safeguard the safety of fostered children, but ignore the rights of parents. The interviews with parents suggest that parents want to have more say in project management.

Conclusion about alternative care protection

This chapter examined an example of specialized foster care as a model of rural community foster care of orphaned children with disabilities to fulfil their right to care and protection in alternative family care in the absence of their birth family (Art. 23 CRPD). In this programme, children in foster care grew up in selected rural villages. The children benefited from the family-like environment, foster parents who loved and cared for them and child-friendly communities. They also benefited from therapy provided by trained foster parents, under the supervision of experienced professionals. The environment in which they grew up is considerably better than institutional care.

The contribution to child welfare was positive – the rights of the children in foster families were respected; they had financial security and personal safety; they were protected against abuse through training and three level supervision; the right to education was fulfilled for most children, except those with access needs; they were physically well developed and covered by medical insurance; and they were mostly healthy and happy. The research of the child welfare conditions suggests that rural family fostered children develop both physically and emotionally, taking into account the characteristics of children with disabilities; that the therapy benefit on the children with disabilities is significant; and that the children formed stable familial relationships with their foster families and communities. The foster relationships were stable, usually only disrupted if the child was adopted.

The weaknesses in the model were access to local school education for children with restricted mobility; support for young adults as they transition to adulthood to avoid reinstitutionalization after the age of eighteen or financial support to the families from other parts of government to continue the adult foster care relationship, as is available in some other Provinces; and the vulnerability of the foster families and foster villages to changes in Institution policies.

The last three chapters have examined rights to care and protection, including rights to life (Art. 10, 16 CRPD); care within the family, including support for mothers (Art. 23); and quality alternative care in the absence of the birth family (Art. 18, 23). They demonstrate that some parts of the state are responding to children and family rights, either under pressure from community demands; from resource opportunities now available through local or regional economic development; or through innovative practice in the context of constrained community resources. The next chapter shifts to the household level and to the right to economic security through earnings or state support (Art. 28 CRPD).

References

CRPD, United Nations Convention on the Rights of Persons with Disabilities (2006) www.un.org/disabilities/default.asp?id=150 [1 February 2012].

Shang, X. (2002) Looking for a better way to care for children: cooperation between the state and civil society. *Social Service Review* 76(2): 203–228.

Shang, X. (2012) Looking for best practice in caring for disabled children: a case of socialized foster care in China. *Asia Pacific Journal of Social Work and Development* 22(1–2): 127–138.

Shang, X. and Fisher, K.R. (2013) *Caring for Orphaned Children in China*, Lanham: Lexington Books.

UNGACC, United Nations Guidelines for the Alternative Care of Children (2009) www.unicef.org/aids/files/UN_Guidelines_for_alternative_care_of_children.pdf [13 July 2014].

8   Right to economic security

The relationship between economic circumstances and disability is multi-directional and affects not only children's right to economic security but also many other aspects of the lives of children and their families. This chapter analyses the practical constraints on economic security in families of children with disabilities compared to other children in China, by focusing on poverty rates, economic activity, access to social security and costs of disability (Art. 28 CRPD). It discusses the economic status of families of children with disabilities, including the extent, severity and causes of poverty and economic participation in terms of family production and employment. It includes the subjective experiences of economic security of families and draws conclusions about the risks of poverty from disability in China.

Data in this chapter are from the Second China National Sample Survey on Disability (SCNSSD 2006) 10 per cent sample (Chapter 1). In addition, case studies from the fieldwork interviews were selected to illustrate the multi-directional relationship between economic security and disability. The details of the case study families are described during the chapter.

Relationship between economic security and disability

The reasons for poverty in families of children with disabilities are intertwined (WHO 2011). Economic security affects and is affected by other household and contextual factors, such as the interdependence of household members, location, sex, and family and community socio-economic conditions. Poverty itself can lead to disabilities. Families living in poverty are more likely to experience disability because of risks from their living conditions, including nutrition, illness, accidents and access to treatment, especially in transition countries such as China (Lygnegard *et al.* 2013). People spoke about examples of poverty causing disability, such as a grandmother who said,

> The child would have been healthy if the family was not so poor, if his mother had not had malnutrition, and if his mother had not had premature labour; even if the child was mute, the situation would have been better. Looking at him, we feel very sad, and we can only try to take good care of him.

The father of another child, Qingqing, was very poor and could not afford to marry well, so he married a deaf woman recommended by the daughter of his uncle. Qingqing inherited her mother's deafness. In one of the fieldwork villages with over 1,000 residents, more than 150 people had disabilities due to poverty and marriage of people with disabilities and genetic conditions. The high incidence of disability further exacerbated the poverty in the village.

The costs of disability can also aggravate economic pressure within a household (Xiong *et al.* 2011). Family members with disabilities and without state support can result in additional costs to families, particularly in a country like China, where families take primary responsibility for the costs of social support in most parts of the country (Chapter 4). Additional costs include direct disability support costs, such as medical expenses, therapy and equipment; daily living costs that are sometimes increased by disability, such as accessible housing, mobility and communications; and in China, the higher costs of larger families (having a child with a disability triggers exceptions to the one child policy). Costs of disability are age-related because of changing support, with younger children dominated by health, therapy and equipment costs; and school-age children's costs dominated by education and training costs.

Disability can also reduce earning capacity due to additional caring responsibilities. There are opportunity costs, such as reduced capacity to work due to caring responsibilities. Children with disabilities can face access barriers to social and education opportunities, which not only affects their childhood, but also their future social and economic participation. Parents of children with disabilities may face fewer employment opportunities and working hours due to additional care responsibility for children with disabilities, thus leading to lower household income.

In a service system such as China's, where families must pay for support in most parts of the country, the experience of poverty determines the realization of many children's rights. The importance of supporting the family unit in China for disadvantaged families and its barrier to service acquisition was explained by Deng and Holdsworth (2007) in their evaluation of the Gansu Basic Education Project (GBEP) in Gansu Province, China. Poor rural families could not prioritize time and resources to participate in disability support for their children. This was both due to cultural beliefs and because their status as a poor family made maintaining a basic standard of living a greater priority than providing disability support for their child.

Poverty and economic security also affect other rights such as education. UNICEF (2006) identifies poverty as one of the key barriers to children receiving an adequate education. Where additional support is not available or is unaffordable, disability can be an impediment to children accessing education, further accentuated in families in poverty (Clarke 2006). In China, this is the case particularly for families living in rural areas. A combination of population mobility, property development and corrupt local officials has led to the dispossession of some rural Chinese families from arable land. For many families in rural China, 'land was not only a means of livelihood, but also a form of security' (Chan, Ngok and Phillips 2008: 180). Land is not only a source of income but an insurance against poverty that increases the risk of economic insecurity after removal.

Incidence of poverty

The first aspect of understanding economic security of children with disabilities is the incidence of poverty. Poverty is higher in families of children with disabilities and highest in families with several children with disabilities. This chapter defines income poverty as where the household income is lower than the local minimum living protection line or poverty line. The analysis assumes that household income changes if under the same conditions it includes children with disabilities, due to the additional expenditures and opportunity costs to parents without the time for income activities. Household income includes annual income of all family members living together. Families of children with disabilities are classified into urban and rural. The children in the analysis are aged less than eighteen and children are divided into three age groups, since expenditures vary by age; for example, education expenditure and the impact of disability may change. Disability has considerable impact on household living standards and average annual household incomes (Table 8.1). The more children with disabilities in the family, the lower the annual household income and living standard. Families of children with disabilities pay additional costs, which reduces their living standard.

Household living standard is lower with an increasing number of children with disabilities in families, the increasing age of the children, and the location of the family. The analysis shows a strong relationship between household living standards and the number of children with disabilities (Table 8.2). The living standard was lower in families where there were more children with disabilities (consistent with Table 8.1). Living standards were higher in urban families and families in the north and northeast of China. Rural families of children with disabilities and families in central, southwest and northwest China were worse off. Living standards were lower the older the children (primary and high school age children compared to children aged 0–5 years). The sex of the child and tertiary education were not significant.

Table 8.1 Living standard and income of households of children with disabilities, per cent

Number of children with disabilities in household	Per cent Living standard			Household income 1000 yuan	Number of children
	Low	Medium	High		
Total	33.29	44.50	22.21	13.18	58,431
None	31.32	44.80	23.87	13.60	48,473
One	41.38	43.91	14.71	11.35	8,627
Two	50.54	38.43	11.03	10.11	1,197
Three or more	68.66	27.61	3.73	7.27	134

Source: Second China National Sample Survey on Disability (SCNSSD 2006) 10 per cent sample.

Table 8.2 Living standards in families of children with disabilities

Variable	Code	Regression coefficient	SD	Significance
Income	Income	0.114	0.001	0.000
Urban/rural	Rural	1.571	0.022	0.000
Sex	Sex	−0.025	0.017	0.148
Education level				
High school or technical secondary school	_Iedu_1	0.271	0.029	0.000
Tertiary education	_Iedu_2	0.586	0.612	0.338
Age group				
6–14 years	_Iagegroup_2	−0.290	0.021	0.000
15–17 years	_Iagegroup_3	−0.562	0.036	0.000
Number of children with disabilities in families				
One	_Idisnum_1	−0.229	0.024	0.000
Two	_Idisnum_2	−0.577	0.062	0.000
Three or more	_Idisnum_3	−1.281	0.203	0.000
Region				
North China	_Iregion_2	0.731	0.030	0.000
Northeast China	_Iregion_3	0.486	0.036	0.000
South Central China	_Iregion_3	−0.446	0.024	0.000
Southwest China	_Iregion_4	−0.742	0.027	0.000
Northwest China	_Iregion_5	−0.371	0.030	0.000

Source: Second China National Sample Survey on Disability (SCNSSD 2006) 10 per cent sample.

Notes: Optimal model of ordered logit regression. Total children = 58,092. Chi-square = 24907.34, P< 0.0000. R2=0.2253. Regression coefficient of income $\beta1$ = 0.105 (odds ratio 0.105 for improved household living standard when the income increases by 1,000 yuan, other conditions remaining unchanged).

The number of children with disabilities in families is used as the disability variable (0 = no children with disabilities in the family; 1 = one child; 2 = two children; 3 = three or more children with disabilities). Explanatory variables were selected depending on the relationship to income and poverty, for example, urban/rural households. Since the dependent variable living standard is an ordinal number variable (low, medium and high living standard), the ordered-logit model was adopted to estimate relationships. Model estimation aims to obtain best equilibrium, so explanatory variables without statistical significance are deleted from the model. After estimating the model, a series of logic sequence variable deletion testing was conducted to obtain the optimal equation. The maximum likelihood ordinal logic was adopted for model estimation.

An example of the economic impact from disability expenses and lost income was the family of Xinxin. He was aged nine and was at a local primary school. He had cerebral palsy, which affected his mobility but not his intellect or speech. When his parents became aware of his disability, they sought treatment, which was very costly. When Xinxin was aged one year, he received daily hyperbaric oxygen therapy at a cost of 80 yuan per day (this is not a scientifically proven treatment for children with cerebral palsy), supplemented with daily injections, each box of injection solutions costing several hundred RMB. The expenses were unaffordable for the family. After one year, Xinxin changed to acupuncture and chiropractic treatment, but again the effects were poor and expensive so they stopped. The last treatment was in Taiyuan when he was four years old. His mother said the treatment in Taiyuan was systematic, but they had to queue up for different service items in a rush and paid more than 10,000 yuan in only one month. She took him home instead because she could not afford such expensive medical expenses.

When Xinxin was eight years old, his mother had a second son. She cared for them full time because Xinxin was dependent on her for mobility and personal care. She had been a salesperson at a retail store, earning a low wage of 300–400 yuan per month before Xinxin was born. His father was a driver with a stable job but low income of less than 300 yuan per month. His mother said, 'A child with disabilities can put a family into poverty.' Although they did not pay for any further costs for treatment, they had many indirect costs. His mother was busy caring for Xinxin and a second child. They could not afford a child carer because no child carer was prepared to work for the low wage they could offer. His mother said, 'If we hire others to look after him, we have to pay the child carer; but if we do not, I have to look after him and cannot work.' The support from their extended family was also limited to a gift from his grandmother of 6,000 yuan when he was born, which was quickly used for medical costs.

Absolute and relative poverty in households of children with disabilities

The income level of children's households influences their wellbeing, development, economic security, education, access to health care and other social support. These needs and associated costs of support are higher in households of children with disabilities and the capacity of households with children and other members with disabilities to earn income is often reduced.

Irrespective of the additional costs of disability, urban and rural households including members with disabilities earned less than other households (per capita income of urban households of members with disabilities 4,864 yuan or 43 per cent of urban household at 11,321 yuan; rural households, 2,260 yuan or 48.8 per cent of rural household incomes at 4,631 yuan; SCNSSD 2006; 10 yuan = £1.1). As a result, the incidence of poverty was higher when more people with disabilities lived in the household and for rural families (Table 8.3; Figure 8.1).

In addition to the living standards analysed above, poverty can also be analysed in absolute and relative terms (Table 8.4). More families were in absolute and relative poverty the more children with disabilities they had. The rate of poverty in urban areas was higher irrespective of whether they had more children because of the higher poverty lines, which does not necessarily mean a lower household living standard in urban areas (see Table 8.2).

An example of absolute and relative poverty was Xiaofeng. She was twelve years old and had cerebral palsy and intellectual disabilities. She needed full support for all care, mobility and communication. Her home consisted of five people, including Xiaofeng, father, mother, older brother and grandfather. Her

Table 8.3 Incidence of poverty for households with children by number of people with disabilities, per cent

	Absolute poverty			Low income			No poverty			Children in survey
---	Rural	Urban	Total	Rural	Urban	Total	Rural	Urban	Total	
None	6.79	1.40	5.24	5.99	1.38	4.66	87.22	97.22	90.11	51,076
One	11.76	3.41	10.11	9.20	3.02	7.98	79.04	93.58	81.91	9,086
Two	18.03	6.48	15.75	11.35	6.88	10.47	70.62	86.64	73.78	1,251
Three	31.68	8.00	26.98	12.87	12.00	12.70	55.45	80.00	60.32	126
Four	35.71	–	31.25	7.14	–	6.25	57.14	100.00	62.50	16
All	7.92	1.70	6.22	6.65	1.65	5.28	85.43	96.65	88.50	61,555

Source: Second China National Sample Survey on Disability (SCNSSD 2006) 10 per cent sample

Note: Significant p<0.0001 except households with four people with disabilities

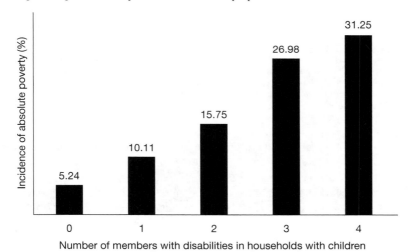

Figure 8.1 Incidence of absolute poverty in households with children by number of members with disabilities, per cent

Source: Second China National Sample Survey on Disability (SCNSSD 2006) 10 per cent sample

Note: Absolute poverty defined as per capita income below 683 yuan; Low income is per capita income within the range of 683–944 yuan; and not in poverty is per capita income above 944 yuan

brother boarded at the township high school because of the distance and only went home during weekends and holidays. Xiaofeng needed full support for all her needs and remained at home all day. Her mother took care of her, including personal care, feeding soft meals and constant supervision. Her mother said, 'The most dangerous situation is when Xiaofeng has very stiff legs and feet that cannot support her body. On flat ground, she can walk some steps, but even a tiny rock may result in trip. We allow her to walk on cement ground but not on soil ground.' As a result of her many falls, she had broken other bones. When she fell she

Table 8.4 Absolute and relative poverty in rural and urban households of children with disabilities, per cent

| Number of children with disabilities in household | Per cent by type of poverty | | | | Not in poverty | | Number of children | |
| | Absolute | | Relative | | | | | |
	Rural	Urban	Rural	Urban	Rural	Urban	Rural	Urban
Total	8.01	15.30	6.75	19.66	85.25	65.04	42,545	15,886
None	6.87	13.33	6.07	18.85	87.07	67.85	34,546	13,927
One	11.92	26.73	9.38	26.31	78.71	46.96	6,932	1,695
Two	18.06	45.19	11.48	18.41	70.46	36.40	958	239
Three or more	33.03	52.00	12.84	32.00	54.13	16.00	109	25

Source: Second China National Sample Survey on Disability (SCNSSD 2006) 10 per cent sample – 2005 income data.

Note: 2005 poverty standards were the absolute poverty 683 yuan and relative poverty 944 yuan in rural areas (Wang *et al.* 2006). In 2005, there were no official data on the poverty line of urban residents, but many scholars estimated urban poverty in China, for example average urban poverty line RMB 1,860 in 2005 (Chen *et al.* 2009). Another method adopted by scholars is the use of relative poverty line, one third or two thirds of the per capita disposable income. The per capita disposable income refers to the median of per capita disposable income among urban residents. According to statistical data from the National Bureau of Statistics, the per capita disposable income of middle-income urban families was RMB 9190.05 in 2005 (National Bureau of Statistics 2007). This chapter uses it as the median of per capita disposable income among urban residents. According to the one-third standard, the relative poverty line in urban residents was RMB 3,063.

could not stand up again without help, so they never left her alone. The mother said, 'Even if we leave home for ten minutes, we have to ask an old neighbour to look after her.' She said, 'Many villagers told me that raising her is as hard as raising three or four other children… it is my fate. Everybody said she was treated badly in our previous lives, so in this life she came to repay me.'

Her parents were both farmers and their land was limited. Her father also often laboured at the stone yard as a stone-worker. Xiaofeng's mother did not work because she provided constant care. The five-person household depended on her father's income of about 2000 yuan per year (400 per person). When her mother left the house, her grandfather cared for her. Her mother could only do limited housework, and an occasional odd job. At home, her mother earned a small amount from peeling sunflower seeds. Many local households collected sunflower seeds from shops, peeled them, and returned them to the shop. In hard times, the family often borrowed money, sold their grains, pigs or chicken, and went without meat. The biggest problems were the cost of maintaining their house and how to secure adequate money for Xiaofeng's future treatment.

Housing security

A third aspect of economic security is housing. Secure housing contributes to the welfare of children with disabilities. Housing conditions and transportation have been found to affect the quality of life perceptions of families of children with disabilities in China (Hu, Wang and Fei 2012). The high owner-occupied housing

Table 8.5 Housing type of rural and urban children with disabilities, per cent

Per cent	Owner-occupied	Rented	Borrowed	Other	Total
All children (n=54,061)					
Rural	96.54	2.08	1.17	0.21	100
Urban	78.52	18.51	2.02	0.95	100
Total	91.62	6.57	1.40	0.42	100
Children without disabilities (n=44,332)					
Rural	96.55	2.08	1.16	0.21	100
Urban	78.53	18.52	2.01	0.95	100
Total	91.61	6.59	1.39	0.41	100
Children with disabilities (n=729)					
Rural	95.59	2.27	1.76	0.38	100
Urban	77.88	18.27	2.40	1.44	100
Total	91.92	5.59	1.90	0.60	100

Source: Second China National Sample Survey on Disability (SCNSSD 2006) 10 per cent sample.
Note: n=58,431 children. P<0.001 urban, rural, but not by disability

rate among all families in China, including families of children with disabilities (Table 8.5), can be attributed to the privatization in the 1990s reforms, prior to which public housing was a key plank of the welfare system. From the 1990s, rural families retained their rights to housing on their land, and urban families could buy heavily discounted housing previously associated with their work (Chen, Zang and Wang 2014).

With the rapid urbanization and commercialization of urban and rural housing markets, however, close attention needs to be paid to future sustainability of such a high owner-occupied housing rate. Already, urban housing security is lower than in rural areas, with a higher proportion of families renting in the cities (18.51 per cent; Table 8.5). The difference is consistent with housing and land ownership policy differences in urban and rural China. Home ownership in urban and rural areas was slightly lower for households including children with disabilities but the difference was not significant. The central government is now aiming for 20 per cent public housing (Chen, Zang and Wang 2014).

Access to social security

The next aspect of economic security is access to social security to provide relief and address poverty and associated risks for eligible families. Access can be through a certificate of disability, participation in social insurance, or access to minimum living protection allowance and relief fund. Each of these is analysed below, considering location, sex and disability.

Certificate of disability

With a certificate of disability, people with disabilities can enjoy preferential policies and disability services, but the possession rate of a certificate is low among children with disabilities, only 13.87 per cent of children with disabilities (SCNSSD analysis, Table 8.6). The consequence of not holding a certificate is that most families of children with disabilities are not entitled to, and do not receive, formal support. The rate of possession of a certificate of disability was very low among children with disabilities (Table 8.6). The rate increased with age, peaking at over one third of older children in urban areas. Children in urban areas were almost twice as likely to have a certificate as in rural areas (20.19 per cent in urban and 12.22 per cent in rural). Girls were more likely than boys to have a certificate in rural areas for all ages, but this was reversed in urban areas. This is probably because in rural areas parents are more hesitant to register for their sons, because the discrimination cost of a disability label would have so few service or benefit returns. In urban areas more services and benefits are available and parents can pay more attention to therapy for their sons.

Reasons for low possession rate include low awareness about its availability, choosing not to apply for it so as to avoid discrimination against children and deciding that government support is limited anyway. For example, Jinbo is an urban child with disabilities who does not have a certificate. His family did not apply for a certificate because,

> We don't need the certificate of disability. Our living standard is good. The certificate of disability only reminds us that our son has disabilities throughout his life. He may have an inferiority complex. Without the certificate of disability, we feel our son is also healthy. I'd like to tell my son to become self-reliant, as self-improvement and confidence are important in overcoming difficulties. In fact, the government only provides limited support. Now, we are earning more money and can address economic problems.

Access to social insurance and social relief

In China, social insurance is the primary component of social security system, followed by social relief as described in Chapter 4. The coverage of social

Table 8.6 Proportion of children with disabilities who have a disability certificate by age, sex and location

	0–5 years old			6–14 years old			15–17 years old			Total		
	Rural	Urban	Total	Rural	Urban	Total	Rural	Urban	Total	Rural	Urban	Total
Male	2.42	5.71	3.14	9.96	24.59	13.01	20.95	37.50	24.82	10.43	22.66	13.10
Female	3.30	4.35	3.51	16.05	16.28	16.10	24.69	35.71	26.32	14.67	16.25	14.98
Total	2.79	5.17	3.30	12.47	21.15	14.29	22.58	36.96	25.43	12.22	20.19	13.87

Source: Second China National Sample Survey on Disability (SCNSSD 2006) 10 per cent sample.
Note: n=1002

insurance is very low among children with disabilities while the coverage of medical insurance is higher than other types of insurance (Table 9.3). This indicates that social relief is not specifically tailored and only provides limited support for families of children with disabilities. Given the high poverty rates (Table 8.4), most children with disabilities living in poverty have no access to government support, particularly in rural areas. As a result, most families have limited capacity to bear the full cost of medical and other disability intervention and all the economic risks and receive no financial government assistance or insurance to do so.

The proportion of children with disabilities receiving minimum living protection allowance and relief fund was also very low, whether they were from families in absolute poverty or low income. The minimum living protection allowance was 4.46 per cent for absolute poverty poor families; 4.49 per cent in low income families and 2.75 per cent in non-poor families. Relief fund was 5.36 per cent in absolute poverty families, 3.37 per cent in low income families and 5.87 per cent in non-poor families; SCNDSS 2006 data). Minimum living protection allowance and relief fund were higher in urban than rural areas, with the highest coverage of minimum living protection allowance among urban boys (7.81 per cent) and the highest coverage of relief fund among urban girls (7.50 per cent). The coverage was not significantly different for minimum living protection allowance or relief fund between children with disabilities irrespective of the level of poverty of their families.

Social security discrimination

As mentioned above, families of children with disabilities only receive very limited social security. This is not only because of the institutional structures, but also because of discretionary resource allocation and discrimination against families of people with disabilities in the provision of social security. A relevant example is the case of Xiaofeng, who did not receive any support or services from the state despite the severity of her disability and the family's poverty. Xiaofeng needed full support for all her care because of her cerebral palsy and intellectual disabilities, yet the certificate of disability from the county Disabled Persons Federation (DPF) only assessed her disabilities as grade 2 intellectual disability, which did not entitle her family to any support. Her family members strongly disagreed with this assessment and insisted that she should be identified as grade 1. The researcher observed that her support needs were greater than another child with intellectual disabilities with a grade 1 certificate surveyed by the researcher.

Equally, the researcher observed that Xiaofeng's household was very poor. Xiaofeng's annual total family income is only 2,000 yuan, with five family members (per capita 400 yuan), lower than the local annual per-capita income. The village where she lives is the largest one in the county and is widely known for its affluence, with an annual per-capita income of 2,705 yuan. The village committee official said, 'Families of children with disabilities in our village have better economic status than other families.' The county DPF had 'optimized' the severity of Xiaofeng's disability support needs and the level of family poverty. As a result, families of children with disabilities in this village did not receive adequate financial support. During the survey, the village committee insisted that their economic conditions were better than others. None of the seven children with disabilities in the village received minimum living protection allowance and other policy support, either because the assessment grading was too low or the child was assessed as not having a disability.

Xiaofeng's parents told the researcher that the family never received support from the government and other departments, including for the high medical expenses described below. They had not been told about the free services at the county DPF therapy centre. The only assistance they received was tokens of 10 yuan in 2008 and 20 yuan in 2009 from the village committee to celebrate the Spring Festival. Xiaofeng's mother complained that their family should have relief but, 'There is no relief for us, even though [other poverty] relief is provided to families without children of disabilities.' Xiaofeng's father twice complained to the township government and the village committee and took her there for informal assessment. The township government replied that, 'We will report your situation to the authority at higher level.' The village committee said, 'She has both parents and is not eligible for relief,' implying that they would only provide relief for an orphan.

In addition to no financial support, the family was also discriminated against by the local government. For example, her mother said, 'I was the only one in the village who has a child with disabilities, and I was forcibly sterilized.' According to the national policy, families of children with disabilities can have another child but she was not given that choice. She said that the village official told her, 'If you do not have the surgery, we will not help you even if your house breaks.' The family attributes the problem to not having 'A village official who cares about' them. The father repeatedly said that, 'A caring official at a lower level is better than unconcerned officials at higher levels.'

It seems that in places such as Xiaofeng's village with a discretionary distribution process, families need resources, power and relationships to obtain state support and relief. Families of children with disabilities that are poor and have no support from officials cannot obtain relief even when they face real financial difficulties.

Impact of the costs of disability

In the absence of state assistance, the family bears full responsibility for all expenditure on disability support and intervention. The case studies demonstrate why some families move further into poverty due to these costs and how they survive under this pressure. In addition to the reduced capacity to earn income due to caring responsibilities discussed above, parents also incur additional disability related expenses. Parents generally try their best to seek support, therapy and treatment for their children, investing considerable human and material resources that drive them further into poverty. The case of Xiaofeng illustrates this. The medical expenses for Xiaofeng were a heavy cost to the family. Her mother said, 'When she was very young, she was so weak physically that we had to send her to hospital every three or fewer days.' She had mild asthma when she was born, and the village clinic diagnosed her with mild congenital pneumonia. On the sixth day after her birth, she was transferred to the county hospital where she lived for nine days. One month later, she was sent to the hospital again and again. She received medical care at the clinics of the village and the neighbouring village and towns. When she was aged four years, she was sent to the county hospital for the fourth time, and the doctor told the parents that Xiaofeng had congenital hydrocephalus, and the surgery would cost over 10,000 yuan, but the treatment efficacy would only be for two years, after which the child would have hemiplegia. The doctor therefore advised them to, 'Let it be, just take good care of her. The surgeries would cost more than you can earn.' The family spent about 30,000 yuan in medical care, which is a heavy economic cost that put the family in almost extreme poverty, when their annual income was 2,000 yuan.

Similarly, Xinxin's family had given up on medical treatment when it proved ineffective and they drained all their resources, as described above. His mother said the primary health problem that she wanted to resolve was Xinxin's eyesight. Other costs were daily living expenses and education. Children with disabilities can be exempted from tuition fees according to the preferential education policy (Chapter 10). But the fees for books and other costs were over 30 yuan per semester. Despite the economic difficulties of families of children with disabilities, they also have to pay additional costs to gain access to education. For example, at the kindergarten, the fee was 100 yuan for each child per month, but the school asked Xinxin's mother to pay 200 yuan because the teachers needed to spend more time on taking care of him. She knew it was unfair and contrary to the policy, but had no choice. If she refused to pay additional costs, Xinxin would have no access to kindergarten because they would have refused to take him.

Employment status of young people with disabilities

A lower proportion of young people with disabilities had any paid work than young people without disabilities (14.22 per cent; 22.09 per cent; Table 8.8; at least one hour paid work in the survey week), despite young people with disabilities of that age also being less likely to be at school (Table 10.1). They experienced this disadvantage in rural and urban areas, although a higher proportion of all young people was employed in rural areas. The sex of the young person was not significant.

The main sources of income for young people who were not in paid work was similar whether they had a disability or not. Over 99 per cent were supported by other family members. Differences were not significant for use of social security (minimum living security – MLS), property income, insurance or other sources.

Most young people not in paid work were school students (92–95 per cent of young people without disabilities; Table 8.7). However, as shown in Table 10.1,

Table 8.7 Economic activity of young people (15–17 years) not in paid work by disability, sex and location, per cent

		School	House-work	Unable to work	Looking for work	Cause of job loss Employer	Self	Other	All
All young people (n=13,766)									
Rural	Men	91.99	0.41	1.12	5.13	–	0.08	1.28	100
	Women	90.46	2.68	1.16	4.51	–	0.06	1.13	100
	Total	91.28	1.47	1.14	4.84	–	0.07	1.21	100
Urban	Men	93.04	0.28	0.67	4.34	0.11	0.22	1.34	100
	Women	94.97	1.13	0.44	2.83	–	0.06	0.57	100
	Total	93.94	0.68	0.56	3.63	0.06	0.15	0.97	100
Total	Men	92.32	0.37	0.98	4.88	0.03	0.12	1.29	100
	Women	91.89	2.19	0.93	3.98	–	0.06	0.95	100
	Total	92.12	1.22	0.96	4.46	0.02	0.09	1.14	100
Young people without disabilities (n=13,534)									
Rural	Men	93.12	0.36	0.18	5.14	–	0.05	1.15	100
	Women	91.60	2.61	0.09	4.57	–	0.06	1.07	100
	Total	92.41	1.42	0.14	4.87	–	0.06	1.11	100
Urban	Men	93.77	0.28	0.06	4.36	0.11	0.17	1.25	100
	Women	95.56	1.02	–	2.86	–	0.06	0.51	100
	Total	94.61	0.63	0.03	3.65	0.06	0.12	0.90	100
Total	Men	93.32	0.34	0.14	4.89	0.04	0.09	1.18	100
	Women	92.86	2.10	0.06	4.03	–	0.06	0.89	100
	Total	93.11	1.17	0.10	4.49	0.02	0.08	1.04	100
Young people with disabilities (n=232)									
Rural	Men	40.48	2.38	44.05	4.76	–	1.19	7.14	100
	Women	36.62	5.63	52.11	1.41	–	–	4.23	100
	Total	38.71	3.87	47.74	3.23	–	0.65	5.81	100
Urban	Men	50.00	–	36.67	3.33	–	3.33	6.67	100
	Women	28.57	14.29	50.00	–	–	–	7.14	100
	Total	43.18	4.55	40.91	2.27	–	2.27	6.82	100
Total	Men	42.98	1.75	42.11	4.39	–	1.75	7.02	100
	Women	35.29	7.06	51.76	1.18	–	–	4.71	100
	Total	39.70	4.02	46.23	3.02	–	1.01	6.03	100

Source: Second China National Sample Survey on Disability (SCNSSD 2006) 10 per cent sample
Note: significant p<0.0001 except within results for people with disabilities

Table 8.8 Young people (15–17 years) in paid work by disability, sex and location, per cent

	Rural	Urban	Total
All young people (n=13,766)			
Men	27.18	8.18	22.10
Women	26.28	9.82	21.80
Total	26.76	8.96	22.00
Young people without disabilities (n=13,534)			
Men	27.32	8.21	22.22
Women	26.53	9.90	21.94
Total	26.95	9.01	22.09
Young people with disabilities (n=232)			
Men	20.00	6.25	16.79
Women	12.35	0.00	10.53
Total	16.67	4.35	14.22

Source: Second China National Sample Survey on Disability (SCNSSD 2006) 10 per cent sample

Note: Significant: $p<0.01$ except sex

Paid job for at least one hour 25–31 March 2006.

fewer young people with disabilities attend school ($p<0.001$). Only 39.70 per cent of young people with disabilities were still at school and school participation was worse for urban young women. The difference in school attendance was almost wholly matched with an equal proportion of young people with disabilities who stated they were unable to work. Sex and location were significant for differences between young people without disabilities ($p<0.001$), but not for young people with disabilities.

Conclusion about the right to economic security

This chapter discussed the right of children to economic security by examining the economic costs of disability (Art. 28 CRPD). It compared poverty incidence between families of children with and without disabilities. The poverty incidence is much higher in families of children with disabilities when measured by living standards and income poverty in absolute and relative measures. The impact is worse in rural than urban areas, and the costs increase with the age of the children. Poverty was directly related to the number of people with disabilities in the household, including children with disabilities. The result is likely to be explained by the capacity of the household to earn income and the additional financial and time costs of supporting family members with disabilities in the absence of government or community support.

The institutional arrangements of social security, including social insurance, poverty relief and medical insurance, did not effectively relieve the economic situation of most families of children with disabilities. The reasons include insufficient coverage, discretionary application of the policies, and inadequate levels of support. Some parents were not even told about what limited free services might have been available to their children. Poverty and inadequate policy implementation excludes children with disabilities from appropriate support, therapy and treatment, affecting their opportunities in childhood and with implications for their future adulthood. Young people with disabilities were less likely to have any paid work, and young women were worst affected in access to education and employment. Each of these differences has a current and future impact on wellbeing, development and security. The implications of a lack of economic security in the examples in this chapter were that it also affected other development rights, such as access to health, education and social participation. The next chapters take up these implications.

References

Chan, C.K., Ngok, K.L. and Phillips, D. (2008) *Social Policy in China: Development and Wellbeing*, Bristol: The Policy Press, University of Bristol.

Chen, J., Liao, C. and Zou, G. (2009) Thinking about the main problems of the minimum living security system for urban residents. *Socioeconomic System Comparison* [Chinese] 4: 76–81.

Chen, J., Yang, Z. and Wang, Y.P. (2014) The New Chinese Model of Public Housing: A Step Forward or Backward? *Housing Studies* 29: 534–550.

Clarke, H. (2006) Preventing social exclusion of disabled children and their families: literature review. *Research Report RR782*, paper for the National Evaluation of the Children's Fund, Institute of Applied Social Studies University of Birmingham.

CRPD, United Nations Convention on the Rights of Persons with Disabilities (2006) www.un.org/disabilities/default.asp?id=150 [1 February 2012].

Deng, M. and Holdsworth, J.C. (2007) From unconscious to conscious inclusion: meeting special education needs in West China. *Disability & Society* 22(5): 507–522.

Fisher, K.R. and Shang, X. (2013) Access to health and therapy services for families of children with disabilities in China. *Disability & Rehabilitation* 35(25): 2157–2163.

Hu, X., Wang, M. and Fei, X. (2012) Family quality of life of Chinese families of children with intellectual disabilities. *Journal of Intellectual Disability Research* 56: 30–44.

Lygnegard, F., Donohue, D., Bornman, J., Granlund, M. and Huus, K. (2013) A systematic review of generic and special needs of children with disabilities living in poverty settings in low- and middle-income countries. *Journal of Policy Practice* 12(4): 296–315.

National Bureau of Statistics (2007) *China City Statistics Year Book 2006*, Department of Urban and Social Economic Survey, Beijing: China Statistic Press.

UNICEF, United Nations Children's Fund (2006) *An Investigation of Families with Children with Disabilities and Relevant Policies.* Unpublished internal document.

Wang, P., Fang, H. and Li, X. (2006) A comparison of poverty standard between China and International. *China Rural Economy* 12: 62–65.

WHO, World Health Organisation (2011) *World Report on Disability 2011.* WHO Press, Geneva whqlibdoc.who.int/publications/2011/9789240685215_eng.pdf [2 May 2015].

Xiong, N., Yang, L., Yu, Y., Hou, J., Li, J., Li, Y., Liu, H., Zhang, Y. and Jiao, Z. (2011) Investigation of raising burden of children with autism, physical disability and mental disability in China. *Research in Developmental Disabilities* 32: 306–311.

9 Right to children's development

Health and therapy services

Most children with disabilities in China do not receive the health and therapy services they need, according to national statistics (63 per cent; Chen and Chen 2008). This threatens their lives, wellbeing and opportunities in childhood and adult life. Access to health and therapy services can contribute to realizing the rights of children with disabilities and can change the experience of families with such children (Art. 25, 26 CRPD). This chapter analyses the efforts of families of children with disabilities to access health and therapy services, in order to understand why most children do not receive the support they need. It uses empirical data to identify the challenges that families face so as to inform changes to policy and service provision.

Medical, health and therapy service system

Free public health care in China is rare. Before the economic reforms following 1978, China had comprehensive health insurance for urban employees, whose children could use half price health care services. The market-oriented reforms between 1978 and 2010 replaced this with a commercialized private health system. Similarly, rural collective organizations (People's Communes) provided preventative and low cost health services before the reforms, which were unsustainable after the dismantling of the collective economy. As a result, during the reform era health care costs for urban and rural children were not covered by public insurance and were the parents' responsibility.

With China's economic growth, the government is returning to a health system with comprehensive coverage for the whole population, including children. Although health care coverage is improving and public health care is more common in wealthier areas, most families of children with disabilities must still pay for it. The costs of health and therapy for orphans is borne by the state and, as a result, most abandoned children have disabilities, as parents are forced into difficult decisions about access to affordable necessary support for their children (Shang 2012).

China has achieved improvements in health outcomes for children, particularly infant mortality, shifting to rates similar to other middle-income countries and equality for girls and boys (from 1990 to 2011, 5.8 per cent reduction in mortality;

UNICEF 2013: 99, 136), which is ahead of international targets (UNESCO 2014). China is developing a comprehensive financial coverage of medical care, which includes three medical care schemes: urban employees' medical insurance, medical insurance for all urban residents, and the New Rural Cooperative Medical Care (NRCMC) in 2011. Among them, the urban employees' medical insurance covers workforce in urban areas, but does not cover children. The other two programmes cover all residents, including children. However, the schemes do not cover all costs if children are seriously sick and the costs are higher than the reimbursement ceilings (Gu 2011). Therapy costs may or may not be included in these programmes depending on the decision made by local governments. Parents sometimes rely on traditional Chinese medicine either because of availability or cost.

The urban employee's medical insurance covers employees in the urban sector, while the health care needs of children are mainly addressed by their families. When children become seriously ill and require medical treatment beyond the affordability of their families, they usually cannot receive such treatment promptly. The situation has not been changed since the medical insurance system is still developing. For instance, according to information from different sources, there are about two million children with leukaemia in China. Technically the cure rate for leukaemia among Chinese children is 80–90 per cent, but the cost is very high (200–600,000 yuan). As a result, 80–90 per cent of Chinese children with leukaemia died without any treatment (Zhongguo Jiaoyuwang 2009). Because of this, parents of many children with disabilities and chronic illness have to abandon their children as they are unable to afford the high costs of treatment and health care services. A few cities developed a system of medical insurance for catastrophic illnesses of school students, which played an important role in provision of medical aid for seriously ill children. Such medical aid does not strictly fall into the scope of social insurance in China; it takes the form of a commercial insurance, with or without government subsidies (Gu 2011).

In rural areas, the NRCMC is developing fast. In theory, a part of the cost of health care and medicine of rural residents can be covered by the programme. The situation of the new programmes is different in different areas since it is a locally run programme. Rural residents, including children, benefit from the programme. Rural residents have to pay a small sum as a premium for being eligible for the benefits of the NRCMC. In most parts of China, the payment from orphans is waived by local governments. Families of children with disabilities, however, have to pay for their children.

The Twelfth Five-Year Programme for the Development of the China Disabled Persons, set goals to provide special assistance for people with disabilities, reduce the access starting points, set a reasonable ceiling for reimbursement costs, and add some new medicine needed by people with disabilities to the list of medicines that are accepted by the health insurance plan for rural and urban residents (CDPF 2006). However, many therapy services provided by NGOs or commercial providers are not in the list.

The medical and therapy costs of children with disabilities remain largely borne by their parents. If the costs are too high to be borne by their families, the treatment and therapy will be delayed. Some areas have special health insurances for children with serious diseases and disabilities (Shang and Wu 2011). These projects are semi-commercial insurance. Because support from the state is not usually available, if operations and treatment are too expensive for families, charity is the only feasible way for children with disabilities to receive the health care they need. Effective health insurance for children has yet to be established, with the result that some children with disabilities die from conditions that could be resolved with medical intervention.

Family experiences of access to services

As a result of this service system, most children with disabilities continue to experience barriers to accessing the health and therapy they need to fulfil their rights as children and as people with disabilities (Fisher, Shang and Xie 2011; McCabe 2008b). Earlier research has demonstrated similar findings for adults with disabilities in Beijing (Yin *et al.* 2007; Fisher and Li 2008). While economic and political attitudes towards social welfare are changing, the family in China is still the primary source of care for children. For the families of children with disabilities this means having no option but to provide disability support without expert knowledge, or if formal support is available, to pay for it themselves. Little is known about experiences of families in this position and what support they believe could help them to provide or access services and achieve their children's rights.

Some policy initiatives to help parents with skills to support their children have been implemented and have met with success. McCabe evaluated one of these initiatives, the Nanjing Child Mental Health Research Center, which began as China's first state-run medical institution for children with autism. The Center provides both clinical support to children with disabilities and training to their parents (McCabe 2008b). The evaluation was longitudinal and looked at the experiences of families and children who had been accessing the Center's services since its inception. It found that while the Center provided valuable support to children with autism and their families and achieved outcomes for the rights of children with disabilities to education and promoting social inclusion, in many cases the service cost was too high to be sustainable for families (McCabe 2008b). In contrast to the autism initiative, Lim *et al.* (2013) and Wang (Wang and Michaels 2009; Wang, Michaels and Day 2011), found that almost all the families in the research had little information about disability, where to find disability support or access to relevant quality support suitable for their children.

This chapter is concerned with children's rights to service support, particularly information about child disability and support; disability support, health and therapy; and children's services (Fisher and Shang 2013). Despite the intentions of the laws and policy, it seems that most children with disabilities continue to experience significant barriers to support that enables their equal participation in their communities. A first step in informing change in this situation is to understand the extent to which families have access to the support they need. The chapter analyses whether children with disabilities receive the health and therapy they need; what prevents families from accessing the services; and the policy implications to support their rights.

The research analysed the 10 per cent dataset from the Second China National Sample Survey on Disability (Chapter 1) and national case studies through observation with eight children and in-depth interviews with members of their communities (Table 9.1).

The sampling unit was the child with disabilities, from which the relevant family members, neighbours, school teachers, social networks and village organizations were selected for interviews (38 interviews were conducted). The case studies looked at the experiences of each family to identify the main factors that prevent children with disabilities from realizing their right to these services. The cases in this chapter include a variety of families with children with disabilities. The families live in different provinces, including middle-class families in urban areas and poor families in rural areas. While the experiences of these families are not statistically significant, they show the difficulties that these families experience seeking health and therapy services for their children with disabilities. The analysis describes the extent of need of children with disabilities aged under 18 years for health and therapy services and their access to these services.

Table 9.1 Case study children for access to health and therapy services

Child*	Sex	Disability	Location
Xiaoqiang	Boy	Autism	Beijing
Yuhao	Girl	Vision	Beijing
Taotao	Boy	Intellectual, hearing and speech	Hubei
Xiaoyi	Boy	Physical	Sichuan
Wenxin	Girl	Hearing and speech	Henan
Qingqing	Boy	Hearing and speech	Jiangxi
Niuniu	Boy	Intellectual	Inner Mongolia
Xiaojie	Girl	Cerebral palsy	Xinjiang

Note: *Alias

Services used or needed by children with disabilities

The findings about national use and need for services are from the National Sample Survey on Disability. The survey categorized services as health care, assistance and support for people with disabilities living in poverty, therapy training and services, educational subsidy or tuition reduction/waiver, assistive devices, daily living services, vocational education and training, culture services, job placement and support and other.

Analysis of the national sample survey showed that the state provides very limited services to children with disabilities. Most children (63 per cent) relied entirely on their families for support and did not receive any government services (Table 9.2).

Children were more likely to receive services if they had physical, emotional, vision or multiple disabilities. Children with speech, intellectual or hearing disabilities were the least likely to receive support. Children in urban areas were more likely to receive support than those who live in rural areas. Service use by sex was not significantly different.

If children did receive services, the most common support was medical (26 per cent; Table 9.3). Less than a quarter of children who received support received poverty relief or therapy training and services, which can be critical for early intervention. This is despite more than twice that proportion of families reporting that their children needed this support. Children in urban areas were more likely

Table 9.2 Children's use of services by disability and location

	Children with disabilities who used any services (per cent)
All children with disabilities	37.4
Disability type	
Physical	51.9
Emotional*	50.0
Vision	45.1
Multiple	39.9
Speech	31.3
Intellectual**	27.8
Hearing	27.5
Location	
Urban	49.0
Rural	34.4
Sex	
Male	37.4
Female	37.4

Source: 2006 Second China National Sample Survey on Disability n=1002

Notes: Significant: $p<0.001$ except sex

*Behaviour, psychosocial; **intellectual, learning, developmental

Table 9.3 Service types by need and received, per cent

	Need a service	Need and receive a service
Health service and assistance	95.8	26.1
Income support for disability poverty	78.0	22.9
Therapy training and service	70.7	22.7
Educational fee reduction or waiver	31.9	12.5
Assistive devices	28.4	10.9
Daily living services	23.9	11.5
Cultural services	11.2	4.8
Other	16.1	7.5

Source: 2006 Second China National Sample Survey on Disability n=1002

to receive therapy support than rural children. Just over 10 per cent received an educational subsidy reduction or waiver, assistive devices or daily living services. These disparities demonstrate that the lack of service use was likely to have been driven by a shortage of affordable support, rather than satisfied needs.

The implications of the quantitative analysis are that many children in both urban and rural areas did not receive the support they needed, including health support and therapy, which are likely to have a serious impact on their lifetime development. The case study analysis contributes to understanding the reasons for that problem. The next section sets out three of these reasons including scarce information about services, a shortage of services and unaffordable services.

Information obstacles

The case studies showed that families did not have sufficient information about disability or disability support (reinforcing the findings of Lim *et al.* 2013 and Wong *et al.* 2004). They did not understand their child's disability support needs, such as identifying that they had disabilities, early intervention and expectations of rights. They were unfamiliar with disability support options, including health, therapy and support. And they did not know about options that children's services should be able to offer them with other children in schools or other children's activities. In the absence of quality information about these needs, they relied on poor quality sources, such as informal sharing and commercial products and services, illustrated below. The poor information reduced their access to support, through delayed, incorrect or no support.

In a policy context of user pays for health care, families invested heavily in the health and therapy support for their children with disabilities. When they found their child had disabilities, or disease possibly leading to disabilities, parents spent whatever they had on health care and therapy. However, because of poor information, they often failed to spend it on effective support.

Confusing information

The case studies found that many families were frustrated by information obstacles. Without accurate information, they made poor decisions about the necessity, goals and costs of therapy for their children. In the absence of useful health and therapy information from government sources, parents paid attention to commercially motivated private businesses, services and therapists.

For example, the parents of Xiaoqiang, a boy with autism, were well educated and had the financial capability to provide early health care and therapy for him. They spent three-quarters of their earnings on interventions, but they missed the opportunity for early intervention due to poor diagnosis and treatment from a doctor. His father said,

> When he was two years old, I noticed that he seldom talked and had trouble communicating and playing with others of a similar age. So I consulted a doctor then at the local hospital. Later I realized that the doctor didn't have the least medical ethics. He didn't even do any assessment of my son, but said it might be a zinc deficiency and recommended a bagged drink for zinc supplementation. My child took the tonic but this didn't make any significant change. I ignored it until my son grew up to school age … he was getting more asocial and eating and even using the bathroom were getting difficult for him – he had almost lost all of his independence. An assessment at [another hospital] found my son had autism.

Yuhao had a very similar experience. Her parents believed that the girl's vision disabilities were an acquired problem due to the doctor's incorrect diagnosis, treatment and advice. Her mother said,

> Because she was so weak at birth, we sent her to … hospital, where the doctor kept her in an incubator for more than 40 days with oxygen … Later when we brought her to an oculist for her eye problem, the oculist told me that … a premature infant should not intake oxygen for more than three days … when we took the child home from the incubator, the doctor told me that the child was all right but advised me to see an oculist in six months for routine inspection … When the child grew up to more than six months old … an ophthalmologist told me that we were too late … Then, although we spent more than 10,000 yuan [£909] for eye surgery, it's too late … she lost the sight of both her eyes.

In addition to misdiagnosis, another common situation was that parents were unaware of appropriate support and hospitals misled them into spending a lot on assessment and treatment in vain. The case studies of children with cerebral palsy illustrated this problem. The mother of a child with cerebral palsy and the director of Angel House, an organization for therapy of children with cerebral palsy said,

Parents of children with cerebral palsy used to consider this as a curable disease, and so they invested lots of money and effort including hyperbaric oxygen, brain tonics or even corrective surgery. But after all of these, when they turned to therapy, they no longer had any money. Almost all of these parents have made such mistakes, which have something to do with our education and knowledge dissemination. Since cerebral palsy is an irreversible condition, rehabilitation training should be introduced as early as possible for better effect.

For children with cerebral palsy, effective therapy needed the participation and help of their parents. Every day rehabilitation training at home was an important step to a good therapy result. Many commercial health and therapy institutions, however, provided therapy services for children with cerebral palsy for profit. They told the parents to rely on the institutions for training their children instead of everyday therapy training at home.

Some parents were not well informed and believed that health and therapy services were useless and so their children missed the opportunity for their development. An example is Taotao, who ceased health care and therapy training when he was aged three. His mother said,

No more therapy is necessary since no change has ever happened in the boy. In addition, we cannot afford it, and we've never heard of any such therapy institution in Daye.

Xiaoyi's parents in Xinjiang were not aware of any therapy service in the area. He did not receive services or financial support and his family could not afford the therapy. A lack of information, confusing or even misleading information about therapy meant that many families were not even aware of the services that could have benefited their children.

Sources of information

The case studies showed that the families had very limited sources of information. They received information from hospitals, TV commercials and personal experiences. When they noticed any difference with their children's development, they sought health treatment first. Hospitals were the most important sources of information for them. Almost all parents received information about health and therapy services for children from doctors. If this source provided incorrect information, they were helpless.

Advertisements were another source of information. For example, when Xiaoyi in Sichuan was old enough, he became interested in looking for information relevant to his condition, mostly from TV commercials. His mother said,

He likes TV commercials very much – I mean those drug advertisements. Whenever he finds any advertised drug for his condition, he will mention it to us.

For example, Xiaoyi saw a local TV advertisement about a drug and said to his mother: 'Look at those people on the TV, they have taken the drug and straighten up their bending fingers.' The boy kept talking about the advertisement, and he kept the TV tuned to that channel for his mother to see the commercial programme. Full of hope, the mother bought the drug for him, which proved to be ineffective.

Other children had similar situations. For example, when Wenxin's parents noticed that she did not respond to sound, they took her to Beijing, Zhengzhou and other localities that were mentioned in advertisements for medical treatment. This cost them 10,000 yuan (£909) but did not lead to any changes. Without other choices, her parents finally bought her a hearing aid.

Some parents did not try to find any information and made the decision about whether their children should receive any therapy service themselves. Qingqing did not receive any health or therapy service because his mother had the same disabilities and they could not afford to pay for support. His parents believed that the boy's hearing disability was inherited and therapy could not help. The boy's father said, 'Qingqing was born with the disease, and therapy training will never be helpful.' He did not have ways of communicating with other people.

Parents were eager for information about health and therapy services. For example, in 2008, Niuniu's mother saw the Shanghai Special Olympics for people with intellectual disabilities on TV and hoped that her son might participate in sport. She took him to a children's activity centre in the town to learn table tennis. The coach admitted him without any charge and the manager of the centre gave him a used table tennis table to practice at home. He went to the gymnasium with his mother twice a day, six days a week and became skilled at playing table tennis. When McCabe and McCabe (2013) organized family support groups in Nanjing, parents in one group insisted on changing its primary function to information and training, rather than parent support, because they had so few other information options.

Lim *et al.* (2013) found that families tried to find information from Chinese internet sources such as chat sites hosted by QQ, but that most of the contributions were about expressing their distress rather than exchanging useful information about support. They were unable to access international internet information because it relied on English fluency.

Impact of information obstacles

Information obstacles had a great impact on families with children with disabilities. Without necessary information, some children with disabilities missed all opportunities for early intervention. For example, therapy in Beijing for Xiaoqiang's autism when he was young was delayed until he reached school age because of incorrect information and the doctor's misdiagnosis. This affected his development.

Sometimes, information obstacles prevented children from receiving any health or therapy service. Taotao in Daye, for example, did not receive any therapy after the age of three years because his parents were not aware of any effective support and were not confident it would make any difference. They did not consider sending him to school because of his disabilities. Similarly, Niuniu in Inner Mongolia had intellectual disabilities. He lived in a small town without information about support. His parents believed that he would remain the same so they kept him well fed and dressed but did not arrange any therapy or school education.

Availability of services

The second set of obstacles to their rights to health and therapy services was the availability and cost of support. The contrast between urban and rural experiences demonstrated in the national survey were even more stark in the examples of inequitable access to health care; disability support and therapy; and education and social activities, either inclusive or segregated. Some rural families did not even ask for their child to attend school because they knew they would be refused; in contrast to some urban families who benefited from income support and free services from birth. Availability and quality of support from both government and nongovernment organizations varied locally (see also McCabe 2013; Sun *et al.* 2013a, 2013b). Yin *et al.* (2007) similarly found that distance from services affected likelihood of service use.

The national survey and case studies showed that availability of health and therapy services was not as problematic in the urban areas. Xiaoqiang and Yuhao in Beijing, for example, had delayed access to health care and therapy due to poor assessment and advice, but with the correct information, they were able to find and use good opportunities for therapy and education.

Yuhao received good therapy training at a school for children with vision disabilities and her parents are satisfied with the school. Xiaoqiang received education and autism therapy at Dongcheng Special School. At the school, 180 children were divided into two departments for children with vision or cognitive disabilities (including autism). Each grade class had eight or nine children. Children older than primary school age attended the vocational education department to learn skills such as computers and cooking. Xiaoqiang's father was satisfied with the services and said,

> The teachers are high-quality professionals in special education. They are very good at communicating with these children, and know how to protect them and how not to hurt their feelings. Therefore, Xiaoqiang has changed a lot since he entered the school. He is doing very well in communicating with his teachers and with other children, and he is very active in learning new things.

In other places, however, especially rural areas, the parents of children with disabilities had very poor experiences trying to access good therapy services. The families of Taotao in Daye and Niuniu in Inner Mongolia had similar stories about support for intellectual disabilities. Niuniu received almost no professional education and therapy services because of his community and family circumstances. First, no therapy centre or special school operated in the town where Niuniu lived and information about where to find the nearest ones was scarce. Second, his family could not financially afford to send him to a special school or therapy centre in a big city.

The national survey found that most families with children with disabilities paid the full or most of the cost of the health and therapy services for their children, without support from the government. The interviews suggested that this situation was changing. In Beijing, Xiaoqiang and Yuhao's families received health and educational assistance from the government. The Beijing government had a preferential policy for children with disabilities, including a free health card, school cost waiver for tuition, books and board and a 100 yuan (£9) living subsidy per month for each child. Other large cities have similar policies.

In some ethnic minority regions, some families also received financial support through preferential government policies. Xiaojie's family in Xinjiang, a Muslim region for example, had been covered by the social health insurance programme since 2009, in which one third of the health cost was paid by the government.

Xiaoyi from Sichuan benefited from subsidies and donations when he travelled to a hospital in Hangzhou for treatment for one year for his physical disabilities. His family could not have proceeded with the treatment without the assistance. The hospital halved the fees for the assessment and treatment and reduced the final payment by another 30 per cent because he was from Sichuan and his family had financial difficulties. Other hospital patients made donations, including an old woman who contributed 1,000 yuan before she left the hospital; and at the factory where his father worked, workers to managers donated 10,000 yuan (£909).

In addition to government support, some nongovernment organizations (NGO) were beginning to offer children's disability services, mainly in the large cities. For example, Angel House is a parent-initiated NGO that provided therapy for children with cerebral palsy. The fees were kept low or free through donations. The NGO provided free assessment and advice and encouraged parents to participate in their children's therapy to make an individual plan and to learn about effective methods and early intervention. Children could continue to use the free training facilities each day after the individual training and ask the support workers for advice.

Disability support and poverty

Despite these new initiatives that made support affordable for some children, most children did not receive the support they needed because the cost would be borne by their family alone. The families' financial position usually worsened due to the three-fold relationships between disability and family poverty demonstrated in the case studies. Some children experienced disability because of the family poverty – they did not have access to basic needs. For other children poverty accentuated their disability – their family could not afford the cost of disability support, as discussed above. Other families lived in poverty due to the cost of disability support and poor information about appropriate support. Yin *et al.* 2007 also found that families were less likely to access support if they were on a lower income.

Many of the children did not receive the health and therapy services that they needed because the families could not afford them, which accentuated their disability. The national survey showed that children with hearing disabilities mostly needed the support with assistive devices. In all the case studies, the parents could not afford necessary assistive devices. For example, Qingqing lost his opportunity for speech training because his father could not afford even the cheapest hearing aid for him. Similarly, Wenxin's speech development was affected by her parents' delay in replacing her hearing aid because it was too expensive. Taotao's parents in Daye spent a lot on ineffective therapy in his early years but not after he turned three years old. They could not afford assistive devices such as a wheelchair so he was almost immobile. They said, 'he can hardly walk but staggers along … and he often falls down, five or six times a day or more.'

In addition, many parents spent whatever resources they had on health care and therapy for their children, which put them further into poverty. For example, the mother of a child with cerebral palsy said her daughter was in the village clinic, village hospital and county hospitals many times when she was a baby. When she was aged four years, they were told she needed surgery that cost 10,000 yuan, which would provide temporary relief. The doctor advised, 'You may take good care of her but forget the surgery … you cannot afford it on your family income' (at the time, annual average income in China was 24,000 yuan – £2,182). After spending 30,000 yuan, the family was under great financial pressure and was emotionally exhausted.

Conclusion about access to health and therapy services

In summary, the families of children with disabilities were often unable to find and use the health and therapy support that their children needed due to no or poor quality information, a shortage of local services and unaffordability of support in the context of fee for service and families living in poverty. While these reasons are common across China (and indeed most countries), the local context, such as government and community resources and policy implementation, affected the degree to which families could obtain the support their children needed.

The national survey showed that although most children needed health and therapy services, less than 40 per cent received any support and less than 25 per cent received the types of support they needed. They were most likely to obtain health care, although in most parts of the country they had to pay for it. The gap between need and use was widest in the rural areas. Sex was not significant.

The central policies for children's health care and disability support commit the provincial and local governments to providing information and services so that children with disabilities can participate equally with their childhood peers. The survey and case studies illustrated the gap between policy statements and local implementation, no doubt constrained by government resources. The case study families had no choice but to use their own resources and contacts to try to find effective support for their children, until their family resources ran out.

The families invested considerable financial and emotional resources in their attempts to assist their children, driving many of them further into poverty. They were forced into this position because they did not have accurate information about their children's needs or effective health and therapy; they could not find services near their homes so they had to add the cost of travel; and the services were expensive. The exceptions were for some children in large cities, although even they struggled to get quality information about best practice support for their children (see also McCabe 2013).

These circumstances will not change until local communities and government policies at all levels prioritize resources for policy implementation to meet the rights of children with disabilities and their families who support them. Accurate information, local services and affordable support are within the reach of policy implementation. The Chinese government is making efforts in this direction (CDPF 2006).

China already has a well developed local structure for information distribution, through the Disabled Persons Federation (DPF), which operates and is funded at all levels of government. DPF should be a reliable local source of information about child disability, children's rights, assessment, service options, best practice for effective support, individual plans, cost of services, support groups and where to get help. DPF engagement with community disability groups, people with disabilities and families of children with disabilities would enhance the reliability and relevance of the information. It would fill the information gap currently taken by commercial interests in the private sector and unscrupulous health professionals who prey on the vulnerability of families who have no way to assess the accuracy of information they receive. Information distribution is not a highly resourced intensive activity, and if supported by a central government policy commitment, could be acted on quickly.

Similarly, access to basic affordable assessment, health care, therapy and equipment during children's early years is critical for early intervention, with implications for development and later life. The wealthier large cities and central government for ethnic minority areas have already recognized the importance of these rights in children's early years and they have begun to make this financial commitment to the availability of affordable services and income support (McCabe 2013). Extending central government resources and local community implement-ation to other less resourced areas is also necessary to meet the needs of the majority of children with disabilities in China. It is implausible to expect that local governments and poorer provinces have the resource capacity to make these commitments without central government resource redistribution.

Local context affects the capacity of families to meet their children's support needs. Without the health and therapy services, their immediate quality of life, implications for development and opportunities for later life are seriously affected (Art. 25, 26 CRPD). Children with disabilities without access to health care and therapy are less likely to experience their rights to meaningful participation and independence, and instead, be forced to rely on their families, the community and the state throughout their lifetime.

References

CDPF, China Disabled Persons' Federation (2006) *A Notice of Issuing the Speech of Senior Officials in the Workshop of Rehabilitation Work for Children with Disabilities,* www.cdpf.org.cn/2008old/kangf/content/2006-10/27/content_75604.htm [10 September 2011].

Chen, X. and Chen, Y. (2008) *The Status Analysis and Strategies of Children with Disabilities in China,* Beijing: Huaxia Press.

CRPD, United Nations Convention on the Rights of Persons with Disabilities (2006) www.un.org/disabilities/default.asp?id=150 [1 February 2012].

Fisher, K.R. and Li, J. (2008) Chinese disability independent living policy. *Disability & Society* 23(2): 171–185.

Fisher, K.R. and Shang, X. (2013) Access to health and therapy services for families of children with disabilities in China. *Disability & Rehabilitation* 35(25): 2157–2163.

Fisher, K.R., Shang, X. and Xie, J. (2011) Support for social participation of children and young people with disability in China, in Carrillo B and Duckett J (eds) *China's Changing Welfare Mix: Local perspectives,* London and New York: Routledge.

Gu, X. (2011) The most difficult task is in cities, not in rural areas for comprehensive coverage of medical insurance, www.zgylbx.com/hvyfuahsnew31230_1/ [11 May 2012].

Lim, F., Downs, J., Li, J., Bao, X.-H. and Leonard, H. (2013) Caring for a child with severe intellectual disability in China: the example of Rett syndrome. *Disability and Rehabilitation* 35: 343–351.

McCabe, H. (2008b) Two decades of serving children with autism in the People's Republic of China: achievements and challenges of a state-run mental health center. *Disability & Society* 23(3): 271–282.

McCabe, H. (2013) Bamboo shoots after the rain: development and challenges of autism intervention in China. *Autism* 17: 510–526.

McCabe, H. and McCabe, K. (2013) Disability and family in the People's Republic of China: implementation, benefits, and comparison of two mutual support groups. *Journal of Intellectual and Developmental Disability* 38: 12–22.

Shang, X. and Wu, X. (2011) Care regime in China. *Journal of Comparative Social Welfare* 27(2): 123–131.

Shang, X. (2012) Looking for best practice in caring for disabled children: a case of socialized foster care in China. *Asia Pacific Journal of Social Work and Development* 22(1–2): 127–138.

Sun, X., Allison, C., Auyeung, B., Baron-Cohen, S. and Brayne, C. (2013a) A review of healthcare service and education provision of Autism Spectrum Condition in mainland China. *Research in Developmental Disabilities* 34: 469–479.

Sun, X., Allison, C., Auyeung, B., Matthews, F.E., Murray, S., Baron-Cohen, S. and Brayne, C. (2013b) Service provision for autism in mainland China: A service providers' perspective. *Research in Developmental Disabilities* 34: 440–451.

UNESCO, United Nations Educational, Scientific and Cultural Organization (2014) *Education For All Global Monitoring Report 2013/4,* 11th EFA, United Nations

Educational, Scientific and Cultural Organization. www.efareport.unesco.org [4 August 2014].

Wang, P. and Michaels, C.A. (2009) Chinese families of children with severe disabilities: Family needs and available support. *Research and Practice for Persons with Severe Disabilities* 34: 21–32.

Wang, P., Michaels, C.A. and Day, M.S. (2011) Stresses and coping strategies of Chinese families with children with autism and other developmental disabilities. *Journal of Autism and Developmental Disorders* 41(6): 783–795.

Wong, S.Y., Wong, T.K.S., Martinson, I., Lai, A.C., Chen, W.J. and He, Y.S. (2004) Needs of Chinese parents of children with developmental disability. *Journal of Learning Disabilities* 8: 141–158.

Yin, Z., Dai, H., Xiao, Z. and Xue, H. (2007) A research study into the requirements of disabled residents for rehabilitation services in Beijing. *Disability & Rehabilitation* 29(10): 825–833.

Zhongguo Jiaoyuwang (2009) *Members of Political Consultant Committee Proposes the Establishment of Funding for the Treatment of Children with Leukaemia,* www.chinaedunet.com/yejy/ziyuan/2009/content_163759.shtml [20 January 2010].

10 Right to children's development

Education policy

Like all children, access to formal education and learning is important for the childhood development right of children with disabilities (Art. 24 CRPD). Failure to protect the right of children to education can have serious negative effects on their childhood and their later opportunities. The next chapters analyse the right to education from two perspectives: education policy and family experience. This chapter focuses on the education system. Chapter 11 focuses on the efforts of families of children with disabilities to enable their children to attend school, the obstacles and challenges for them, and the support they sometimes receive. Apart from formal education, families are also major providers of education for children.

China has made considerable progress in nine years compulsory education law (free universal basic education) to middle school level (up to sixteen years of age) (Compulsory Education Law 2006). But few support resources, such as teacher training, teacher assistants or equipment are available in schools to enable children with disabilities to attend (McLoughlin, Zhou and Clark 2010). The obstacles for the realization of right of children with disabilities to education include accessibility, availability and affordability of education services, and whether the education environment is inclusive.

This book refers to inclusive education as the process of equitable access to education with other children in their local community (Article 24), such as supported education within a mainstream classroom or school (Runswick-Cole 2011). Inclusive education is also articulated in the UN Convention on the Rights of the Child and the Salamanca Statement and Framework for Action on Special Needs Education (UNESCO 1994). The definition used here is in contrast to special education in a segregated environment and exclusion from formal education altogether.

The Ministry for Education claims that China has over 90 per cent school enrolment and young adult literacy (UNICEF 2013), yet the analysis in these chapters shows that many children with disabilities are actively excluded from school. The SCNSSD data in 2006 showed that the school enrolment rate of children with disabilities was far lower than other children. Only 62 per cent of children with disabilities aged 6–14 years received the free compulsory education (Chen and Chen 2008). Even this enrolment rate for children with disabilities looks optimistic compared to the stories of exclusion in these chapters. Barriers to children's access to education include government approach (policy, funding and organization of education); school conditions (physical, curriculum, teachers and communication; social attitudes; and socio-economic factors (UNESCO Bangkok 2014). This chapter examines the first two barriers (government approach and school conditions).

Education policy for children with disabilities

The Chinese government has prioritized universal free education (referred to as compulsory education in China) since 1986, concentrating on nine years of school education. The progress is consistent with one of the UN Education For All (EFA) 2000 goals, which is to provide free and compulsory primary education for all (UNESCO 2014). The other five EFA goals are: Expand early childhood care and education; Promote learning and life skills for young people and adults; Increase adult literacy; Achieve gender parity (likely by 2015 in China); Improve the quality of education. EFA largely ignores the right to education of all children with disabilities (e.g. see UNESCO 2014); except through the separate UNESCO 2004 EFA Flagship Initiative, The Right to Education for Persons With Disabilities: Towards Inclusion. Some researchers and policy makers are attempting to return the focus to a human rights model and promote engagement between EFA and inclusive education goals to overcome this separation (Miles and Singal 2010; Peters, Johnstone and Ferguson 2005).

China has not yet prioritized early years, upper high school or tertiary education. Its school age priority has enabled rapid improvements in general enrolment and literacy, especially in contrast to other lower and middle income countries (UNICEF 2013). Despite an estimated 97 per cent enrolment, it has more than a million children still out of school (UNESCO 2014). This is partly explained by its large population, but also partly explained by disability exclusions. Roughly 90 per cent of children with disabilities worldwide are excluded from education (UNESCO 2014). The proportion excluded in China is discussed in this chapter. Education opportunities for children with disabilities in China consist of support within mainstream schools and special education, but not all children are entitled to attend school.

Right to free basic education

Mainstream education in China is a right to education for all children. The core of mainstream school education is the free nine-year compulsory education determined in 2006 and launched as of 2007. The state began to implement a compulsory education system in 1986, formalized in the Compulsory Education Law in 2006. Article 2 states,

> Compulsory education is the education which is provided by the state and must be received by all children of the specified age; it is part of the public interest arrangements that must be ensured by the state … No tuition or miscellaneous fees shall be charged for compulsory education.

The Compulsory Education Law is also the legal basis for special education, which focuses on learning in regular classes or in special schools. In the policies released in 2008 and 2009, the education of children with disabilities, the inclusive education approach with Chinese characteristics was reiterated, and the target school enrolment rates of school-age children with disabilities was defined.

Education levels of children with disabilities

The goal in the developed areas is to achieve a school enrolment rate comparable to that of other children, although the SCNSSD figures demonstrate the challenge of achieving that goal. Almost all children without disabilities attend some schooling (more than 97 per cent in both rural and urban areas; Table 10.1). In contrast, over a third of children with disabilities had no schooling, and surprisingly, this was worse in urban than in rural areas (36.0 per cent urban; 32.12 per cent rural). Sex was not significant.

The difference in educational attainment between children with and without disabilities worsened further for higher levels of education. No rural or urban children with disabilities in the survey had attended higher education; and no urban girls with disabilities had even attended senior high or technical college, in contrast to 16.06 per cent of urban girls without disabilities. This shocking exclusion is examined further in Chapter 11.

Access to education is worse for any children in rural compared to urban areas, and before the 1986 universal basic education policy, rural enrolments for children with disabilities were worse still (Deng and Holdsworth 2007). Following the

Table 10.1 Education levels of school-age children (6–17 years) by disability, sex and location, per cent

	Illiterate, no school		Primary		Junior high		Senior high, technical		Junior college and above	
	Rural	Urban	Rural	Urban	Rural	Urban	Rural	Urban	Rural	Urban
All children (n=45,061)										
Boys	3.21	3.21	55.10	50.94	34.07	30.61	7.58	15.10	0.03	0.14
Girls	3.60	3.04	54.55	48.51	34.67	32.23	7.14	15.90	0.03	0.31
Total	3.39	3.13	54.85	49.81	34.35	31.37	7.38	15.47	0.03	0.22
Children without disabilities (n=44,332)										
Boys	2.72	2.76	55.13	51.04	34.40	30.88	7.72	15.19	0.04	0.14
Girls	3.05	2.71	54.64	48.47	35.03	32.45	7.24	16.06	0.03	0.31
Total	2.87	2.73	54.90	49.84	34.70	31.61	7.50	15.60	0.03	0.22
Children with disabilities (n=729)										
Boys	28.27	35.48	53.87	44.09	16.96	11.83	0.89	8.60	–	–
Girls	37.45	36.84	49.38	52.63	12.35	10.53	0.82	–	–	–
Total	32.12	36.00	51.99	47.33	15.03	11.33	0.86	5.33	–	–

Source: Second China National Sample Survey on Disability (SCNSSD 2006) 10 per cent sample

Note: Significant: p<0.01 except sex

1980s economic reforms, schools received greater autonomy and the responsibilities of the central and local governments' towards education decreased (Chan, Ngok and Phillips 2008). This led to a greater disparity in access to, and quality of, education, particularly for children living in rural Western provinces of China (Deng and Holdsworth 2007). Rural areas are the most densely populated area for the school-age population, yet schools in rural areas were allocated only 38 per cent of total basic education funding (Chan, Ngok and Phillips 2008). This is particularly important in view of the demographic profile of families of children with disabilities in China, the majority of whom live in rural areas (PED JICA 2002).

If the 2006 SCNSSD data were correct, the relative disadvantage between rural and urban children with disabilities might have changed now that mainstream enrolment has become more likely in rural areas. Worsening access to education in urban areas now, also contrasts with improved urban access to other health and support services (Chapter 9), suggesting that urbanization itself is not further disadvantaging access to education for children with disabilities.

Disability education policy

Historically, education for children with disabilities was established in public special schools after 1949, primarily for children with hearing, vision and other disabilities. For a full history of special education in China see Ellsworth and Zhang (2007). Education policy for children with disabilities has had major enhancements in the past decade. Most children with disabilities who receive education attend mainstream schools (87.0 per cent in mainstream, 7.6 per cent at special schools, and 5.4 per cent in other institutions; Chen and Chen 2008: 90). The recent laws and regulations about education of children with disabilities include:

- National Education Commission (2001) *Measures for Implementing Learning in Regular Class for Children with Disabilities.*
- Compulsory Education Law (1986, 2006).
- State Council (2008) *Opinions on the Development for Persons with Disabilities.*
- Law on Protection of People with Disabilities (1990, 2008).
- State Council (2009) *Opinions regarding Further Accelerating the Development of Special Education.*

These policies define the key institutional arrangements for the education of children with disabilities. Guided by these national laws, local areas have developed their own measures. Some local areas reinforced the development of special education through their attempts to implement compulsory education, by adding special education classes in mainstream schools and inclusive regular classes in mainstream schools. At a practical level, inclusive education is the only feasible option for enrolling children with disabilities in rural areas and particularly mountain areas, border areas and remote, poor areas (Hua 2003). The 1995 survey of Daba Mountain area in Sichuan Province showed that some rural primary schools had enrolled local children with disabilities since the 1950s. More recently, rural governments implementing the compulsory education laws have unconsciously taken the same inclusive approach. When combined with additional training and support, such as in the Gansu Basic Education Programme, this unconscious approach has been extended to improve the quality of education so that any children with learning or other disabilities are more likely to not only be able to enrol in local schools, but also to have a positive learning experience (Deng and Holdsworth 2007).

The motivation for these changes has been a recognition of the institutional barriers to inclusive education and lobbying from the disability movement concerned about their rights. As in many countries, China's basic education is elitist, relying heavily on hierarchical examinations and screening. This approach is institutionalized through exam-oriented education, and is reflected in the inequality of government financing for education, which favours urban areas, higher education, a few elite schools and high academic achievement students within them. A public focus on privileged opportunities through elite examination screening exceeds their concerns for children's rounded development. Most parents and schools concentrate on the competitive position of the individual children in the exam-oriented education, and the consequent further education and employment opportunities this will facilitate. Schools and teachers are judged against the academic performance outcomes of the students in their classes. Children with disabilities can be excluded even more in better schools because of these performance targets.

With such a narrow education focus, the institutional arrangements in mainstream education are not conducive to the development of most students, before even considering suitability for children who need additional support. Students who cannot adapt themselves to exam-oriented education can be harmed and ignored. Even non-academic students without disability can be marginalized, when the ranks are determined by the examination scores and at least 49 per cent of students are ranked at the bottom and labelled with poor academic performance. Since the economic reforms started in 1978, the public and policy makers have been exposed to alternative approaches to education, including recognising the rights of children with disabilities to attend inclusive education. However, against the inertia of this history of elite, exam-based education, most schools have extremely limited resources and understanding about inclusive education.

Gradually, the education system is emerging as a 'three-track system', similar to international trajectories, in which learning in mainstream schools as a primary approach is the policy goal, special schools remain the dominant players, and special education classes in mainstream schools supplement the other two. Although the three-track system in China has provided valuable educational opportunities for many children with disabilities, others remain excluded from all parts of the education system, as described below. They have no education options, unless their family is able to pay for education not provided by the government.

The remainder of this chapter describes the policy experience and case studies of inclusion and exclusion from mainstream, special education and non-government education.

Mainstream state schools

The government has promoted inclusive education in mainstream classes since the 1980s, facilitating new educational opportunities for children with disabilities. Access to mainstream schools achieved higher school enrolment to meet the goals of the universal free education at low cost. The policy aim of learning in regular classes is to enable children with disabilities to receive education and acquire knowledge and skills in an environment with minimum constraints, and promote their all-round development in morality, intelligence, physical health, aesthetic appreciation and labour, to help them to participate equally and independently in social life (McCabe 2003).

The Ministry of Education first proposed the three-track system in 1988. The National Education Commission took the lead in 1989 by piloting inclusive mainstream classes, running dissemination conferences and encouraging national implementation (1989 pilots in Beijing, Hebei, Jiangsu, Heilongjiang, Shanxi, Shandong, Liaoning and Zhejiang for children with vision or hearing disabilities; 1992 pilots in Beijing, Jiangsu, Heilongjiang and Hubei for children with hearing or speech disabilities; from 1990, five national, provincial and city field conferences or workshops on learning in regular classes; 1994 national conference on children learning in regular classes in Yanchen, Jiangsu Province to review the experiences of promoting learning in regular classes). Following the 1994 conference, the National Education Commission released the Measures for Implementing Learning in Regular Class for Children with Disabilities in July for national implementation. The China-UNICEF project on 'Education of children with special education needs' and the 'Golden Key Project for Promoting Learning in Regular Class for Children with Impaired Vision' also contributed to the replication of learning in regular classes (Hua 2003).

The policy of learning in regular classes did not, however, allow all children with disabilities to enter mainstream schools, only 'school-age children with disabilities with the capacity to receive regular education'. Local governments have detailed definitions, for instance, Shanghai stipulates eight categories of children with disabilities allowed to learn in mainstream classes: children with vision, hearing, mild intellectual, physical, learning disorders, speech and verbal, or mental and behavioural disabilities, and children with an illness. They include children who have attended special education and have become capable of learning in regular classes, and children with mild disabilities who have been enrolled in primary or high school, and children who find it difficult to learn.

Mainstream learning poses new requirements on schools – teachers must provide education to all students in the class; and they are expected to provide the additional education support specifically designed for the students' disabilities to promote their therapy, functional recovery, and effective development of potential and social integration with other students. Some schools, particularly in urban areas, have good support for teachers to enable them to implement this new approach to the benefit of the children with and without disabilities in their class (e.g. Dyson 2012). Without these additional resources and training, the teachers can struggle to achieve these goals.

To address this problem, from 2013 Beijing requires that all mainstream schools must accept any child with disabilities, and the school can receive support from the expertise in the former special education schools. Teachers' attitude to inclusive education is also critical. International research, including in China, has shown that teachers most likely to have an inclusive attitude to children with disabilities in their classroom are those newest to teaching, those with actual experience with these children and those with training about inclusion (de Boer, Pijl and Minnaert 2011).

Apart from the education provided according to central government policies, some local initiatives have emerged. An example since 2010 is that some wealthier areas provide free education delivered in the homes of children with disabilities (e.g. Tianjin, Fujian, Beijing and Shanghai).

Example of mainstream learning

Implementing mainstream inclusive education faces many implementation challenges, despite its initial attraction as a low cost method of access to universal education. This section takes the example of a primary school teacher who has students with disabilities in regular classes to illustrate some of the challenges at the local level (Anqing City). It complements the next chapter about the children's experiences of mainstream classes. The fieldwork researcher was a local resident postgraduate student, so the teacher was comfortable reflecting on her wariness about inclusive teaching. She had doubts about educating children with disabilities in a mainstream class.

She was a rural teacher with ten years' teaching experience. Her school had several students with disabilities, whose needs varied, in each class. She also commented that the teaching and management approach was to treat them the same as other children, but they faced challenges. The impact on her class was that some students performed well, but others disturbed the class sessions, particularly the students around them. She commented on their behaviour and social skills. She said some of them were well-behaved and followed teachers' instructions; some were naughty, and several of them were violent. She said maybe they were just naïve; some of them did not know how to express their intentions and views, and were unaware of their violent body motions; when they play with other students, they could make trouble for their peers. Some students complained that the students with disabilities bullied or hit them. She said most students, but not all, fitted into the classes and got along with other peers. Some students with disabilities voluntarily helped others. A few students behaved poorly, for example taking others' articles, nice clothes or interesting stationery, probably because they did not know how to express themselves. So they did not get on well with peers.

She said communication with the parents was not frequent because it is a rural school. One of her students was deaf, aged ten, older than the other students in the class. She always followed teachers' instructions and was well-behaved; but she found it challenging to attend class sessions, because she could not hear or express herself. She just did written transcription or handwriting, but could not participate in other learning. The teacher had tried to contact her parents many times, but they were migrant workers in another region. She was cared for only by her grandfather who had another young child to look after, so he did not have time to visit the school even if he was invited by the teachers.

The teacher did not think the arrangements for learning in regular classes were appropriate for children with disabilities. She did not believe her school was suitable for them. She thought a special school was the better choice for them, and the government should allocate more resources to special schools to enable the children to obtain the same education and achieve the same growth as other children.

Her comments reflected that although the rural school enrolled children with disabilities, it did not have the additional arrangements or the resources that could have improved the educational and social experiences of the children. As a result, some of the children's support needs were not met, and their access to education was limited to what they could pick up without assistance. The implications of her comments included the need for facilities, equipment, specialist teachers or teacher assistants, and training for teachers and peers.

Special education schools

Special schools in China are for children with vision, hearing and mild intellectual disabilities. Mainstream schools now enrol some of these children too, as discussed above. The Law on Protection of People with Disabilities 2008 stipulates that,

> Special education institutions at junior high school level or lower levels and special education classes of regular education institutions [mainstream schools] shall provide compulsory [free] education to children with disabilities who are incapable of receiving regular education. Institutions providing special education shall possess the places and facilities appropriate for the learning, therapy and living of people with disabilities.

Special education schools and the special education classes in mainstream schools are designed to provide education to children with specified disabilities whom the schools deem are incapable of learning in mainstream schools. Yet few special or mainstream schools accept any children with cerebral palsy, autism, moderate or severe intellectual disabilities or other sensory, physical and cognitive disabilities that require significant support.

Example of special education

The effectiveness of laws and policies about inclusive education relies on adequate implementation. The example in this section illustrates the implementation process in a moderately developed city. The information is from the field research interviews (Chapter 1) with the chairman and management staff of the local Disabled Persons Federation (DPF), except where otherwise stated. The city is a typical model of special education in China in a small low-developed area.

Gao'an City is in northwest central Jiangxi Province. It was upgraded from a county to a city in 1993. It has two districts, 22 townships and two farms, with a total population of 830,000 (including 600,000 farmers). In 2006, the per capita net income of farmers was 3,827 yuan, making it a relatively developed city in the province (Gao'an Government 2010).

City education policies

The municipal DPF is responsible for services to the 54,000 people with disabilities in the city (SCNSSD). It had an employment service centre and general office, with ten staff members (30–59 years; one of the staff was a person with disabilities), three rooms and a meeting room. Its funds were from the municipal government budget and employment security funds for people with disabilities.

The exact number of children with disabilities was unknown to the DPF. According to the survey findings of the local education authority in 2006, there were about 533 school-age children with intellectual, hearing or vision disabilities in Gao'an City (Table 10.2). The school enrolment rate is over 80 per cent for children with vision and intellectual disabilities and 72 per cent for children with hearing disabilities. All children with vision disabilities were in mainstream schools. These rates are likely to be an overestimation of school attendance, because the number of children with these disabilities is far lower than would be expected in a city of this size, probably because it does not include any children the government defines as incapable of benefiting from education.

Special education had a short history in the city. In 1988, a class for urban children with intellectual disabilities was set up in one of the urban primary schools, but the class only enrolled students intermittently because of the shortage of trained special education teachers. The development of special education

Table 10.2 Level of school enrolment of children with disabilities in Gao'an City

Disability	Children with disabilities	Mainstream school Primary	Junior high	Special school	School enrolment Total	Per cent
Intellectual	348	250	36	9	295	85
Hearing	115	40	4	39	83	72
Vision	70	56	10	0	66	94
Total	533	346	50	48	444	83

Source: Gao'an Education Authority field survey 2006. Children aged 7-16 years

expanded in 2004 when the Gao'an City Special School was established, for children with hearing, intellectual and other disabilities. The primary special school was for children with vision, hearing and mild intellectual disabilities. Children with physical disabilities attended mainstream schools and most children with more serious disabilities did not attend school. The DPF officials said enrolment improved in 2007 and 2008 (the 2008 DPF work report mentioned that school enrolment was 93 per cent; 72 children in local special school or special education classes; four children in other special schools and 350 in mainstream classes in other areas; five students in colleges and universities; Gao'an City Disabled Persons' Federation 2009).

The city set new objectives for the education of children with disabilities in 2008: 1) achieve a school enrolment rate of children with disabilities who are capable of receiving regular education in the city approximately the same or no lower than other children; 2) reform the special education classes and develop a Gao'an City Special School; 3) achieve an average school enrolment rate of children with disabilities in the city of 85 per cent (95 per cent for urban areas, 90 per cent for rural areas, and 75 per cent for remote and mountain areas); and 4) enhance the quality of education, targeting short- and medium-term training to children with disabilities.

The city policy on disability policy did not reduce or exempt children from the cost of therapy and medical interventions, but families in extreme difficulties could obtain medical relief for families in poverty (not specifically for families of children with disabilities). The city did not have a dedicated institution for the therapy of children with disabilities. The public rehabilitation institution within Gao'an City Orthopedic Hospital was for people with physical and intellectual disabilities. The facilities were very limited, primarily including single and parallel bars designed for mobility exercises. It did not have a professional rehabilitation doctor. Several children with mental illness had received treatment there. Their parents took them to the institution for diagnosis and medication during psychotic episodes. Very few children received services from the institution.

Gao'an City Special School

As a county-level city, Gao'an City has funding for a primary special school up to grade four. The school had 48 students, ten teachers and two carers in 2010. It is in a pleasant location and had reasonable facilities (dormitories, canteen, and rooms for rhythm exercise, computers, multimedia and entertainment). No tuition fee was charged. The mission of the school was to:

> Enable the students to support themselves by their own labour, based on the human-oriented vision of functional supplementation, survival, adaptation to the social life, and reintegration into the mainstream and [guidelines of] enhancing internal capacities and external image, and fully implementing the government policies for education.

At its peak, the number of students reached 72. Some students learned to communicate sufficiently to transfer to other schools to learn in mainstream classes, with the assistance of the special school. At the time of the survey in 2006, the school had 48 students, including 39 deaf children and nine children with intellectual disabilities. The students were divided into four grades and five classes. The nine children with intellectual disabilities were in one class, including six girls and three boys; and the 38 deaf students were divided into four classes, including eight girls and 31 boys. These small classes contrast with mainstream schooling, which the fieldwork found could be up to 52 children (consistent with Callaway's (1999) earlier findings in schools for deaf children).

Most students came from rural areas (80 per cent), holding rural registered permanent residence. Most of their households were in poverty, but the school enrols any eligible children sent by parents (aged six to sixteen years, status and types of disabilities). A deaf student who was aged 20 was still enrolled, because he was keen to attend the school and supported in his decision by his parents. The school interviews children with intellectual disabilities before enrolling them due to the limited teachers and other resources. This excludes some children. Most students lived far away so that they boarded at the school during term-time and returned home during vacations.

The principal was previously a senior teacher at a mainstream primary school. His field survey about education of children with disabilities in the city spurred the government to support his proposal to establish the special school. The school started with seven teachers and the principal, who were transferred from mainstream schools. It then employed three teachers with special education diplomas and experience. Of the ten teachers, one had a bachelor's degree, nine had graduated from junior colleges, and two were studying for a bachelor's degree. None of the teachers had disabilities. The teachers exchanged peer training such as sign language and special education. All teachers must learn sign language through in-service training for the more than 30 deaf students in the school. Teaching was in sign and spoken language, although teachers usually communicated with students in sign language. Many students learned sign language after they entered the school. The carers were primarily responsible for assisting the students with their daily life activities when they were not in class.

The curriculum in the special education is defined by the central government (Chinese, maths, verbal training, computer application, fine arts, handwork and moral education). The teachers used a combination of sign and spoken language for the deaf classes. The deaf children sit mid-term and final examinations in each semester, and students who exhibit good academic performance are granted certificates of merit. The curriculum for the intellectual disabilities class differed from the mainstream curriculum, and focused on independent living skills. They received only simplified tests without requirements.

The school has a short history and was small. It did not arrange for students to participate in graduation examinations. If students wished to continue to junior or senior high school, the school intended to extend the opportunities or refer them to the special school in the neighbouring city. It was seeking support from the city government to develop an occupational junior high school (e.g. some special schools offer training skills for blind massage therapy). The school had leveraged its social connections to help three older students to secure jobs.

When the school first opened, parents were wary about the benefit of special education. Some parents thought education for children with disabilities was not necessary and did not send their children to school. The teachers visited the communities to disseminate information and seek potential students. When the parents saw the effectiveness of the education, they began to trust the school. Enrolments decreased as the number of school-age children declined; the improvement in living standards and medical technologies meant that fewer children were born deaf; and better opportunities emerged in mainstream classes. In some years, the grade one class was full, but when they reached higher grades, the number of students decreased significantly.

Learning in regular classes remained the primary approach for education of children with disabilities. The special school was less prioritized: the government resources were inadequate for special education; teachers at special schools were in short supply; and education quality was compromised. School facilities were not sufficient for the mainstream curriculum requirements of children with disabilities in the city, not even offering classes beyond grade 4.

Special school management

Since its establishment, the school gradually developed its management system and regulations, and earned a government city-level advanced, safe and civilized school award according to the school principal. The school funding was from the special fiscal budget of the government. Prior to its establishment, the City government agreed to allocate a fixed annual amount from the fiscal budget (the principal declined to disclose the amount). The school is a public school; teacher salaries are similar to teachers at mainstream schools; and the sources of funds are basically the same.

In addition to funds for the school, the government also funded support for the living expenses of students through urban minimum living security to all students at the school, regardless of their origin, which is higher than the rural minimum living security and can be used to support living expenses; and the 'Two exempts and one allowance' treatment from the education bureau, including exemption of tuition fees and miscellaneous fees, and allowance for boarding. The boarding fee standard was equal to junior high school students (500 yuan per student per year). The students did not have to pay any fees. Although, the principal said the funds fall short of the expenses for training, facilities, expenses and enrolment of more students. Government support for the operation of the special school included routine funding and ad hoc support, such as medical insurance for the students and official visits to the school. In the Chinese political context, such visits play a key role in driving the development of the school.

Gao'an is a small city with less developed economy and few donations to the city. Local small businesses sometimes fund support to children with disabilities.

For instance, the local DPF connected a potential donor with staff at the special school to visit and donate stationery, free services and lectures; and connected a hearing aid company to donate free hearing tests and hearing aids.

The school was a locked facility, which was supported by the parents. Before it was locked, a stranger entered the school and kidnapped a deaf child. The child was found and no harm was done, but it frightened the staff and parents. A consequence of the locked facility was that the students were isolated from their local community. The principal said that the risk was too great. People were welcome to visit by invitation, such as students from a local primary school. Teachers also accompanied students to shop in the supermarket to learn about community skills. Sometimes the children went into the community to clean the roads and pick up rubbish to strengthen community responsibility and win praise from the local residents by contributing to the environmental sanitation of the community.

Non-government special schools

Some families of children with disabilities have the capacity to seek education from the market. Some non-government and private organizations provide education to children who are excluded from public school education. Some of the schools were established by parents whose children were excluded. Where parents demanded special education for their children and state schools failed to meet their rights, some privately-run special schools have emerged. The number of non-government schools is limited and they face numerous challenges to meet the children's needs. They are now an important part of the Chinese education system for children with disabilities, but compared to public special schools, they have greater trouble securing funds. This section analyses the experience of a private special school for deaf children.

Private school for deaf children

The school in this example was the only special school in the local city, established in an urban area in 1998. The school had 27 students at the time of the research and usually had between 30 and 40 students. From 1998–2009, 200 students had attended the school. The school aims to provide basic education to students and help them integrate into their community. Most students were from the local district and some were from counties in the city. The girl to boy ratio was less than 1:10, because parents preferred to send boys to the school, especially when they were in poverty (consistent with Callaway's (1999) findings about government schools for deaf children). Each month the teachers communicated with parents two or three times, including follow-up visits and record management. The parents were grateful to the teachers, because many of the children had learned to speak.

The school provided speech training and literacy courses in Chinese and maths. Speech training was rhythm exercises (mimic the mouth shape and actions without moving body) and tongue exercises (to strengthen the flexibility of tongue). The students were in four classes according to their level of speech ability, so that no class had more than eight children. The children sat at an arc-shaped table, so that they could all observe the mouth shape of the teacher. During the visit, the children played together in groups of up to five. They did not have the opportunity to play with children with hearing and those that were boarding were also isolated from their families. The teachers said that their social development was limited because they did not have augmented communication, but the teachers would not talk about this with the parents, because the parents disagreed.

The school did not offer certificates of graduation. It was basically a therapy centre. When children became better able to speak, they left the school. Sometimes they transferred to a mainstream school (only one girl had done so, because her family could afford her schooling) to check if they could keep up the progress of learning there; sometimes they came back to the special school. Sometimes students discontinued any education and lost contact with the school; or they continued to learn skills while earning a living in skilled labour.

Private school management

The school is small (land 200 square meters, building over 600 square meters), with eight classrooms, and rooms for meeting, exercise, observation, bedroom for younger children, and dining. The operation relied on parent fees, because it had no government funding. The annual tuition fee was over 2,000 yuan, plus 30 yuan per month for board. Fees were reduced for families in extreme poverty. The fee income was low and costs were high. The principal established the school with his own money in response to a proposal from a special education teacher and raised income through business with friends to cover the gap in costs. The school could only afford a basic salary to teachers and used student teachers to save costs. It tried to serve nutritional meals within its limited income.

The school had six staff, including four teachers and two carers, none of whom was deaf. Callaway (1999) notes that the formal requirement for qualified staff decreased the number of deaf teachers in schools). The speech training teachers had graduated from special schools, mostly holding a technical secondary school diploma. The literacy teachers were student teachers from a local college, who received a small remuneration from the school. One teacher was aged under 30 years and had been teaching at the school since it was established. She had graduated from a Special Education Secondary School. While teaching, she studied junior college courses by herself, and finally obtained her junior college diploma.

The school registered as a private school in 2004 with the support of the local DPF. Staff from the DPF visit the school, donate stationery, food and coal in winter. The local government is not involved in supporting the school, despite the lack of any alternatives in the city. The principal said he has to visit the government officials several times before he can secure any small amount of government support. The school was valued by the parents and children, facilitating many children to obtain valuable skills and their first opportunity for education. Without government support, however, the survival of such schools faces great challenges.

Conclusion on education policy and development

This chapter explored the policies and implementation supporting the right to education of children with disabilities (Art. 24 CRPD). The Chinese government has made progress in protecting the right to education through the implementation of free universal school education for some children. However, the education system does not yet even aim to meet the rights of all children with disabilities.

The policies primarily cover children with vision, hearing and mild intellectual disabilities; and some children with physical disabilities if they can get to school and are independent in self care. The right to education of all other children with disabilities is not protected – including children with cerebral palsy, autism, moderate and severe intellectual disabilities and other physical disabilities requiring greater support. These children generally have no access to schooling or only receive education at home or in the few non-government, private schools. Very few families in China have the financial capacity to educate these children.

Most children with disabilities rely on the inclusive education policy of learning in regular classes. While this approach is advocated in education and disability research and ensures the right to school-based education, the implementation in the context of few or no additional resources and incompatibility with the elite, exam-oriented academic education can lead to exclusion within a mainstream school. The more competitive the school, (e.g. urban schools with good college entrance results), the less feasible it is for children with disabilities to enter. Enrolment in mainstream schools is a good first step towards the realization of their right to education. Substantive realization will require greater resources, new approaches to education and changed attitudes of teachers, managers and peers.

References

Callaway, A. (1999) Considering sign bilingual education in cultural context: a survey of deaf schools in Jiangsu Province. *China Deafness Education International* 1: 34–46.

Chan, C.K., Ngok, K.L. and Phillips, D. (2008) *Social Policy in China: Development and Wellbeing*, Bristol: The Policy Press, University of Bristol.

Chen, X. and Chen, Y. (2008) *The Status Analysis and Strategies of Children with Disabilities in China*, Beijing: Huaxia Press.

Compulsory Education Law (1986, 2006) www.gov.cn/flfg/2006-06/30/content_323302.htm [9 July 2012].

CRPD, United Nations Convention on the Rights of Persons with Disabilities (2006) www.un.org/disabilities/default.asp?id=150 [1 February 2012].

de Boer, A., Pijl, S.J. and Minnaert, A. (2011) Regular primary schoolteachers' attitudes towards inclusive education: a review of the literature. *International Journal of Inclusive Education* 15(3): 345–346.

Deng, M. and Holdsworth, J.C. (2007) From unconscious to conscious inclusion: meeting special education needs in West China. *Disability & Society* 22(5): 507–522.

Dyson, L. (2012) Strategies for and successes with promoting social integration in primary schools in Canada and China. *International Journal of Disability, Development and Education* 59: 157–172.

Ellsworth, N.J. and Zhang, C. (2007) Progress and challenges in China's special education development. *Remedial and Special Education* 28(1): 58–64.

Gao'an City Disabled Persons' Federation (2009) *Annual Report of the Gao'an City Disabled Persons' Federation 2008*, Gao'an: Gao'an City Disabled Persons' Federation.

Gao'an Government (2010) *Entering Gao'an*, Gao'an City Municipal Party Committee, www.gaoan.gov.cn/system/2011/12/22/011859232.shtml [11 July 2014].

Hua, G. (2003) The situation and development of inclusive education for children with disabilities. *Education Studies* [Chinese] 24(2): 65–69.

Law on the Protection of Persons with Disabilities (1990, 2008) China Disabled Persons Federation, www.cdpf.org.cn/english/laws1documents/200804/t20080410_267460. html [2 May 2015].

McCabe, H. (2003) The beginnings of inclusion in the People's Republic of China. *Research and Practice for Persons with Severe Disabilities* 28: 16–22.

McLoughlin, C.S., Zhou, Z. and Clark, E. (2005) Reflections on the development and status of contemporary special education services in China. *Psychology in Schools* 42(3): 273–283.

Miles, S. and Singal, N. (2010) The Education for All and inclusive education debate: conflict, contradiction or opportunity? *International Journal of Inclusive Education* 14(1): 1–15.

National Education Commission (2001) *Measures for Implementing Learning in Regular Class for Children with Disabilities*, National Education Commission and CDPF, www. cdpf.org.cn/jiaoy/content/2001-07/19/content_75922.htm [29 October 2010].

PED JICA, Planning and Evaluation Department, Japan International Cooperation Agency (2002) *Country Profile on Disabilities, People's Republic of China*, Tokyo: Japan International Cooperation Agency.

Peters, S., Johnstone, C. and Ferguson, P. (2005) A disability rights in education model for evaluating inclusive education, *International Journal of Inclusive Education* 9(2): 139–160.

Runswick-Cole, K. (2011) Time to end the bias towards inclusive education? *British Journal of Special Education* 38: 112–119.

State Council (2008) *Opinions on the development of welfare for persons with disabilities*, www.gov.cn/jrzg/2008-04/23/content_952483.htm [28 January 2012].

State Council (2009) *Opinions regarding further accelerating the development of special education*, www.gov.cn/zwgk/2009-05/08/content_1308951.htm [28 January 2011].

UNESCO, United Nations Educational, Scientific and Cultural Organization (1994) *Salamanca Statement and Framework for Action on Special Needs Education* www. unesco.org/education/pdf/SALAMA_E.PDF [3 May 2015].

UNESCO, United Nations Educational, Scientific and Cultural Organization (2004) *EFA Flagship Initiative, The Right to Education for Persons With Disabilities: Towards Inclusion* http://unesdoc.unesco.org/images/0013/001378/137873e.pdf [3 May 2015].

UNESCO, United Nations Educational, Scientific and Cultural Organization (2014) *Education For All Global Monitoring Report 2013/4*, 11th EFA, UNESCO. www. efareport.unesco.org [4 August 2014].

UNESCO Bangkok, United Nations Educational, Scientific and Cultural Organization Bangkok (2014) Barriers to inclusive education, www.unescobkk.org/education/ inclusive-education/what-is-inclusive-education/barriers-to-inclusive-education/ [6 August 2014].

UNICEF, United Nations Children's Fund (2013) *The State of the World's Children 2013: Children with disabilities*, www.unicef.org/sowc2013 [2 May 2015].

11 Right to children's development

Education experiences

This chapter discusses the perspective of children with disabilities and their families of their barriers to education. It complements the findings of the previous chapter about the ambitious government education policies and the challenges to implementation through mainstream and segregated education in government and non-government schools. China has made progress in access to inclusive education, but barriers in the education system and resource distribution across China prevent many children with disabilities from attending school (Table 10.1). For most children, access to education is generally better in urban areas, but this is not necessarily so for children with disabilities.

While the government and schools continue to improve education policies and implementation for children with disabilities, the public remains largely unaware of the shortfall in education to children with disabilities, the frustration experienced by children and their families, and the barriers that prevent them from attending school. This chapter examines these experiences using the interviews from the 52 case families (Chapter 1) to understand the education needs of children with disabilities and the barriers they face.

As introduced in Chapter 10, barriers to children's access to education include the government approach (policy, funding and organization of education); school conditions (physical, curriculum, teachers and communication; social attitudes; and socio-economic factors (UNESCO Bangkok 2014). Chapter 10 analysed the barriers in the first two factors – government policies and implementation in schools. It described how China has invested in inclusive education for children with vision, health and mild intellectual disabilities, but other children generally have no access to school education and usually only receive informal education at home, if at all. Families experience various barriers to seeking formal education opportunities for their children. Some families are confident in the future since their children have access to education. Others struggle to address the barriers that prevent their children attending school. This chapter focuses on families' experiences with the barriers from these school conditions, social attitudes and socio-economic factors.

School conditions

Many barriers to education that families face are at the local level of how schools interpret their obligations to offer inclusive education. Barriers within schools include physical access to getting to school and around the school; the adaptability of the curriculum to the child's needs; teachers' attitudes, skills, support and resources; and the school's willingness to offer communication suitable to the child in terms of language, and augmented communication (UNESCO Bangkok 2014). Many of these barriers are driven by the higher government policy and funding discussed in Chapter 10, particularly the centralized education policy control and distribution of financial resources. Other barriers have remedies in the approach taken by local schools and teachers. Families identified several barriers at the school level – school and teacher capacity, physical conditions, curriculum and communication assistance.

Local school and teacher capacity

The central government policy is that schools cannot refuse to enrol children who have local registered residency, including children with vision, hearing and mild intellectual disabilities. Preferential policies are available for these children with disabilities, including an exemption from miscellaneous expenses and fees for books and the provision of living allowances.

School conditions, analysed below were an important factor preventing some children from continuing in school, including inadequate coverage of the current education system and the exclusion of eligible children with disabilities from education. Many children with disabilities need additional support, assistance or equipment for interpersonal communication, self-care, social skills and learning methods, whether they are learning in regular classes in mainstream schools or in special schools. The families said they had problems finding out what support their children could expect; and receiving the support in a mainstream school or a special school.

Information about support for learning

The families described difficulties knowing where to find appropriate education and what support their children needed to make the education opportunity effective. The school or other local government did not give them information about what they were entitled to according to central policies, such as their right to enrol their child in school, free education, exemption from miscellaneous fees and support in the classroom. They were not told about possible education approaches for their child, such as whether to choose a local school, special school, private school, home schooling or no education. They did not know what support they could expect or ask for to make the schooling accessible, such as physical access, communication support, and personal care support. And they did not know about government and non-government welfare opportunities to make the education affordable and accessible.

Many families, especially in rural areas, had limited capacity to find relevant and timely information about educational opportunities, which affected their children's access to support and education. For example, a deaf child, Xiaoxin, lived in a county city, which had good information available to families. She received language training at an early age. As a result, she could communicate with other children and was able to study in a regular class in her local primary school. In contrast, Xiaobao, who was also deaf, lived in a rural area in the same province but only received language training when he was eight years old. Consequently, he was studying at a special school for deaf children, where he mainly used sign language and did not have opportunities to use spoken language. He only spoke short words rather than sentences. Neither Xiaobao or Xiaoxin's family was rich, but Xiaoxin had an advantage since her family lived in an urban area. Other parents spoke about reading an advertisement in a national newspaper for free surgical treatment for deaf children and hoped their children could be assisted. They would then find that the surgical treatment was not for local children because priority was given to children with disabilities in large cities.

Similarly, some parents did not know they could apply for a disability certificate so that their child was eligible for welfare benefits and concessions on school costs. Parents gave examples about randomly finding out that they were eligible for assistance:

> Two days ago, I read the [local newspaper] and became aware of the 'Plan for Supporting Children with Hearing Disabilities' that distributes hearing aids. We have submitted the application and are waiting for the approval.

Schools refusing enrolment or offering conditional enrolment

Many of the children had been excluded by schools. For example, Juanjuan's parents were migrant workers who lived in a city away from her. When she was seven years old, her grandmother took her to the local rural school, but the principal recommended a special school for deaf children. The school principal told her grandmother that if Juanjuan attended the local school, her performance would affect the learning achievements of the other students. Her grandmother did not have the capacity to argue so took Juanjuan home. The special school was far from Juanjuan's home and charged high fees, which her grandmother could not afford. Consequently, Juanjuan did not attend any school. Juanjuan lost interest in learning. Since she did not go to school, she did not have any friends and stayed home with her grandparents all the time. She could not speak, communicate, read or write. Her mother said,

> This [school exclusion] will have lifetime impact on Juanjuan. I wonder how will she communicate with others in the future? ... I worry about her future very much.

Other children with disabilities excluded from school education faced a similar situation. Parents said,

> When I took my child to the primary school at the very beginning, the principal refused to enrol him due to his weak health and lisp.

> My child now doesn't go to school due to his inability to care for himself and lack of care from others in the school.

> My child went to the school for only one semester because he entered a regular school and seldom played with other children due to physical inconvenience. Teachers also paid little attention to him.

> When our child reached school age, we sent him to the local primary school, but the principal advised us to send him to a special school rather than a regular school since he could not speak and would affect teaching achievements in the regular school. The special school is far from home and charges high fees. Our family is poor and has to give up the special school.

Another boy, Mingming, was refused enrolment to all the public primary schools, so attended a private school paid for by his parents who said,

> Children without disabilities can enjoy the nine-year compulsory education, but our child is excluded from it. Since no public schools are willing to enrol our child, we have to send him to this private school with high fees.

One mother tried to enrol her child in many schools, but they all insisted that if she enrolled her child she would have to be there with him or provide full-time care at the school. The schools were afraid to bear any responsibility if an accident occurred affecting the child or other students. For example, the teachers told Hongmei to leave school after one month because she needed assistance to care for herself. The teachers said that she could be in danger without the protection of an assistant. For example, she might get hurt when classmates quarrelled or fought noisily. Other children might bully her because of her disabilities. The family took her out of school, but tried to seek other education opportunities. They tried to send her to a special school, but it was only for children with vision and hearing disabilities (which she was not) and the quality was not good. Other children in her community had a similar experience of no access to school education.

Some schools allowed the children to enrol only if the family went to the school during breaks for personal care such as eating and toileting. For example, Xiaoyi started school in grade one after medical treatment. The mother carried Xiaoyi to the school on her back after breakfast, and then returned home to do housework, until she carried him home again after school. Xiaoyi could not go to the toilet during the day, because the school would not provide support and his mother could not attend. From grade three, Xiaoyi had difficulty walking. When his mother went to the school to pick him up the other children had left and Xiaoyi was crying, walking by holding the wall. He told his mother, 'I don't want to go to school.' By the time he was ten years old, it was difficult for his mother to carry him. He was forced to give up school education due to the lack of support from the school for his physical needs.

Mainstream schools

Many schools failed to provide the support their child needed to learn and participate with their peers. The capacity of teachers to teach according to the particular needs of each child was limited by their training, the size of their classes, and the resources, assistance and equipment available to them. Most schools in the fieldwork communities did not have any special services needed by children with disabilities, as described by the families,

> My child could not understand what teachers teach and was often sick. The school had no means to provide additional support and care. Finally, she left the school.

> [without any support from the school], due to a hearing disability, my child cannot keep up with other children.

> My child often cannot find his schoolbag and books and doesn't know what homework is assigned by teachers. Being asked what he learns during the school, he knows nothing. He is studying at grade two now after six years of schooling, but often gives a wrong answer for such simple calculations as one plus one.

> Dongdong learnt nothing in the school and doesn't know simple songs, Chinese phonetic alphabets and numbers. He also dislikes the school himself.

For example, Xiaoyu was receiving mainstream education like the other children of her age. On average, at her school there were about 50 students in each class, including one or two children with disabilities. Her teachers could not spend extra time addressing the needs of the children with disabilities in her classes. Her mother had no complaints about the school. She believed that teachers had tried their best and the family had no right to ask for additional care from the teachers for Xiaoyu. She was deaf and could not keep up with other children because she had no assistance in the classroom. As a result, she progressed slowly in understanding new knowledge and her school results were poor. Her mother had reported this to the local DPF several times but they had taken no action to organize or fund support. Instead, her mother hoped to find a more appropriate special school for Xiaoyu to improve the quality of education she was receiving and to enhance her education achievements.

Most of the fieldwork areas did not have senior high schools or tertiary education for young people with disabilities, yet most of them remained excluded from mainstream schools and colleges. A principal of a special school suggested establishing one senior high school in each province or regions, although this continues the history of segregation, rather than addressing the wider question of inclusive education at all levels (Chapter 10).

Special schools

The special schools were also restricted by the equipment, teacher resources and teaching facilities available to them. Nearly half the case study children who were at school attended public or private special schools. The schools did not have national guidance on how to adapt the mainstream curriculum or implement suitable teaching support. As a result the quality of the education and support in special education varied widely in different areas, as described by principals in special schools,

> There are no national criteria for the education of people with disabilities, such as achievements of students and performance assessment of teachers. Different schools follow their own practices.

> The schools design [graduation] examinations by themselves... and report students qualified in the examinations to education authorities. Education authorities directly examine and approve graduation certificates.

> Teachers design questions by themselves. Generally, students successfully graduate as long as they can read and take care of themselves. Graduation certificates for primary schools are issued for these children.

The special schools also faced serious understaffing, finding it difficult to recruit any teachers, with or without qualifications. The principals said,

> [The school] recruits [teachers] in the community, but seldom attracts qualified teachers.

> The school cannot afford the recruitment of professional language training teachers to provide special education for these children. Graduates from kindergarten teacher colleges are all eligible [instead].

The fieldworkers observed that special school teachers taught to an average level in their classes rather than to the specific needs of each child. One school explained that it had no eligibility criteria for enrolment or sorting students into compatible groups, which led to a wide range of student needs in the same class, but without teacher capacity to teach to the range. For example, they observed that in the classes, some children could easily understand the teachers and were sitting around bored, while the teachers were not able to offer suitable support or curriculum to other children. The school was proposing to introduce entrance examinations in the new year to improve this problem, which would have the impact of excluding children, rather than addressing their education support needs.

Teachers in the special education classes said that students were usually older than in the same grade in regular schools. Children were asked to leave the school when they were aged eighteen years, even if they had not completed the nine-year compulsory education. For example, Xiaoxing's support needs were high even in his special education class, especially his vision. His teachers said he had progressed far in his learning, but they only treat him like the other children, rather than giving him relevant support. Xiaoxing stayed grade one until he was twelve years old in a special education class because of his lack of basic skills. At the age of fifteen he was studying in grade three. Xiaoxing may be asked to leave the school after completing grade six because he was unlikely to achieve a higher grade before he turned eighteen. The impact of encouraging children to stay in school but at a lower grade than their age was that at least they were gaining formal education. The cost of this approach though was that they were not in social groups with children of a similar age with opportunities for friendship and social engagement.

An extreme example of this age disparity was Hong Yang, who was fifteen years old and had restarted school in grade one in a special school. Before attending the special school, he went to a regular class in his free local school from the age of nine, where he completed grade five. His family's preference would have been a free special school rather than the local school, but it was not available and they could not afford to pay for special education. They paid close attention to any information about neighbouring special schools and heard of a school for blind and deaf children in a city nearby, but the fees were too high for the family. When the special school exempted students from all fees in 2008, they moved him to the special school. The principal recommended Hong Yang start again from grade one. The mother emphasized that Hong Yang was already fifteen years old and should start grade six. The principal explained that mainstream schools paid little attention to the actual learning needs of children with disabilities and Hong Yang could start from grade one to learn sign language in the special school. His parents still shouldered a heavy economic cost for his education and development including borrowing money from whomever they could. Although the special school did not charge tuition fees, they still needed to pay for boarding (250 yuan per year) and meals (ten yuan per day).

The private special schools emerged in response to the market demand in areas where there were no public special schools (Chapter 10). The school and teacher capacity in these private schools was generally even worse because they did not have government funding or supervision. For example, one private special school had not secured a permanent location. The principal was very frustrated because the semester had to be delayed while the construction of the school buildings organized by the education bureau was completed. Previously, they had lessons in a free building from the education bureau. It was located in an army family member's courtyard, where retired officials lived, such as school principals and Party secretaries. They had to leave because the residents complained when the teaching activities affected their daily lives.

Social attitudes

Access to education affects both learning and social inclusion. Children with disabilities are often excluded from activities of social inclusion such as education (Holroyd 2003). Social attitudes from the local community, schools, teachers and peers can all be barriers to education. Most of the families invested heavily in overcoming the expectation that their child did not have the right to education.

Discrimination from school and teachers

The families of most of the case study children in regular classes at mainstream schools (11/13) said their children had experienced explicit discrimination. For example, they were refused enrolment or their parents were asked to sign letters of guarantee to exempt schools from any obligations for the children while at school and to exclude them from participation in examinations and some school activities. In addition, personal discrimination led to some children leaving school or not learning to their potential. Some parents said,

> My child went to the school for only one semester because he entered a regular school and seldom played with other children due to physical inconvenience. Teachers also paid little attention to him.

> When he was six years old, we sent him to the pre-school class, but he refused to attend the class. When he was seven and half years old, he was sent to a primary school. Subsequently, he stayed at grade one for two years. Teachers are unwilling to enrol him because he is disobedient and may affect other students. He is hyperactive. The teachers reach an agreement with us that he will not participate in any examinations.

In another case, the school allowed all classes two lessons at the audio-visual teaching room. When Xinxin was at grade three, he was excluded from this opportunity and no seat was arranged for him. His mother was angry when she found out. She sent Xinxin to the audio-visual teaching room and questioned the teachers about why he was excluded. She forced them to arrange a seat for him, but the discrimination continued. Again, his mother went to the school during the time when the teachers and other students were all in the audio-visual teaching room, and only Xinxin was left behind, in tears. In another example, the mother of Jinbo complained that her son had to leave school,

> Prior to leaving, he was studying at grade four in a local regular school … He didn't want to go to school by himself. During the stay at school, he hoped to participate in labour and sports, but teachers refused him due to his hand disability. Gradually, he was unwilling to attend the school.

The striving for elite achievement worsened the discrimination of children with disabilities. For example in a famous 'education town' that achieved nineteen 'number one scholars in college entrance examinations', a parent of a child with disabilities complained that the experience of his son, Junjun, in the school was that, 'The school only posed harm to him rather than bringing any benefit to him.'

Discrimination from peers

In addition to discrimination from the school and teachers, the case studies also revealed widespread discrimination from peers in the schools. Social relations with peers are important for social development, yet the social experiences of some of the children at the school were very negative. In these cases, the schools had not educated the school mates about non-discriminatory attitudes towards children with disabilities or taken other steps to create a welcoming environment for the children to reduce discrimination.

Discrimination from school mates led to some of the children leaving school. For example, according to his father, Dongdong refused to go to the kindergarten after one month. His father thought he should go to kindergarten to learn basic Chinese characters and maths, so he paid to send him to a private kindergarten. Other children at the private kindergarten would not play with him and he was left to stand alone. The teachers also paid little attention to him. During lunch, other children took his food from him, but when he cried about it, the teachers ignored him, so he went home hungry. Instead, Dongdong left the kindergarten and stayed at home because of the discrimination from his peers and because his family could not afford to pay for education.

Socio-economic factors

The final set of barriers to education are socio-economic factors in the family household and community; and affordability for the family of the cost of education. Social and education policy to overcome these barriers requires not only central policy initiatives but also local resources and motivation to implement them.

Expectations of families

The literature and some of the case studies revealed how some families had low expectations about their child attending school, due to their household poverty and cultural norms in their communities. Some parents did not know that schools could be suitable for their children and so they did not seek education opportunities at all. They made comments such as,

> My child is eight years old and has severe language problems. He can only say 'mom', 'bye bye' and other simple words, and cannot express his feelings and thoughts.

The child cannot take care of himself and has no means to stay at the school.

Children like him have no school to attend. There is no special school here. We can take care of him throughout his life. No regular schools will enrol him. He cannot take care of himself and needs our help for such simple activities as eating.

Some poor families of children with disabilities living in rural areas are reluctant to send their child to school, preferring instead for them to learn to farm or work in the cities to help support their families (Deng and Holdsworth 2007; Chan, Ngok and Phillips 2008). For the family of children with disabilities, cultural norms also play a significant role in supporting their children's right to education. Parents' own experiences of disability within their cultural context can also be a barrier (Ellsworth and Zhang 2007), such as family shame about disability. A study in Hong Kong revealed that families with a child with epilepsy were unwilling to tell people that their child had a disability for fear of the shame and social stigma they might experience as a result (Holroyd 2003). Families sometimes viewed their child's disability as a result of some personal failing, and were unwilling to send them to school to study with other children. An interviewee to Deng and Holdworth's (2007: 515) research summarizes the impact of families' culture on education, 'The local culture doesn't value education, and kids learn to farm or work in the cities to support their family at an early age instead of going to school'.

Cost of education

Since 2006, the government policy is that schools must provide free education for children with disabilities and exempt them from miscellaneous fees (Chapter 10), but this was not always implemented at the local level. The additional costs of education were too much for some families to bear. Some of the case study children did not attend school due to economic difficulties. For example, Xiaoyi did not go to school for one year because his family could not afford it (96 yuan per semester), although his younger brother continued to attend pre-school classes (125 yuan). His mother said,

We were too poor after spending a large amount of money for treatment for Xiaoyi. I had to send Xiaoyi to his grandma and I went to other places for jobs. He stopped attending school in that year due to our poor household situation.

The case demonstrates the formal fees still charged to parents despite the central policy; and the difficult choices that families make about how to spend their scarce resources between family members with or without disabilities.

In a more positive case, when Qingqing attended school it was a proud moment for her small village of 1,531 people, including more than 100 people with disabilities. The children were usually cared for by their parents rather than attending school, because their families were very poor and they could only just make ends meet. Qingqing was the youngest child with disabilities in the village and the first one ever to attend the school. The school partly applied the compulsory education policy. Her family did not pay any tuition fees, but they did pay for exercise books (10 yuan) and living expenses to board at the school during the semester (900 yuan for four months). She only returned home during holidays, when her father picked her up.

An example of a city that had fully addressed the affordability of education was Daye. The special school in Daye City had gone one step further in addressing the economic barriers that might prevent children from attending school. All students with disabilities received free school education, without boarding or miscellaneous fees and the city had allocated their families the minimum living security. The civil affairs department provided funds for school meals. If the civil affairs funds were inadequate, the schools supplemented them with community donations. The school provided students with free necessities such as bedding, clothes and boots in winter. Most of the children were from rural poor families.

Positive impact of quality education

The fieldwork included a case study of Yangli, who had a positive experience of quality special education. She had been marginalized in her regular classes and her education needs were not met. Her family learned about a public special education school and shifted her there. Her family is from a rural county in Yunnan Province, southwest China. In the county in 2008, of the 182 school-age children with disabilities, the 26 children who were not educated in school were all in rural households; 119 children were in mainstream schools; and the other 52 children were learning in the special school for children with vision or hearing disabilities, according to the county DPF.

Yangli was seventeen years old, of Yi nationality and deaf. She was probably born with mild hearing loss but her family did not have information about, and could not afford to find, treatment, so that by the time she started school, her speech was also affected. Her family had five people – her father, mother, grandmother and younger sister. Her family earned a middle income for the village (more than 5,000 yuan per year) and was building a new house. Her father was a migrant worker and her mother was a farmer. Her sister attended the village primary school. Yangli also attended the school until grade three. She was discriminated against by her peers, according to her family and friends, for example her uncle said, 'Her classmates called her dumb and refused to play with her,' and he visited the classmates' parents asking them not to bully her. When she was bullied by a boy and fought with him, the teacher visited her father to pay the cost of fixing a window they broke. The bullying in the small village put a lot of strain on the family and community relationships.

Her uncle found out from a friend (whom the uncle match-made with a deaf woman) that if Yangli could get a disability certificate, she could get preferential treatment, including education. He made contact with the civil affairs department through the village committee. Yangli was given permission to transfer to the special school of Dali City restarting from the first grade. The cost of tuition and books were free, but the expenses included meals, pocket money and fares. Donations and DPF sometimes paid the extra costs and the costs of the parents when they picked up the children.

Yangli's academic grades at the special school were good and she was confident and optimistic about the future. Lively, optimistic, enthusiastic and ambitious were the words people used to describe her. She had good friends in the village and school because she was no longer bullied. Her academic achievement in the local school had been lower because she could not hear the teacher and was not provided with support. The school offered the same curriculum as mainstream schools, but the exams were not as demanding – primary school students only sat school exams and junior high school students could only sit vocational exams. The school laid emphasis on practical ability, such as embroidery, planting camellias and barbering for deaf students and musical instruments and massage for blind ones. When she was at school, her aunt in the city was her main guardian. Yangli stayed with her on weekends and short vacations and the aunt attended parent meetings. Yang had argued with the school and her family for greater independence, such as travelling home unescorted (the school had cases of student abduction by criminal groups).

She aimed to study in senior high school, which the school hoped to offer in the future. She wanted to find a job to remain living in the city, with the help of the school. Her father and uncle agreed that the greatest government help would be to find a job.

Conclusion on education and development

This chapter discussed barriers to the right of children with disabilities to education, including school conditions, social attitudes and socio-economic factors (Art. 24 CRPD). In the most positive cases, local governments have adopted the intention of the central government policies for inclusive education and allocated resources to make that happen. In these cases children are attending their local school without additional cost, receiving support in the classroom to attain their learning capacity and engaged in social friendships in their local community.

Many children do not have the benefit of that experience and their families struggle with overt discrimination – the schools refuse to enrol their children, they do not provide the support to make the classrooms an accessible learning environment, and they condone discriminatory attitudes of teachers and peers. Some families can resolve the problems if they have the opportunity and capacity to send their children to segregated special schools at great financial and social cost to themselves and their children. In the good cases the special school is a safe supported environment for the children to learn academically and socially; in other cases these schools too are under-resourced and further isolate the children from inclusive social experiences. Exclusion from school also has broader implications for other social exclusion, such as friendships and leisure. The remaining case study chapters discuss these social inclusion rights.

References

Chan, C.K., Ngok, K.L. and Phillips, D. (2008) *Social Policy in China: Development and Wellbeing*, Bristol: The Policy Press, University of Bristol.

CRPD, United Nations Convention on the Rights of Persons with Disabilities (2006) www.un.org/disabilities/default.asp?id=150 [1 February 2012].

Deng, M. and Holdsworth, J.C. (2007) From unconscious to conscious inclusion: meeting special education needs in West China. *Disability & Society* 22(5): 507–522.

Ellsworth, N.J. and Zhang, C. (2007) Progress and challenges in China's special education development. *Remedial and Special Education* 28(1): 58–64.

Holroyd, E. (2003) Chinese cultural influences on parental caregiving obligations toward children with disabilities. *Qualitative Health Research* 13(4): 4–19.

UNESCO Bangkok, United Nations Educational, Scientific and Cultural Organization Bangkok (2014) Barriers to inclusive education, www.unescobkk.org/education/inclusive-education/what-is-inclusive-education/barriers-to-inclusive-education/ [6 August 2014].

12 Right to social participation

Social institutions of support

Chapter 12 addresses the final set of rights to social participation (Art. 8, 30 CRPD). This set is discussed last because families' experiences of social participation are affected by the other sets of rights to care, economic security and development. In the context of childhood, analysis of the right to social participation includes age-specific experiences of social networks and activities within the family, neighbourhood and community with peers and adults, including play and friendship.

The chapter examines the experiences of three dimensions of social participation – communication, social relationships and interest representation. It analyses the effect of the mix of social structures in children's lives, including their family, community, schools and informal and formal organizations. New local connections are emerging as families, organizations and children and young people themselves take initiatives to build social relations and opportunities for participation.

In addition, the chapter analyses the impact of child disability on other family members' social participation, including the aspects listed for children and other citizenship rights such as channels to articulate opinions, interests and complaints. It particularly scrutinizes the experiences of mothers with children with disabilities, to see under the double disadvantages of sex and disabilities, how mothers deal with the barriers facing their children and their families.

Social participation is analysed in terms of the impact of barriers and facilitators on experiences of social inclusion and exclusion, such as physical access, social isolation, policies, social attitudes and discrimination. The analysis explores variation of experience, such as by location (urban/rural), age, sex, socioeconomic status, family structure and support needs. The analysis relies on fieldwork because the SCNSSD does not include these data.

Social participation and an ecological model

Without doubt many children and young people with disabilities in China do not have the same opportunities for social participation as their peers. Social interaction in their family, neighbourhood and community can be a positive aspect of a child's quality of life and can affect their social experiences in later adult life. This chapter looks at the social experiences of children with disabilities in China and which social institutions facilitate positive social experiences. It investigates the experiences of children and young people with disabilities (hearing and speech disabilities, blind, and mentally disabled) in rural areas and middle-sized cities. It applies an ecological model of childhood to ask which social institutions support their social participation; to what degree does that rely on the agency of the child and their family; and what are the implications for social policy change in China?

Systems to support children with disabilities and their families are under pressure in many developed countries because of service gaps, cost and unfulfilled child rights to inclusion (Clarke 2006). The purpose of the study is to understand the experiences of these children with disabilities in the context of their families and communities to inform social policy change and support their rights as citizens of China.

A key aspect of children's rights is social participation in the social contexts in which they live – their family, neighbourhood and community. It is particularly relevant to children with disabilities who are at risk of exclusionary practices that prevent their equal participation. In many respects, social participation can be reflective of the cumulative experiences of other core rights to care and protection, economic security and development. In the context of childhood, analysis of the right to social participation includes age-specific experiences of social networks and activities within the family, neighbourhood and community with peers and adults, including communication, social relationships and interest representation. Child disability can also affect the social participation of other family members.

In this study, we focus on the groups of social institutions that might affect child social participation and the changes as the children age. While the research questions examine the rights of children, the study focuses on children within the context of their families and other social institutions (Banks 2003; Jenks 2005; Kelly 2005; Case 2000; Baker and Donelley 2001). This follows the ecological approach to childhood, which recognizes the social context of development (Bronfenbrenner 1979; Dowling and Dolan 2001). We extend application of this approach to analysing the experience of rights and outcomes, how the social institutions in a child's life contribute to or negate experiences of social participation. We adopt a recent application of the ecological model which groups social institutions as: family; residential and relational community; programmes and services; regional and national; and global (Irwin Siddiqi, and Hertzman 2007; refers to these groupings as spheres of influence). Most relevant to the findings are the first three groups, although this background section places the analysis in the context of the last two.

Life history case studies

This study analyses the life history of four children with disabilities via semi-structured observation about the living environment of their families and in-depth interviews (Table 12.1). The sampling method for the in-depth interviews was

Table 12.1 Case study children for social participation

Child*	Sex	Age	Disability	Ethnicity	Household	Location
Hongmei	Girl	17	Physical and intellectual disability	Bai	Parents, brother	City, Yunnan
Xiaohua	Girl	18	Low vision	Zhuang	Parents, siblings	Town, Guangxi
Jiahuan	Boy	17	Deaf	Han	School or parents	City, Guangxi
Hengheng	Boy	17	Deaf and speech	Han	Parents, brother (sister in city)	Town, Jiangxi

Note: *Alias

snowballing and opportunistic sampling, by interviewing several families of children with disabilities at first, then including other people from their social networks. The advantage of interviewing them at the end of their childhood (seventeen to eighteen years) was that they could recall changes over their lifetime and the impact of early childhood experiences on later ones.

The researchers interviewed these children, their family members and other people connected with their life. The social institutions include families, peers and informal and formal organizations. For these children with disabilities, supports were provided by their parents, peer groups, and other organizations including community-based activity groups, schools, and the local disabled persons federation (DPF). We also conducted repeat interviews with the staff of local schools, DPF and examined the relationship between DPF and the informal community group, and local people, such as neighbours, doctors and other people who know these people with disabilities.

The data were analysed with the intention of developing a comprehensive picture of social participation of the children with disabilities and their families, strategies and difficulties they experienced and the social support they received. The information from different interviews and observations were critically analysed against the rights framework, from the perspective of children with disabilities' social participation. A life history from the perspective of the children's experiences and each of the social institutions with which they had contact was developed from the repeat interviews and observation data.

The findings about the opportunities for social participation are presented chronologically because of changes probably due to the children's ages. The types of social participation are divided into communication, social relationships and interest representation. The roles of social institutions that might affect each of these dimensions of social participation are analysed. In this analysis, the social institutions in which children and young people interact and communicate include family, peers, community groups and government organizations, reflective of the ecological approach described above.

Hongmei

The first young woman was Hongmei, who was aged seventeen and from the Bai ethnic group in a city in Yunnan Province. She had an intellectual disability. She lived with her parents and a younger brother. Her parents could have a second child because their first child had disabilities. Hongmei got on well with her brother. Whenever he teased her about her disability, their mother said, 'You would not have come to this world, if not for your sister's disability.'

Hongmei's father supported the family by working as a security guard at a small hotel. Her mother was unemployed for more than ten years in order to care for Hongmei at home; occasionally she did an odd job for a couple of days. The family was in extreme poverty and was one of the poorest families within the community, which was one of the poorest communities within the city. Hongmei received a minimum living security (220 yuan per month – £20, which was the standard amount in the city) together with other support from the government including the DPF.

Hongmei was born with congenital heart disease and over ten years had frequent heart attacks that threatened her life. The family visited many hospitals in the community, city, region and provincial capital. She received cardiac and brain surgery, which stabilized her condition and reduced the frequency of their hospital visits. They paid 80,000 yuan (£7,273) for the treatment, which was completely unaffordable for the already poor family. They lived in small and shabby rooms so that they could rent out their house for ten years to repay the debt for the surgery. The DPF organized regular therapy and Hongmei gained the ability to speak clearly and acquired skills for her daily living, such as cooking, cleaning, dressing and eating.

The family's income was from her father's earnings, Hongmei's minimum living security and other irregular subsidies for the girl, and renting out the house. Their financial conditions were harsh, with a surplus of 5–600 yuan (£45–54) per year after saving every penny. The financial condition improved when her condition stabilized, which reduced the medical costs, and once the government began to give financial support. Her mother said every family has difficulties and it was better now her family could manage their life. She wished the government would pay more attention to the therapy of children like Hongmei and help them plan for a sustainable future since her parents could not care for her forever.

Hongmei did not attend school. Before she was school age, her grandparents often cared for her, until they died. She went to a primary school at the school age, but left after a month at the school's request because she could not care for herself. The school argued that she might be in danger at school without a dedicated care-giver – for example, she staggered and tended to fall down; she could be hurt by other romping children; and she might be teased by some children about her disability. Her parents sent her to a special school, where the children were friendly, but the school only educated children with hearing and vision impairment. This city was actually better than most in the province, even with only the one special school. No other schools were available. The family was very disappointed that she did not have the opportunity for formal education. Her mother said, 'At least let her know how to use money,' meaning that she wished her to be taught to do simple things, have basic life skills, and to be able to survive after her parents died.

Xiaohua

Xiaohua was aged eighteen. She had low vision and could walk freely with only a trace of light. She lived with her father (Han ethnicity), mother (Zhuang ethnicity), younger brother and younger sister in a town in Guangxi Province, about 30 kilometres from a city. She attended a government school for deaf and blind children. When Xiaohua was born with low vision, they took her to Nanning, but the doctor said the condition could not be treated. Xiaohua was the first daughter. Her sister did not have disabilities, but her brother developed the same condition as Xiaohua. Her parents were told their son could be treated at a hospital in Guangdong Province, but they could not afford the treatment and travel costs.

Xiaohu's school fees were a large cost for a low-income farming family. She achieved a fee waiver for her good school performance until 2008, when fees were waived for all children. She still had to pay the annual boarding and food fees (550 yuan), which her parents had to borrow from friends. They could not afford any extras such as a piano, but she visited a neighbour grandfather with an electronic musical keyboard to practice what she learned at school.

Jiahuan

Jiahuan was aged seventeen and of Han ethnicity. He was in the senior college at a school for the deaf in a large city. He was the president of the student union and a deputy secretary of the Youth League general branch of the school. He usually lived at the school and during winter and summer vacations returned home to visit his parents. His parents were teachers at a local high school. He became deaf from an illness when he was a baby. His parents took him to a Beijing hospital that told them treatment would not be effective. They tried traditional medicine but they stopped the treatment because of the cost and it was not effective. His parents never considered having another child because they regard Jiahuan as a perfect child and they did not want him to feel ignored or marginalized with a brother or sister. Jiahuan's parents wanted him to have self-esteem.

Hengheng

Hengheng was seventeen and of Han ethnicity (Fisher, Shang and Xie 2011). He had hearing and speech impairments. He had left school and lived with his parents and brother. His sister lived and worked in a city. Hengheng's father is a carpenter with junior middle school education background and his mother is an illiterate housewife. Hengheng also has an older brother and sister who work in Guangdong and Zhejiang respectively. They both left school after graduating from junior middle schools. The income source of the family is from the father and an older sister. The family has lived for the past 20 years in an old, single storey 40m² unit that is attached to many other small units that are in very poor condition, partly because of the costs of paying for Hengheng's support.

Hengheng was found to be deaf when he was three years old, probably from a severe fever when he was one-year-old. After identifying the hearing loss, his family actively sought treatment. The family went to hospitals in Nanchang and Shanghai many times for examinations and treatments, costing them RMB20,000–30,000 (3–5 times an average annual rural salary in Jiangxi). When they found that one of Hengheng's ears had retained 30 per cent hearing, they spent over RMB3,000 on an imported hearing aid. The doctor said that with this much hearing, if Hengheng received good education, he could learn to speak and to hear people. The family did not receive any support and benefits from the government or organizations in the process of diagnosis, treatment and therapy.

Hengheng's parents loved him very much. They not only cared for him in daily life but also placed great emphasis on helping him master the means to communicate with people who could hear. Hengheng was the youngest in the family and disabled so his parents said they spoilt him often. If they had a difference of opinion with Hengheng, they usually gave up. They said Hengheng could usually make decisions for himself. Because of this, the parents said they had difficulty disciplining him.

Schools were also an important in Hengheng's childhood for meeting peers and teachers. After he temporarily left school the first time at the age of fifteen, he met other people with hearing and speech impairments and adults in the community and in informal and formal organizations with common interests, work or support. The effect of these social institutions – family, schools, community and organizations – in each dimension of participation (communication, relationships and interest representation) are analysed below.

Communication

The first dimension of social participation analysed is communication. With adequate communication support, children with disabilities can develop social relations within their family, with friends and with other members of their community. Support can include individual therapy, communication aids, group activities and school education. Many children only receive this assistance informally from their families, unless their parents can afford to pay or they live in cities where services are free.

Hongmei could not speak and used body language to communicate. She had not attended school and did not have augmented communication assistance, such as speech therapy or visual aids. According to her mother, Hongmei had a positive perception of herself, others and her community from the encouraging environment in her family and at the DPF children's activities that she attended. She did not retaliate when people were rude and could express herself sufficiently to engage them positively, such as saying thank you.

Xiaohua's spoken communication was not affected by her low vision and her skills were enhanced by attending a special school. Xiaohua, Jiahuan and Hengheng all used text and social media to communicate with some friends (for a discussion of internet use, see also Guo *et al.* 2005). Hengheng made new friends and chatted with them online. Internet and texting were the main ways he communicated with his sister, to whom he was closest in the family. Xiaohua liked animated cartoons and listening to radio dramas. She performed at school and community events, such as reciting part of *Di Zi Gui* (Standards for Being a Good Student and Child) and sang a song to the researcher. Her mother was proud, 'The child is clever and good at speech, and she knows how to greet others properly.'

Jiahuan's parents focused on developing his verbal communication and confidence once they learned that treatment would not fix his hearing. While he was young, his mother spent every evening doing the communication exercises (during this period she lost connections with all her friends but they recovered when he was older). At the primary special school, his classes were in sign language and he used sign language with teachers and other children. His parents did not learn sign language because they thought it was important that he could speak confidently with hearing people. He spoke and wrote with them when he could not make himself clear. Technologies like SMS were useful tools for him to communicate with his parents when he was at school, his friends and in the community.

When he was very young, Hengheng used only body language and gestures to communicate with his family. Because he could not speak to anybody before he went to special schools, he did not have contact with peers or have any friends during that time. Hengheng's brother said that Hengheng played simple games with him and their sister when he was little. He was quiet, shy and stayed alone. As he grew up, he wanted more sophisticated means of communication. Hengheng and his parents soon had difficulties communicating with each other, causing frustration for all of them. His family did not have the knowledge, means or education to learn sign language themselves. Instead, they did their best to invest in Hengheng's education, with the expectation that he would learn skills to communicate with people who can hear. His family could not communicate well with him until Hengheng learned to read and write at school. Neither could he talk with his family by writing unless they were with each other during school holidays. Hengheng's mother, who was unable to read, could not communicate with him directly. Observation during the research found that the family did not actually communicate a lot with paper and pen, Hengheng's written language structure was only suitable for relatively simple concepts.

During the interview, Hengheng's father continuously expressed his anxiety about communicating with Hengheng. He thinks he cannot communicate with his child, and most of the time he does not know what is going on in his son's mind. And together with the child's determination, he cannot give his son any instruction using his experience. His father is afraid that once Hengheng leaves home, he might be vulnerable to abuse or exploitation by other people. Hengheng not only receives love and care from his family, he also loves them and tries to contribute to the family. Through his experience of working, Hengheng has greater confidence about his ability to contribute to his family and care for himself. When he returned he brought gifts for his parents. He said he is now saving to reconstruct the family home and to prepare for marriage.

The case study children varied in their capacity to communicate, depending on their disabilities, assistance and therapy when they were younger. The resources and finances of their family, community and local government affected their access to communication support. The children who had early communication intervention had improved their communication and this affected other aspects of their development, including confidence, social relations and education. As young adults they were then able to use SMS text and social media to supplement spoken language.

Social relations

The second dimension of social participation is relationships. Most children could be expected to have relationships within their family, with peers, in their local community and in formal settings such as school. Children with disabilities may experience barriers to these opportunities if they do not receive the support to participate and communicate with other children. The case study children each had close relationships in their families and extended families. Some of them had wider social relationships with friends, with and without disabilities, depending on their social experiences, including school and disability organizations.

Family and local community

Hongmei liked to be with other people. Her main social connections were with her parents and brother, after her grandparents died. She had limited opportunities outside her family because she was denied access to school, where she would have met other children and teachers; and other children and adults often discriminated against her, so she had very few friends in the community, except children at DPF activities. She relied on her mother to take her out. When the researcher visited her home, Hongmei came in slowly from another room. Her mother explained that she was not shy, but she did not go out often. At home she watched TV. Occasionally, her mother took her out or to free DPF therapy activities with other children with disabilities. She liked to go anywhere there was a crowd, and she was excited whenever her mother took her to visit other people. Her mother said,

> She often goes to the park, where she is very happy to see those dancing in the evening and tries to dance among them. Most of the park-goers know her and befriend her. She received a rattle stick used for dance from an aged dancer frequently seen there, and she likes it very much and often uses it in her dancing.

The other children were also close to their families. Xiaohua was the oldest of three children and was responsible for caring for them when she was at home. Jiahuan had close connections with his family and extended family. During his childhood they visited his maternal and paternal grandparents each weekend. At boarding school, he would send text messages each night to his mother telling her that he was all right.

Jiahuan and Hengheng's families did not learn sign language, which limited the depth of their interaction. Jiahuan parents taught him to speak and write, but Hengheng's mother could not write. As Hengheng's need for social participation increased with his age, he sought other meaningful relationships with people outside the family, as other children do as they grow older. In Hengheng's case the need was more urgent since he needed to find people who could use sign language. Hengheng's family told stories about how their communication difficulties had caused them great stress and placed Hengheng in vulnerable situations about which they were unaware and where they were at a loss as to how to assist him. First, Hengheng's father told us a story about how helpless he felt when Hengheng had a three-day break from school and was due to come home. Hengheng was sixteen years old and had asked his tutor to telephone his father and tell him that he would be home by the end of the day. But the parents waited till midnight and still he had not returned. To get back home Hengheng had to change trains. His father wondered that Hengheng might have missed the second train. It was bitterly cold and Hengheng did not have extra money. The next afternoon, Hengheng finally turned up, looking very upset and he refused to have dinner. His father, who had been worrying for a whole night, was enraged by his behaviour and told Hengheng to get out if he insisted on not having dinner. To his great disbelief, Hengheng left the house immediately. His father followed him for several hundred metres and stopped him by pulling his clothes. The father told us he felt extremely helpless because he did not know how to make himself understood by his child. They remained in this stalemate for half an hour. They finally calmed down and the father suggested to Hengheng that they should go home and talk by writing everything down. Only through this process did the father find that Hengheng had not attended classes for two months; the tutor did not care about him; and that his teacher was on leave and the surrogate teacher did not offer a special class for him. Hengheng's father said that he still does not know what happened to Hengheng that night.

They also told a story about another time when Hengheng suddenly left home when he was fifteen years old. Hengheng's father returned home and found Hengheng was not at home. He thought Hengheng was just playing outside, and he did not care about this too much until he found a piece of paper on the bed: 'Dear Papa and Mama, I am so bored at home! I want to find a job and earn some money. Please do not worry, I will return.' Seeing this, Hengheng's parents were very afraid. They went to the railway and bus stations to look for their son. They also contacted the school and his classmates. They spent every day in a state of anxiety after Hengheng left home, especially when they saw on TV some crimes about forcing handicapped people to do illegal things. After about 20 days,

Hengheng's older sister, received a strange phone call. There was no sound on the other side. The same number soon called again but still no-one spoke. She guessed it might be Hengheng. Hengheng's father reported the case to the police. But because the phone call was from Hubei Province, the case required cooperation with the Hubei Police which was difficult to obtain. Finally, three months later, by the time Hengheng's parents had become extremely pessimistic, Hengheng returned home. According to the parents, he arrived home at 10pm, with lots of packages in his hands. He brought back his salary (RMB1,000, equivalent to an annual rural salary) and he bought his father cigarettes and his mother fruit. Hengheng told his father later that he had been with a middle-aged man, who also had a hearing and speech impairment. They earned RMB800 per month by selling handicraft articles. Since then, he has gone away to work three times. At sixteen, Hengheng suddenly said he would like to return to school. His father asked why but Hengheng would not say. The school very reluctantly accepted him back but isolated him from the other students in his living arrangements so that he would not influence them. His father was very angry about this discrimination and of course Hengheng resented the conditions.

The young people's close friends were mainly from special school or within the disability community, discussed below. Xiaohua had some friends in her local community from her neighbourhood. Jiahuan's main social relations were limited to family and school. Like Xiaohua, he was socially confident, 'I like communicating with others, and now I have many friends.' His mother was anxious when, for example, he played badminton. He mostly played with his family and when his parents asked their students to play badminton with him, they remained no more than acquaintances. They were worried he would not have the social connections to find a job. His parents worried about his safety when he went out since there were so many cases of fraud towards deaf children in China. His mother said,

> We often feel sad about this. We normal people have many friends from different areas including our primary schools, high schools, universities and workplaces. It a pity that the children like him have very few friends.

Friends from special schools

In contrast to Hongmei, the other children had attended special schools, which gave them a wider range of opportunities to develop social relationships. Xiaohua and Jiahuan achieved well at school and were popular with other students and teachers. They both held leadership positions at school. Attending school was important to Xiaohua. Most of the students were deaf, so she was in the only class for blind students of all grades. The school did not pay much attention to her class because it was too small. Helped by the school, she set a goal to become a singer and pianist. She hoped the school would purchase a piano for the blind class. Xiaohua liked school and aimed to enter university. Her parents supported her education goals as long as they could afford it. When asked what she liked best,

Xiaohua answered without hesitation – 'making friends'. At school the teachers encouraged her to assert herself, for instance asking for extra music practice and lessons and requesting a piano for the class.

Jiahuan's experience with school friends was similar to that of Xiaohua. His parents did not expect him to reach the same academic achievements as children without disabilities but they wanted him to give his best effort. The school was an important part of Jiahuan's life. In the preschool year, the focus was on speech training, and his teachers and parents worked to reinforce each other. He went to his local city special school for ten years until the end of junior high. He continued to visit his junior school teachers and friends from school, but he had few relationships outside this family and special school. His mother was pleased with the quality of the teachers at the school. He moved to one of the country's best special schools in Wuhan to prepare for university. When his parents called the school each month his teacher commended his academic performance, school record, and role as president of the student union and a deputy secretary of the Youth League general branch at the school. He was determined to enter an ideal university. His parents looked forward to the day when their son became a university student.

Hengheng's entry to education was delayed. Most children start school aged six or seven years old in his community. Like many other children with disabilities he was not welcomed to attend his local mainstream school because they did not have the skills and resources to support his communication needs. When he was aged ten his parents took him to a special school in another city, 250 km away from his home, hoping he would recover speaking skills with the help of the school. The school was famous for its qualified teachers and high teaching quality. Hengheng's development, education and social skills improved there.

When he was aged thirteen, his father heard about a new special education school closer to his home. Because of its impressive new buildings, geographic convenience and low tuition fees, Hengheng and his father reached agreement to transfer to this school. However, soon after the transfer, Hengheng's father found the school did not have classes in lip reading and speech training because of its limited finances. In addition, this school did not offer education after grade five, which meant Hengheng would need to transfer again to attend grade six. At the new school, Hengheng's academic development did not improve and he stopped speaking. He chose to leave the second school when he was fifteen so that he could work. He returned to the first school when he was sixteen to finish grade five. He did not want to complete any further grades.

Hengheng's father thinks that although the family is not wealthy, they have offered their son the best education they could. His father wished Hengheng would finish junior high middle school (grade 6–9, usually for children aged thirteen to sixteen, Hengheng started school education three years later than normal children), but Hengheng did not want to return to school at such a late age. At this stage of his life, what the parents want is assistance from the government, such as training with professional skills, allocating them into state-owned enterprises with safe, stable work posts and fringe welfare benefits.

In his first school, training included teaching speaking skills to children with some hearing capacity or teaching sign language to children without any hearing capacity. In the second school, no speaking was taught. In school, he learned basic sign language, reading, writing and computer skills. He is able to use sign language to communicate with other deaf children, young people and adults who use sign language. He also uses the internet to connect with friends and his sister. These capabilities have helped Hengheng to develop a social life outside the family, in his school, with peers and in the community. He has had less opportunity to develop his speaking capability and currently cannot speak.

Seven of the ten people with disabilities associated with the hair salon Hengheng attended received formal special education. The other three were illiterate. They informally teach each other through gatherings and chatting. They share new skills or improve their proficiency in formal sign language. In this way, Hengheng improved his command of sign language and corrected errors acquired through formal education. The hearing interpreter at the hair salon has similarly developed his signing skills from starting with simple sign language and progressing through learning with the hair salon members to reach a higher level of sign language.

Once Hengheng started school, he was able to seek opportunities for social interaction with people who shared his communication skills, initially through the school communities and then through informal disability groups. Besides friends at school, Hengheng also made new deaf friends from the local community. Students in the special education schools that he attended all have hearing and speech impairments. When Hengheng was at school, he could communicate with teachers and students, and established social relationships with them. He made many new friends in both schools. His father said that Hengheng used to visit his classmates by himself in holidays and his friends also went to his home to play with him. Most of his friends are deaf children who use the same language, share common interests and face similar difficulties in their daily lives. After he left school, he kept up these relationships by meeting people in person and on the internet. Only Jiahuan had attended a special school in his local community and he had moved away for senior high school. They continued their relationships remotely when they were not at school.

Disability community

Hongmei's mother became an active volunteer in DPF activities, which provided Hongmei with opportunities to meet other people. At the DPF activities she regularly met other children and she got on well with them. They play, dance and perform shows. The DPF asked her to be a mother volunteer at the weekly activities and to encourage more parents to bring their children. Some of the families refused, but others joined in the training and physical exercises. Hongmei's health and abilities improved from the ten years of attending the DPF therapy training and other activities. She did not meet with these friends except at DPF activities. Xiaohua also participated in sports and performances. 'Now all people at the municipal DPF know me well,' she said proudly.

When Hengheng was fifteen years old, he met a deaf handicraftsman named Ying, Hengheng's family do not know how they met. The DPF director reflected that often initially coincidental meetings between people with similar impairments lead to longer-term social connections. Through his friendship with Ying, Hengheng found another group of peers in the hair salon, which became an important place for Hengheng to develop his social connections in the local community. More than ten people with hearing impairments often come to the hair salon. Their average age is over 30 years. In addition two teenagers come, including Hengheng. The salon was started by the owner and his wife, who were deaf.

Before the salon opened, local deaf people had already formed a small group. This informal group was originally founded by three couples with hearing and speech impairments in the county town. Their families were relatively rich and were able to afford formal special education for them. After they grew up, their families also supported them to learn crafts and to start their own businesses. Since they had stable shops and had more contact with various people in the community, they became well known. As they were the same age and all communicated through sign language, they became good friends. They responded to the needs of the growing number of people with hearing and speech impairments in the county town, attracting more and more friends. The organization became bigger, including members without disabilities.

After the salon opened, this group used it as a place for activities. They gathered in the salon every day to chat and play card games and mahjong. The interviews, conversations and observation data showed that the primary function of this organization was that it provided a public space for people with hearing and speech impairments to know and communicate with each other. Hengheng's father said that after meeting the members of the hair salon, Hengheng had grown to know many other people with hearing and speech impairments. Since then, Hengheng had become more outgoing. In the past, he used to watch TV at home, but now he went out to see his friends at every opportunity and often came back home late at night. Hengheng told us that he liked to go there because the people often discuss news and tell stories, which he loved. The research process confirmed his positive approach to the salon. So that he could be interviewed, Hengheng's father brought Hengheng home from the salon, but after only half an hour, Hengheng was in a hurry to return. He was eager to be with his friends because only in this community could he understand others and express himself fully.

Another function of the salon, described further in the next section, was that its members supported each other. According to the members and comments from neighbours, doctor and the DPF director, if one person had a problem, others helped to solve it. For example, a doctor at the county hospital said if a person with hearing and speech impairments came to hospital, other members of the hair salon accompanied them. One who could write was in charge of communicating with the doctor, while the others helped to care for the sick person, pay for the fees and manage the medicine. The doctor said they were very warm-hearted to each other and hospital staff are all impressed whenever they visit. The mutual help also included introducing work opportunities to each other when one member had work information. The DPF director said that a similar organization in the county set up by people with physical impairments had about 40 members.

Interest representation

The third aspect of social participation analysed is interest representation. When they were young, the interests of children with disabilities were represented by their families. They sought out a diagnosis, treatment and therapy; and education choices and suitable schools. For some children, without a political voice, government support or information, their only choices were attempting to select appropriate, affordable services available in the paid market. In Hengheng's case this was restricted by his parents' own education; balancing the limited family resources among all the family members; and the lack of exposure to information about the options to best meet the needs of children with disabilities. Hengheng's parents' made a large financial investment in these choices, thinking that it might maximize his skills to interact with people who can hear. His parents and siblings have provided significant support and representation for Hengheng during his childhood. In addition, his parents had a limited capacity to understand Hengheng's wishes and preferences because they could not fully communicate with him. For example, when Hengheng was mistreated in his second school, he could not tell them the whole story. Because of this, his parents could not articulate or support his rights in the school context effectively. Although his father complained to the school about the treatment he received there, he did not have sufficient power to protect Hengheng's rights. Once Hengheng returned to school after a period working, the school did not want him in case he had a negative influence on the other students. Our data collection did not extend to interviewing staff from the schools so we cannot comment on the role of schools in expressing or protecting the interests of children with disabilities.

The other case study families had the capacity to represent their children's interests to the special schools and DPF. They knew how to negotiate and advocate to meet their children's needs. For example, despite the poverty of the family and the forced unemployment brought about by the need to care for Hongmei, her mother developed strong relations in the community, the DPF and other relevant organizations, to the benefit of her daughter's opportunities with other children. She told the researcher that she had to work hard to get support for her daughter and other children, 'I try my best to overcome my difficulty. When I cannot manage it, I turn to the community; and this is usually a way that works.' For example, the criteria for the disability allowance and minimum living security were different so not all families got the income support they needed, despite the high medical and care costs that created problems for the families. Hongmei's mother reported this situation to the community director, who issued her a disability certificate so that she received recurrent benefits from the community and DPF including income support, materials, the minimum living security and free therapy training. This benefit was possible, not because they were educated or wealthy, but because they lived in an urban area, where they had easy access to information and easy walking distance from the DPF. Her mother was especially patient and even-tempered, and she nurtured her relationships with her neighbours, the community and the DPF. In addition to benefiting her own daughter, she also advocated for other children, by volunteering and encouraging other families to participate. The other case study young people had started to advocate for themselves and other young people with disabilities, through their special school leadership positions (Xiaohua and Jiahuan) and their association with friends with disabilities, including Hengheng's case.

Some people with disabilities register with the DPF as disabled. In Hengheng's county, they generally only registered if they wanted assistance such as tax benefits, a licence to attend a special school, or a fee subsidy when compulsory education schools charged fees. The DPF did not provide assistance such as support to families or training such as sign language to children or family members. They charged for the use of equipment. The other case study children were in larger urban areas that could provide more support, such as Hongmei's case described above.

Informal groups are a necessary bridge from people with disabilities when the DPF wants to gather information about the interests of people with disabilities. Hengheng's county DPF director admitted to us that it is difficult for the DPF to work without the informal groups. The people with disabilities and their families we interviewed spoke about how the formal government organization and informal groups mutually support and complement each other's functions. The DPF relied on the hair salon to communicate with its members. Because it did not have anyone with hearing and speech impairments, the county DPF often asked two core people from the hair salon for help when it needed to contact people with hearing and speech impairments or provide information to them. The DPF director said that if it needed to inform them of something or hold an event, it asked the hair salon to assist. Another more formal function of the hair salon was to gather and express the common interests of its members. The local DPF director reported that usually if a person with disabilities came to DPF for help, if they had not joined an organization, they came alone, or with one or two relatives. In contrast, people with hearing and speech impediments in the county worked collectively. He gave the example of one occasion on which the DPF office was filled by seven or eight deaf people who came in support of someone who wanted to consult about the application for the minimum living security benefits.

In order to enhance the cooperation between the hair salon and the DPF, the DPF validated the status of the core members of the informal group by inviting them as representatives of people with disabilities in the county to attend a Civic People With Disability Congress at the county and city levels. Compared to the other members of the hair salon, these two representatives had the higher level of education, fluent writing skills and sign language for communication with both people with and without hearing and speech impairments.

The hair salon was an informal group, independent from the DPF, formed spontaneously and operated without assistance. On the other hand, it also cooperated with the DPF. From the perspective of members of the informal group, it was impossible for people with hearing and speech impairments to have a politically effective voice without the DPF. With help from the DPF, people with hearing and speech impairments were able to use formal channels to express their interests or affect decisions. This was also of benefit to the DPF, because it helped it to establish contact with people with disabilities and represent their interests locally and politically through the informal groups. Without the informal groups, the DPF director said it would not have the means to make contact with people with disabilities. He said this would weaken its function to represent the interests of people with disabilities. As an official organization, DPF is required to provide a communication platform and aids for people with disabilities, but it could not do this without the assistance of organizations set up by people with disabilities.

However, the support from the DPF to informal groups was very limited. For example, in 2004, another physical disability organization asked the DPF for support to register as an NGO, but was rejected. Without that support, the government regulations prevented it from gaining a legal status and its opportunities for further action, such as receiving funding, were therefore restricted. The hair salon did not intend to register as an NGO because it functioned primarily as a social group.

These examples of cooperation illustrate how people with disabilities and their families used both informal and formal channels to articulate their interests. The formal government organizations, informal community groups, and parents, played important roles representing the interests of people with disabilities. By working with the DPF, families and informal groups had more access to relevant information. The case also illustrates how the interest representation by the informal community group was limited. It was difficult for an informal group to become formally recognized or supported financially or organizationally by the DPF.

Conclusion about social institutions

This chapter analysed the right to social participation (Art. 8, 30 CRPD) of children with disabilities in China by examining the cases of four children. The analysis indicated that even children with strong family resources like Jiahuan are marginalized in key opportunities for social participation, such as local mainstream education. Children in more isolated locations and poor households, such as Hengheng, are even more ignored by the state.

In all the cases, their families did their best to pursue their children's interests, committing their time, financial resources and advocacy with the local schools, local government, DPF and community services. As the children became older, some of them were able to act independently to enhance those opportunities, such as Hengheng finding the local deaf community. All the children had limited friendships outside the family when they were young, because they could not attend the local school or because of discrimination from other children. Three of the children attended special schools away from their home towns, where they became friends with other children boarding with them. They also found and maintained friendships through social media and texting.

The different experiences of the children reflect the capacity of their local community, family and support needs. Children in the larger cities had more government resources available to them, even when their families were poor, as in Hongmei's case. Presumably, access to this government support will continue to expand in terms of income support, therapy, medical intervention and education.

The findings showed that families of children and young people with disabilities advocate for opportunities for social participation through communication assistance, social relationships and interest representation within each of the expected social institutions. The social participation was primarily with families, school friends and schools during childhood years; and with other children with disabilities through schools, DPF and informal community groups as they grow older.

It was the families who organized and paid for access to special schools where their children could meet other children who used the same communication skills as they did during their childhood. They were not able to attend local mainstream schools, which did not have the resources or skills to support children with disabilities or refused enrolment (as in Hongmei's case). As they reached teenage years, it was through their own social interactions that they found other young people and adults with disabilities. Hengheng's story was strongest in this respect because he had already left school and through local informal contacts he found a vibrant social network that gave him access to socialising, discussion, support and communication to access the hearing community, further informal training about communication skills for people with hearing and speech disabilities and information about job opportunities. These opportunities were not available to him through the local Disabled Persons Federation. Xiaohua and Jiahuan continued to rely on school connections and their families. Hongmei was most isolated because she did not have independent support to communicate, schools refused to enrol her and she depended on her mother if she wanted to leave the house, despite her gregarious personality.

The implications for social policy changes to fulfil the rights of children with disabilities to social participation relate to support for social institutions at each level in the ecological approach. Families currently bear the full cost of diagnosis, treatment, therapy and education of children with disabilities (Shang and Wu 2003). If they cannot afford the support, the child does not have access. In a poor rural context, if they can bear the cost, there is economic disadvantage to the whole family. Families also do not have access to information about what support might best meet the social needs of their child. Hengheng's family, for example, did not have information about communication skills that would help him within the hearing and non-hearing communities. They might, for instance, have learned sign language themselves or taught writing skills to his mother so that she could communicate with him directly. Such reliance on the family in early years can risk abuse and neglect in the home (Shang 2008). If other family members are not people with disabilities, they often consider the needs of children with disabilities only from the perspective of people without disabilities. Other needs of some children with disabilities may be neglected, such as sign language education by parents and schools in China. Hengheng's family situation was probably eased by having three children, with the benefit that the older children financially contributed to the cost of supporting Hengheng's education.

The second social institution supporting children's participation is school. Rural mainstream schools do not have resources, teachers or skills to support children with disabilities within the local community. The impact for children with disabilities is that they face the risk that they miss out on local connections with children in a school environment. All the case study children had this experience. They might attend school but without additional assistance their education and social outcomes suffered, including bullying and abuse, such as Xiaohua at her local school (Shang 2008). Their entry into school may be delayed; they do not have formal support to develop communication skills unless their family can afford to send them to specialist schools; and at worst, they do not attend any formal education, such as Hongmei.

Alternatively, their family might have the information, commitment and resources to access special schools outside the community. While this has the advantages of social contact with children with similar disabilities, education and communication skills development, it dislocates the children from their family, community and other children without disabilities. None of the case study children had close relationships with other young people without disabilities. The quality of the education also relies on the resources of the school, as illustrated by Hengheng's experience in the second school, which did not teach speaking skills.

The third set of social institutions is the community and local informal organizations. As children grow older they might acquire agency to find these themselves, as in Hengheng's case, or some families or other social contacts introduce children and young people directly, as in Hongmei's case. This introduction requires both that the families have information about them and that they understand the benefit to their child about contact and support from other people with disabilities. While the informal organization in Hengheng's community provided direct benefits for social participation in all three dimensions (communication, relationships and interest representation), it was entirely self organized. It was not supported by the government with formal recognition of the organizations or resources to facilitate the activities that complemented government functions. These organizations which were established by people with disabilities themselves to meet their participation needs to play an important and irreplaceable role in fulfilling the participation rights of people with disabilities, including children and young people. However, the informal organizations lack government resource support, funding and formal channels to express the interests of their members.

The fourth social institution at the government level, Disabled Persons Federation relies on the informal organizations to fulfil its formal functions of contact into the disability community. Many local DPF neither employ people with the necessary communication skills nor organize the support to facilitate social participation of people with disabilities (Kohrman 2005). The DPF has official responsibilities and stable financial and administrative resources. The cooperation between the formal and informal organizations is beneficial to both levels to fulfil their own missions and serve the interests of people with disabilities. While they cooperate well in Hengheng's county, development into sustainable support for children and young people with disabilities was hampered by the rigidity of structural support. Partly this reflects a central policy limitation on the regulation of NGOs. But even within that regulatory framework, the local government seemed to lack the will to formalize established community groups into incorporated NGOs.

In summary, the implications for improved social policy change are the establishment of direct government engagement with people with disabilities and the provision of information, support, resources and formal structures to assist children and young people with disabilities, their families, communities, schools, local informal and formal nongovernment organizations. Tangible steps would be to provide access to government-supported diagnosis, treatment and therapy; information, teachers, training and resources in mainstream and specialist schools; and processes to register and support the development of local nongovernment organizations.

Understanding family experiences of child disability and informing policy development, would contribute to furthering the rights of children in China and improving the wellbeing of families and children with disabilities. It is vital information to support the efforts of the Chinese government and nongovernment organizations to establish effective child disability policy. The findings are also a basis for further research, such as evaluating models of support policies in China; comparing them with those in other countries to identify models of good practice; and analysing disability experiences in the Chinese population. The findings offer new insight into policy and add to theories of children's rights in the context of the relationships between parents and children, and between the state, the family and civil society.

References

Baker, K. and Donelly, M. (2001) The social experiences of children with disabilities and the influence of environment: a framework for intervention. *Disability and Society* 16(1): 71–85.

Banks, M.E. (2003) Disability in the family: a life span perspective. *Cultural Diversity and Ethnic Minority Psychology* 9(4): 367–384.

Bronfenbrenner, U. (1979) *The Ecology of Human Development*, Cambridge: Harvard University Press.

Case, S. (2000) Refocusing on the parent: What are the social issues of concern for parents of disabled children? *Disability & Society* 15(2): 271–292.

Clarke, H. (2006) Preventing social exclusion of disabled children and their families: literature review. *Research Report RR782*, paper for the National Evaluation of the Children's Fund, Institute of Applied Social Studies University of Birmingham.

CRPD, United Nations Convention on the Rights of Persons with Disabilities (2006) www. un.org/disabilities/default.asp?id=150 [1 February 2012].

Dowling, M. and Dolan, L. (2001) Families with children with disabilities – inequalities and the social model. *Disability & Society* 16(1): 21–25.

Fisher, K.R., Shang, X. and Xie, J. (2011) Support for social participation of children and young people with disability in China, in Carrillo, B. and Duckett, J. (eds) *China's Changing Welfare Mix: Local Perspectives*, Routledge, London and New York.

Guo, B., Bricout, J.C. and Huang, J. (2005) A common open space or a digital divide? A social model perspective on the online disability community in China. *Disability & Society* 20(1): 49–66.

Irwin, L.G., Siddiqi, A. and Hertzman, C. (2007) *Early Child Development: A Powerful Equalizer*, Commission on the Social Determinants of Health, World Health Organisation.

Jenks, E.B. (2005) Explaining disability: parents' stories of raising children with visual impairments in a sighted world. *Journal of Contemporary Ethnography* 34(2): 143–169.

Kelly, S.E. (2005) 'A different light': examining impairment through parent narratives of childhood disability. *Journal of Contemporary Ethnography* 34: 180–205.

Kohrman, M. (2005) *Bodies of Difference: Experiences of Disability and Institutional Advocacy in the Making of Modern China*, Berkeley: University of California Press.

Shang, X. (2008) *The System of Social Protection for Vulnerable Children in China*, Beijing: Social Sciences Academic Press.

Shang, X. and Wu, X. (2003) Protecting children under financial constraints: the case of Datong. *Journal of Social Policy* 32: 549–570.

13 Interrelated rights and social exclusion

This final case study chapter brings together analysis of the cumulative effect of discrimination against the rights of children with disabilities. By socially excluding children, their experience of discrimination affects multiple, interrelated aspects of their lives. The chapter presents findings about families of children with disabilities in a disadvantaged, rural case study community. The primary focus of the findings is on the experience of one family from the perspective of the child, family members, other children and community members. Data about the focus family is supplemented with data about other families and locations to draw implications beyond the case. The findings about the families' experiences are presented against the four rights domains of children with disabilities introduced in the earlier chapters – care and protection, economic security, development support and social participation. It draws together the arguments in the book in terms of impact on children, families and communities, before the final chapter on social policy implications.

Social exclusion and discrimination

One measurement of children with disabilities' experience of their rights is the extent of discrimination compared to children without disabilities (CRPD 2006; Stein 2010). The UN definition of disability discrimination is,

> Discrimination on the basis of disability means any distinction, exclusion or restriction on the basis of disability which has the purpose or effect of impairing or nullifying the recognition, enjoyment or exercise, on an equal basis with others, of all human rights and fundamental freedoms in the political, economic, social, cultural, civil or any other field. It includes all forms of discrimination, including denial of reasonable accommodation. (Article 2, CRPD)

Discrimination, or breach of rights, affects children both now and in the future. A rights framework has the advantage of emphasizing that child development is dynamic and cumulative: disadvantages experienced by children with disabilities at any age have an ongoing effect during childhood and adulthood. In relation to government responsibilities, this includes both positive discrimination in institutionalized processes, such as social support; and prevention of discrimination by other citizens towards children with disabilities and their families (Article 4, CRPD). This chapter analyses evidence about the cumulative effect on families and children of discrimination in both institutional processes and people's attitudes and behaviour towards children with disabilities and their families in their local communities.

It follows a case study of a disadvantaged, rural community. A focus family of a child with disabilities Maomao (alias) provides an in-depth investigation, around which other findings in the case study community and related locations are presented (Shang, Fisher and Xie 2011). The research gathered and analysed data about the lived experience of the focus family in relation to the impact and responses of the child and family to discrimination. Data collection included semi-structured observation in the living environment of the family and in-depth interviews about the life history with people in the child's life in 2007 (extended family, neighbours, teachers, other children). We supplemented the case study method with other interviews and secondary data described in Chapter 1. For the purpose of generalising beyond the focus family, at the same case study site we also conducted repeat visits with five other families of children with disabilities, which included in-depth interviews with the children's parents, teachers, classmates and other relevant people. At some of the interviews, the children were present and contributed to the conversation, with the permission of their parents.

The case study site was chosen because it is a disadvantaged, rural community, where we could expect to observe restrictions on the rights of family and children with disabilities. The county is located in Jiangxi Province. The county has been on the list of national poverty counties since 2001 – the per capita net income of rural households was 70 per cent of the national average (2,598 yuan compared to 3,587 yuan (£236 to £326) Bureau of Statistics of County H 2007, 2008).

In addition, we used secondary data to identify the main trends and common problems facing families of children with disabilities in China. The secondary data include both published data, and programme reports provided in the fieldwork by local agencies and UNICEF or written by Dr Shang for other social policy projects. UNICEF (2006) commissioned the unpublished report referred to in this chapter to inform their programme to prevent the abandonment of children with disabilities. They gave the report to Dr Shang as part of a policy consultation process. The UNICEF survey data was collected by a team led by Chen Zhonglin. The survey was with families of children with disabilities in five Chinese cities (Tianjin, Huangshi, Datong, Haerbin and Yibin) in 2006. It included economic status, parenting difficulties, support services and expectations for future policy progress.

Right to care and protection

The first rights domain is the right to care and protection, including the right to life and right to live with their family (Art. 10, 16, 18, 23 CRPD). Maomao suffered abuse and neglect both in his family and in his community, described in this and the later sections. Maomao was a fifteen-year-old boy who lived with his parents. He had physical disabilities and epilepsy. His older brother was a soldier. The family were socio-economically disadvantaged because neither parent had a fixed job. When they worked, his father was a carpenter and his mother had small businesses.

According to China's family planning policy, a family in a rural community whose first child had a disability was permitted to have a second child. Since his older brother did not have a disability, Maomao's parents did not have permission for a second child. They gave birth to him secretly and he was born with a physical disability. This was a double blow to the parents because they violated the one-child policy and the child had a disability. They were not only ineligible to apply for any special treatment for children with disabilities, they also faced fines and other possible penalties.

Because of Maomao's disability and the fear of being fined, they sent him to his paternal grandmother on the outskirts of the county. Although Maomao received care and love from his grandmother, he did not have access to early support and treatment for his disability. When Maomao was five years old his grandmother died. Because no one else in the countryside could care for him, he returned to his parents' home. The family had to first cope with avoiding fines for a child born outside the birth-control plan, rather than concentrating on support for his disability. Out of the fear of being found out, Maomao's mother hid the child. She locked him at home each day when she went out. Predictably, this neglect of his basic needs had a severe negative mental impact on the five-year-old child. Eventually, they were discovered and the family was fined. The family was already poor because his mother had lost her job in 1996, while he was still with his grandmother. She tried to contribute financially through small business activities. She did not cope with the combined economic pressure and the failure to hide him and eventually vented her distress by beating him. As he grew older he began to hit her back. His parents argued about the mother using corporal punishment.

The mother's attitude toward Maomao was ambivalent. As soon as the first interview began, she said, 'If we had not had this son, we could live a much better life. But the reality is he is alive and there is nowhere we can send him to. We cannot but face the reality.' She regretted that he had a disability, rather than that the birth was illegal. Maomao knows that his parents favour his brother, saying, 'You just love my brother.'

Most parents support their children with or without disabilities within the family unit. However, the research found that discrimination within families against children with disabilities was not uncommon. For example, in another interviewed family near the county, the parents left their son with disabilities with his sick grandparents, while they took their other son without disabilities when they migrated to the city for work. The grandparents cared for this son with disabilities for six years without any support until the grandmother became completely blind. Another family in the county revealed that they had considered abandoning their child with disabilities because they could not support him. These findings are consistent with the findings about families abandoning children with disabilities from interviews with service providers and the literature (Shang and Fisher 2014). Lim *et al.* (2013) also found stigma within the family (from grandparents, parents, extended family and nannies) as well as externally (Chiu *et al.* 2013).

Right to economic security

The second rights domain is economic security through family economic activity, social security and welfare provision for the child and family now and in the future (Art. 28 CRPD). Families' economic vulnerabilities are exacerbated by the responsibility of caring for a child with disabilities without formal support. They may have unstable income and sole responsibility for the cost of the child's disability related support needs.

The first aspect of economic security is cost related to childhood and disability support. After she lost her job in 1996, Maomao's mother made a living with small business activity, selling food in the street. Maomao's father worked as a carpenter when he could get work. In this context of unstable income, Maomao's parents also took the full economic cost of his disability support needs. Costs included treatment such as medical expenses. The family's biggest financial cost was compensation when Maomao caused trouble in the community. His mother said,

> Counting the fine of his birth and the compensation costs, the money we have paid is countless ... The expenses on food and clothes are not large, but once he makes some trouble, the amount of money that I have to pay equals to the amount for his whole year food ... I do my business around the clock, once he makes trouble outside, it will dry out the money that I have accumulated for several months, can you say that I am not angry!

His family were not able to pay for special education and disability support, which may have contributed to Maomao's failure at school. This was in contrast to another family at the case study site, who paid for their child to attend a special school near his home. They paid for medical care for his hearing impairment during his childhood (30,000 –£2,727); miscellaneous fees, school fees, accommodation fees and travel expenses Their annual cost of approximately 4,000 yuan per year was over 150 per cent of an annual rural household income in the county (2,598 yuan). This family had three children, with two earners – the father and oldest sister.

Poverty is common among families of children with disabilities. Four of the five other families of children with disabilities in the same county also experienced economic difficulties. A UNICEF (2006) survey of children with disabilities in five Chinese cities found that parents were responsible for additional costs for their children's education. Special education was the largest part of family expenses in household expenses in Tianjin, a large city, and the second largest part of expenses in middle and small cities (where food and clothes were the largest part).

The second aspect of economic security is future economic needs after childhood. When asked about her expectation for Maomao's future, his mother hoped that he could learn a craft. She said, 'In future, we parents will die and he could not rely on his brother to feed him. I have told him that he should not trouble his brother.' Furthermore, the mother also feared that his brother may have difficulty in finding a wife because of his responsibilities for his brother. 'Even if his brother agrees to accept him, his sister-in-law will refuse.' The UNICEF survey found that most families of children with disabilities were low-income households and they had similar experiences to the families in the case study site in respect of implications for future economic security (UNICEF 2006; also Kohrman 2005).

Rights to developmental support

The third rights domain is the right to support for child development (Art. 24, 25, 26 CRPD). Formally, children with disabilities in China have the same rights as other children to support and services necessary for development, including the right to attend a public school. The state also has preferential policies for children with disabilities through the exemption of miscellaneous fees, textbook fees and by granting living subsidies. However, in practice, schools refuse to accept local children. This section presents findings about discrimination in access to schooling. The following section on participation rights extends these findings to the impact on child development outcomes.

Maomao experienced discrimination in attempting to exercise his right to education, reflected in the following ways, including access, assistance and at worst, neglect. His mother said she tried her best to provide Maomao with necessary care, education arrangements and protection, including arranging for her son to attend the local school. However, Maomao was discriminated against in this access to education.

Maomao often encountered difficulties during annual enrolment and registration at school. Almost every year, he was deliberately impeded with difficulties during registration. On the day of registration, he was almost always the last one to be registered. Maomao said,

> When I go to school for registration, the teachers don't accept my money or pay attention to me. They just handle other students' application. I would not dare to return home for fear of being scolded by my mother.

According to his mother, one year Maomao did not return home after registration, so she went to school to look for him. She succeeded in enrolling him only after quarrelling with his teacher. In the most serious incident, Maomao's father found out about the registration difficulty after he had been drinking. He went to the home of the teacher with a kitchen knife to threaten him if the teacher refused to grant registration. The teacher was frightened and finally agreed.

Maomao also suffered discrimination at school. In severe cases, he could not enter the classroom to study. Once a new student was transferred to the class and the teacher took Maomao's desk and chair for the new student. When the teacher ignored Maomao's request for the return of his desk and chair, he feared that his mother would scold him so he pretended to go to school each day, but just sat in the playground. After a month a classmate told Maomao's mother, who went to school to argue with the teacher until Maomao could return to the classroom.

Discrimination by the school also deprived Maomao of his right to enjoy education assistance. Since 2003, China has a policy of 'exemption of miscellaneous fees, textbook fees and a subsidy for boarding' for the students with disabilities for the nine-year compulsory education in rural areas. Children with disabilities are eligible for the benefits. Maomao had the benefit for two semesters, but the teacher revoked it after Maomao caused trouble at school. His mother went to the head teacher and found that teacher had not applied to the school for Maomao's exemption and because the deadline had passed, he lost his eligibility. His mother had to pay all the fees to keep his education going.

Maomao was also denied access to curricula and teaching support to match his ability. After the unsupportive attitudes in the school, Maomao lost his interest in learning and received low marks. His learning level remained at grade two. His teachers refused to teach him in higher grades even when he was in their classes. He completed second year middle school but because he could not keep up with other students and suffered discrimination, he left the school.

One reason that Maomao experienced discrimination at school was that the performance management of schools and teachers is based on student scores. This system disadvantages students with disabilities with poor academic performance. Their scores affect the performance results of teachers. In examples such as Maomao, when his mother wanted him to repeat a grade, the teacher would not want to accept him. A school strategy was to offer only opportunities that were unattractive to his continuing at the school. Another family in the case study site found that whenever the school had an important test, the teacher encouraged poorly performing children with disabilities 'to go somewhere else', and refused to allow them to participate in the exam so as not to lower the average scores of the class.

In other examples at the same site a child with hearing and speaking difficulties was not able to start until he was aged ten years old (instead of six or seven years old for children without disability) because the local school refused to accept him. Another child in the community had never gone to school owing to his disabilities, although he was not affected intellectually. The UNICEF (2006) survey found that it was difficult for many children with disabilities to attend their local school, due to a lack of facilities and teachers with training in how to support children with disabilities.

In addition to educational support, children with disabilities may need other developmental support, such as health services, rehabilitation, income support and special education. Maomao's family did not receive assistance with either the basic child developmental support needs of other children in the village or the additional needs related to his impairment and illness. The UNICEF (2006) survey found that other developmental support was available to most children with disabilities only if parents arranged it and have the capacity to bear the costs as discussed in the right to economic security. An interviewee who provided services to families of children with disabilities in Kunming used the term 'at the edge of collapse' (both financially and spiritually), to describe the situation of her clients.

Social participation rights

The last child disability domain analysed is the social participation rights of children and families (Art. 8, 30). Rather than experiencing positive social contact with other children, the research revealed discrimination from children, adults and family members. Maomao said he had no friends. He said that because his left hand and leg are affected, many children called him 'cripple' at school. They also called him names that he was not willing to disclose because they were too upsetting for him. He said that he would do things alone at school and just watch TV at home, without communication with other classmates. Maomao's mother also said that he was very introverted. He said that it was much easier to make friends with other children with disabilities.

Due to the frequent mistreatment from his classmates and fear of beating and scolding from his mother, Maomao seldom told his parents about abuse at school. Sometimes, however, his parents guessed at his problems from observing his torn clothes or injured body. For example, Maomao's father once found Maomao's face was severely swollen on one side, with clear scratch marks. His father became very angry knowing that Maomao had been beaten by others. Maomao initially refused to admit the beating by one of the classmates. His father immediately went to argue with the teachers, until the student and his parents came into the office, where in presence of teachers and parents, Maomao's father forced Maomao to slap the face of the student.

In the second meeting between Maomao and the researcher, he spoke about abuse from his classmates. He said that because his mobility was limited, students sometimes robbed him and ran away to irritate him. If he got angry and chased them, students would laugh at his way of running, which made him even angrier.

Evidence of discrimination from peers was a common experience of Maomao and the other children with disabilities at the case study site. At school, children with disabilities experienced humiliating nicknames, were isolated from others and even abused by classmates. These experiences had a negative impact on their school work, interpersonal relationships, mental health and personal development. For example, two boys whom a child with intellectual disability identified as friends refused to acknowledge the friendship to the researcher. Other students told the researcher that it was these 'friends' that bullied the child with disabilities most violently. One student said the two 'friends' played tricks, beat and teased the child.

Maomao and his mother also recounted social stigmatising from adults. Most upsetting was an incident where he was accused of stealing after playing with a shopkeeper's daughter. On one occasion, the two children played together in the store. They were the same age. The shopkeeper's daughter took out a purse and wanted to buy some food to share with Maomao. The girl's mother found that purse was missing after they returned. The mother asked the girl who had taken the purse. The girl was frightened and said Maomao had stolen it. Maomao said no matter how he had defended himself, no one would hear his story. The shopkeeper detained Maomao and went to his home with several men. They told his mother that Maomao had stolen all the US and Hong Kong dollars in the purse (about 1,500 yuan) and if she did not repay the money, they would smash the house. Maomao's mother was so worried that she borrowed money from two relatives. In anger, she beat Maomao on the way home.

The second aspect of social participation rights is the social participation of the family members affected by their responsibilities. Parents discussed the enormous social pressures they face raising a child with disabilities. In the case of Maomao, when he had problems such as refused registration by school, or being accused of theft and abused by his classmates, his parents solved the problems by negotiating with the school, the neighbours, the police and the parents of his classmates.

In addition, community opinions also affected his parents. People covertly talked about the parents as having illness, bad genes or having done things that have incurred the retribution of bearing a child with disabilities. In another family at the case study site, the parents refused to take their child outside, and insisted on asking him to stay with the grandparents, because they thought 'others would mock them', and 'they dared not face the reality'. Other research with Chinese families about internalized stigma has found similar results (e.g. Lim *et al.* 2013; Chiu *et al.* 2013; Mak and Kwok 2010). They found that some parents avoided social contact or restricted where they went, while others became used to it and were encouraged by positive interactions with neighbours or members of the public.

Impact on children's development

The findings about the experiences of the families of children with disabilities from the children, families, community members and professionals illustrate a number of levels of discrimination and failure of support for the rights of children with disabilities in the four domains of care and protection, economic security, developmental support and social participation. Without addressing the basic or specialist needs of Maomao, the impact on himself, his family and community became more negative and more difficult to resolve. His mother regretted not receiving adequate support, particularly education and social support for her son.

Denial of their rights can have a negative impact on children's educational, physical, cognitive and social development; and capacity for future independent opportunities. Discrimination and abuse against Maomao affected his development in respect of his cognitive and possibly physical development. Persistent educational discrimination resulted in only grade two educational achievement and leaving school early. Other children with disabilities at the case study site either had not attended school for the same number of years as other children or attended special schools for a limited period paid for by the family.

Maomao was born with a physical impairment and has since developed epilepsy, for which he took medication, paid for by the family. Other children with disabilities at the research site only received medical and other treatment if their parents could pay.

At the age of fifteen, Maomao had poor socialization skills and limited social contact. His communication was limited to his family. He had no friends inside and outside school. During the research, communication with him was difficult – he spoke with his head down, sometimes uttering ambiguous, undistinguishable words and in other time answering beyond the question. These social outcomes were common to the other children in the research. If they had social contact, it tended to be within the family or with other children with disabilities. Their communication skills reflected this limited social contact.

Unlike the other children included in the research, Maomao had also developed aggressive behaviour, presumably in reaction to physical and emotional abuse from his mother and classmates. Now that he was older he hit back and yelled at his mother. Of wider consequence, he began to play with fire in the community, which led him to have police contact, when he threatened further arson and possible threats to life.

The longer time impact of discrimination against children with disabilities denying their access to developmental support is the lifetime affect. Not only does discrimination have an immediate developmental impact during their childhood, it can also affect their future opportunities. In Maomao's case, his failure in education and poor social skills were likely to affect his future employment, leading to lifelong poverty.

Impact on families

In addition to the impact on the children, the impact on the families from the discrimination towards children with disabilities was evident in their economic situation, family relations, social status and isolation. Many of China's rural families of children with disabilities have low income and their educational level is not high. In addition, the number of children in the family is usually more than that of the common family. Without a formal social support system, the families of children with disabilities bear the caring and economic responsibility. Because the families have no formal support for their children's disability support needs, their economic situation was worse than other families in this disadvantaged community. Family members work harder to financially support the child, paying for the additional health care and educational expenses for children with disabilities. In Maomao's case, the family was already in poverty and the sole financial and social responsibility for his additional needs exacerbated the pressure on the family, culminating in neglect and violence towards him. In addition, they worried about the future earning capacity of the parents or child in his adult life.

In addition to the financial cost, the research found that the impact of discrimination and lack of formal support strained family relations, threatened their social status and resulted in social isolation of children and their family in the community. Maomao was isolated and bullied by class mates, teachers, without social networks outside the family. His family endured social pressure from community members who did not understand the impact of his disabilities on his vulnerability to discrimination. The social and economic position of the family had probably been permanently affected by this discrimination. All family members of children with disabilities shared the pressures caused by the lack of social support (Ma 2002). Sun (2004) holds that such pressure may be misdirected towards the child, as seen in Maomao's case.

Impact on the community

The third effect of failing to meet the rights of children with disabilities is the impact on the community, including social justice, future social safety and social harmony. The detailed findings from Maomao's case illustrated the disharmony within the family, social networks, school community and potentially wider community from Maomao's threats of arson. Without adequate social support for Maomao or his parents, his life was full of discrimination, violence and injustice at home, school and the community. The effect of the multiple disadvantage and discrimination was that he had developed anti-social behaviour, which as he grew older, presents more serious risks to himself and others. The opportunities and capacity of Maomao to contribute to his community in the future were likely to be compromised.

In contrast, another child with disabilities in the same research site found a group of adults with disabilities who are assisting him with education and economic opportunities to remedy the past neglect from formal services. At the most optimistic, perhaps in the long term, this self-help approach of community groups of people with disabilities might mitigate the personal, family and community cost of failure to meet the rights of children with disabilities.

Conclusion about interrelated rights and social exclusion

Research in this case study rural community showed that some families of children with disabilities in China experience discrimination in the four rights domains of care and protection, economic security, developmental support and social participation. The lack of institutional processes to secure formal support exacerbates the pressure on some families, further increasing the risk of social exclusion and neglect of children with disabilities. The effects of the failure to meet their rights as children with disabilities were negative outcomes for the children, their families and their communities. These findings support the more general research from wider descriptive national surveys of children with disabilities and the other case studies in this book.

The policy implications relate to the full range of social policy fields, including child, family, education and disability policy. The final chapter draws conclusions for social policy reform to address these rights of children in the context of their families.

References

Bureau of Statistics of County H (2007) *Statistical Yearbook of County H, Jiangxi*, unpublished.

Bureau of Statistics of County H (2008) *Overview of Socioeconomic Development of County H, Jiangxi Province in 2007*, unpublished.

Chiu, M.Y.L., Yang, X., Wong, F.H.T., Li, J.H. and Li, J. (2013) Caregiving of children with intellectual disabilities in China – an examination of affiliate stigma and the cultural thesis. *Journal of Intellectual Disability Research* 57: 1117–1129.

CRPD, United Nations Convention on the Rights of Persons with Disabilities (2006) www.un.org/disabilities/default.asp?id=150 [1 February 2012].

Kohrman, M. (2005) *Bodies of Difference: Experiences of Disability and Institutional Advocacy in the Making of Modern China*, Berkeley: University of California Press.

Lim, F., Downs, J., Li, J., Bao, X.-H. and Leonard, H. (2013) Caring for a child with severe intellectual disability in China: the example of Rett syndrome. *Disability and Rehabilitation* 35: 343–351.

Ma, H.L. (ed.) (2002) *Social Welfare for China's Disabled Persons*, Beijing: China Social Press.

Mak, W.W.S. and Kwok, Y.T.Y. (2010) Internalization of stigma for parents of children with autism spectrum disorder in Hong Kong. *Social Science & Medicine* 70: 2045–2051.

Shang, X. and Fisher, K.R. (2014) Social support for mothers of children with disabilities in China. *Journal of Social Service Research* 10.1080/01488376.2014.896849.

Shang, X., Fisher, K.R. and Xie, J. (2011) Discrimination against children with disability in China: a case study in Jiangxi Province. *International Journal of Social Welfare* 20(3): 298–308.

Stein, M.A. (2010) China and disability rights. *Loyola of Los Angeles International and Comparative Law Review* 33(7): 7–26.

Sun, Y. (2004) Welfare demand analysis on China's children with special difficulties and the due intervention strategies, *Youth Study* [Chinese] 1: 9–13.

UNICEF, United Nations Children's Fund (2006) *An Investigation of Families with Children with Disabilities and Relevant Policies*. Unpublished internal document.

14 Child and family disability policy in China

This final chapter draws conclusions from the earlier chapters about implications for the role of the state in implementing the rights of children with disabilities (CRC 1989; CRPD 2006). It informs directions for social policy change to support family, community and state efforts to improve the fulfilment of the rights of children with disabilities in China. It focuses on the ways state policy can strengthen the agency of children and family networks, rather than exclude families from the child disability policy process. In this, it takes a broad approach to policy implementation by acknowledging the policy role of the state, non-government agencies including international agencies, communities and citizens.

The significance of the conclusions stems from the policy evidence gained from studying the experiences of families of children with disabilities and disability policy in China. This offers a different perspective of disability from other sources that inform policy, namely officials and the public. Systems to support children and their families are under pressure in many developed countries because of service gaps, cost and unfulfilled child rights to inclusion. The book offers new insight into policy and adds to theories of children's rights in the context of the relationships between parents and children, and between the state, the family and civil society within east Asia.

Social policy reform

Social welfare provision for children with disabilities in China has developed fast in the past decade. The policy development covered many aspects of lives of children with disabilities. Principles about the rights of children with disabilities, social participation and inclusion were reinforced in China by international organizations and Chinese people educated internationally. When these principles are combined with the governing principles of the Chinese government, such as 'people-centred' development and 'harmonious society' (Blaxland, Shang and Fisher 2014; Fisher, Shang, Blaxland 2011), the influence on policy processes has been a deep change to policies to promote the rights of children with disabilities. Although there are still many gaps in welfare provision to families of children with disabilities, it is likely that they will be addressed over time in the context of economic growth, and the development of a welfare system across the country. A child welfare system, which provides comprehensive support and services to families of children with disabilities, is slowly emerging.

Any changes in governing principles and social policies, however, have to be based on social consensus and accepted and supported by a majority of its citizens if it is to be fully implemented. It is more difficult to change social attitudes towards people with disabilities than to change social policies. The government needs to take a leading role in terms of establishment of a new social consensus, to reduce social exclusion and discrimination against children and other people with disabilities, in order to create a more inclusive, harmonious social environment for children with disabilities and their families. From this perspective, the framework of human rights could be useful.

Significant efforts have to be made in the following aspects for the development of welfare support to families of children with disabilities in China: first, policy changes – new policies have to be made in order to fill in policy gaps or to improve where the old policies are not effective enough to support families of children with disabilities in China. Second, policy implementation and creating and sharing good practices has become a focus. Third, these changes are in the political context of promoting a social consensus of social inclusion, to create a harmonious environment for people and children with disabilities. These policy developments are summarized below in relation to the four sets of rights of children with disabilities.

Right to care and protection

Examples of the policy implications emerged in the four rights domains. The analysis of experiences of right to life of children with disabilities in Chapter 5 suggests that on the one hand, there was no effective policy to protect the life of children with disabilities in China. The death or life of children with disabilities almost entirely depended on the attitude and decisions of parents, who were not well supported in that process. When parents decided to give up the lives of their children with disabilities, they received sympathy and were supported by many people, who had deep misunderstandings about the lives of people with disabilities. Social interventions to change the attitudes of medical professionals and community members towards people with disabilities would be necessary to overcome this barrier to protecting the right to life of children with disabilities.

In relation to rights to care and protection, the family planning policy shaped parents' decisions about who would care for their child with disabilities and where, to avoid penalties, yet in the short term this meant some children did not have access to support services and some were denied the opportunity to live with their parents. Some innovation focusing on early intervention, inclusive practices and financial support were evident in some wealthier areas and some State Child Welfare Institutions to enable some families to continue to care for their children with disability support needs.

Right to economic security

The analysis about the economic status of families of children with disabilities in Chapter 8 suggests that families of children with disabilities are more likely than other families in their community to live in relative and absolute poverty. The central government has policies to address this problem, but implementation is limited by local government resources and attitudes. It is important for the central government to intervene to implement the existing policy more effectively in order to improve the economic situation of families of children with disabilities.

Family experiences of the right to economic security have implications for poverty relief policies. In the absence of specific income support or government-provided disability support services, families that are already under economic pressure, also currently bear the additional cost of disability support. If they cannot bear that cost, their children cannot access support.

Right to child development

Addressing child development rights, Chinese government has policies to establish universal systems of health care and education to children with disabilities. The coverage of medical insurance is expanding, and hopefully problems of access, particularly in rural and poorer areas, will be solved gradually, although it will take time for all children with disabilities to benefit. Of particular importance will be universal free access to early medical intervention and therapy for children born with disabilities so that the impact on their other rights is minimized and their families are not forced further into poverty in their attempts to find and pay for effective intervention. The absence of government funded or provided disability support services for families and children with disabilities prevent them from achieving the same developmental outcomes as other children.

Similarly, central government universal free education policy is inclusive of children with disabilities, relying on the three strategies of learning in regular classrooms, special education and home education. Although the written education policy is inclusive of children with disabilities during the compulsory education years, in practice, many of these children are excluded because of the lack of school resources, facilities and training, and a performance measurement system based on test results. The experience of children and their families is that inclusive education policy implementation is weak, depending on the local resources and attitudes. Where they live means that many children are excluded from mainstream education, must pay for special education (which is only available for children with particular disabilities) or are excluded from education altogether.

A core limitation to the Chinese educational system is that it is clearly characterized by elite oriented examinations and streaming at all levels of education, and at almost all age groups of children. Government education investment is biased towards urban areas, higher education and elite schools, colleges and education. In fact, rather than a focus on equal education to all children, current practice focuses on an examination streaming process. Many parents and teachers pay more attention to students achieving a good ranking in examinations, than a rounded development. In this context, non-elite students, especially students with learning disabilities, are marginalized.

Right to social participation

Finally, the research revealed that policy responses are needed to fulfil the right to social participation of children and families through supporting children, families and communities with resources and information that facilitate inclusive opportunities for children of all ages. Equally, public education about social inclusion and social attitudes towards children with disabilities would contribute to achieving these rights.

Discrimination against children with disabilities is expressly prohibited by Chinese law but without formal support for families, children are placed at risk of serious neglect and a lifetime of social exclusion. The implication for policy development is that a combination of support for families, access to mainstream services and specialist support is required for children with disabilities to experience rights equal to other Chinese children.

Children and their families experienced significant discrimination in the four child disability domains of rights of care and protection, economic security, developmental support and social participation. The impact was both direct in terms of poor support for the children and families; and indirect in terms of cumulative pressure on families, which accentuated the social development disadvantages of the children.

Improving the implementation of policy to address the rights of children with disabilities in China requires a new consensus among the state, communities and families of children with disabilities, in order to allocate resources and promote real inclusion for children with disabilities in all communities.

References

CRC, United Nations Convention on the Rights of the Child (1989) www.ohchr.org/en/professionalinterest/pages/crc.aspx [2 May 2015].

CRPD, United Nations Convention on the Rights of Persons with Disabilities (2006) www.un.org/disabilities/default.asp?id=150 [1 February 2012].

Blaxland, M., Shang, X. and Fisher, K.R. (2014) People oriented: a new stage of social welfare development in China. *Journal of Social Service Research* 10.1080/01488376.2014.923801

Fisher, K.R., Shang, X. and Blaxland, M. (2011). Review Article: Human rights based social policies – challenges for China, *Social Policy & Society* 10(1): 71–78.

Appendix

Articles relevant to child disability in the UN Conventions

The extracts from the Articles of the UN Convention on the Rights of the Child 1989 and the UN Convention on the Rights of Persons with Disabilities 2006 below have been selected as most relevant to understanding children's rights in China. The full Conventions include other relevant rights, particularly for older children and young people: CRPD at www.un.org/disabilities/convention/conventionfull.shtml and CRC at www.ohchr.org/EN/ProfessionalInterest/Pages/CRC.aspx

UN Convention on the Rights of the Child 1989

Article 23

1 States Parties recognize that a mentally or physically **disabled child** should enjoy a full and decent life, in conditions which ensure dignity, promote self-reliance, and facilitate the child's active participation in the community.
2 States Parties recognize the right of the **disabled child** to special care and shall encourage and ensure the extension, subject to available resources, to the eligible child and those responsible for his or her care, of assistance for which application is made and which is appropriate to the child's condition and to the circumstances of the parents or others caring for the child.
3 Recognizing the special needs of a **disabled child**, assistance extended in accordance with paragraph 2 of the present chapter shall be provided free of charge, whenever possible, taking into account the financial resources of the parents or others caring for the child, and shall be designed to ensure that the disabled child has effective access to and receives education, training, health care services, rehabilitation services, preparation for employment and recreation opportunities in a manner conducive to the child's achieving the fullest possible social integration and individual development, including his or her cultural and spiritual development.
4 States Parties shall promote, in the spirit of international cooperation, the exchange of appropriate information in the field of preventive health care and of medical, psychological and functional treatment of **disabled children**, including dissemination of and access to information concerning methods of

rehabilitation, education and vocational services, with the aim of enabling States Parties to improve their capabilities and skills and to widen their experience in these areas. In this regard, particular account shall be taken of the needs of developing countries.

UN Convention on the Rights of Persons with Disabilities 2006

Article 3 – General principles

The principles of the present Convention shall be:

a   Respect for inherent dignity, individual autonomy including the freedom to make one's own choices, and independence of persons;
b   Non-discrimination;
c   Full and effective participation and inclusion in society;
d   Respect for difference and acceptance of persons with disabilities as part of human diversity and humanity;
e   Equality of opportunity;
f   Accessibility;
g   Equality between men and women;
h   Respect for the evolving capacities of **children** with disabilities and respect for the right of children with disabilities to preserve their identities.

Article 7 – Children with disabilities

1   States Parties shall take all necessary measures to ensure the full enjoyment by children with disabilities of all human rights and fundamental freedoms on an equal basis with other children.
2   In all actions concerning children with disabilities, the best interests of the child shall be a primary consideration.
3   States Parties shall ensure that children with disabilities have the right to express their views freely on all matters affecting them, their views being given due weight in accordance with their age and maturity, on an equal basis with other children, and to be provided with disability and age-appropriate assistance to realize that right.

Article 8 – Awareness-raising

1   States Parties undertake to adopt immediate, effective and appropriate measures:

a   To raise awareness throughout society, including at the **family** level, regarding persons with disabilities, and to foster respect for the rights and dignity of persons with disabilities;

b   To combat stereotypes, prejudices and harmful practices relating to persons with disabilities, including those based on sex and **age**, in all areas of life;

c   To promote awareness of the capabilities and contributions of persons with disabilities.

Measures to this end include:

a   Fostering at all levels of the education system, including in all **children** from an early age, an attitude of respect for the rights of persons with disabilities;

Article 10 – Right to life

States Parties reaffirm that every human being has the inherent right to life and shall take all necessary measures to ensure its effective enjoyment by persons with disabilities on an equal basis with others.

Article 16 – Freedom from exploitation, violence and abuse

1   States Parties shall take all appropriate legislative, administrative, social, educational and other measures to protect persons with disabilities, both within and outside the home, from all forms of exploitation, violence and abuse, including their gender-based aspects.

2   States Parties shall also take all appropriate measures to prevent all forms of exploitation, violence and abuse by ensuring, inter alia, appropriate forms of gender- and **age-sensitive** assistance and support for persons with disabilities and their families and carers, including through the provision of information and education on how to avoid, recognize and report instances of exploitation, violence and abuse. States Parties shall ensure that protection services are age-, gender- and disability-sensitive.

5   States Parties shall put in place effective legislation and policies, including women- and **child-focused** legislation and policies, to ensure that instances of exploitation, violence and abuse against persons with disabilities are identified, investigated and, where appropriate, prosecuted.

Article 18 – Liberty of movement and nationality

2   **Children** with disabilities shall be registered immediately after birth and shall have the right from birth to a name, the right to acquire a nationality and, as far as possible, the right to know and be cared for by their parents.

Article 23 – Respect for home and the family

1   States Parties shall take effective and appropriate measures to eliminate discrimination against persons with disabilities in all matters relating to marriage, family, parenthood and relationships, on an equal basis with others, so as to ensure that:

    a   The right of all persons with disabilities who are of marriageable age to marry and to found a family on the basis of free and full consent of the intending spouses is recognized;

    b   The rights of persons with disabilities to decide freely and responsibly on the number and spacing of their children and to have access to age-appropriate information, reproductive and family planning education are recognized, and the means necessary to enable them to exercise these rights are provided;

    c   Persons with disabilities, including **children**, retain their fertility on an equal basis with others.

2   States Parties shall ensure the rights and responsibilities of persons with disabilities, with regard to guardianship, wardship, trusteeship, adoption of children or similar institutions, where these concepts exist in national legislation; in all cases the **best interests of the child** shall be paramount. States Parties shall render appropriate assistance to persons with disabilities in the performance of their child-rearing responsibilities.

3   States Parties shall ensure that **children** with disabilities have equal rights with respect to family life. With a view to realizing these rights, and to prevent concealment, abandonment, neglect and segregation of children with disabilities, States Parties shall undertake to provide early and comprehensive information, services and support to children with disabilities and their families.

4   States Parties shall ensure that a **child** shall not be separated from his or her parents against their will, except when competent authorities subject to judicial review determine, in accordance with applicable law and procedures, that such separation is necessary for the best interests of the child. In no case shall a child be separated from parents on the basis of a disability of either the child or one or both of the parents.

5   States Parties shall, where the immediate family is unable to care for a child with disabilities, undertake every effort to provide alternative care within the wider family, and failing that, within the community in a family setting.

Article 24 – Education

2   In realizing this right, States Parties shall ensure that:

a   Persons with disabilities are not excluded from the general education system on the basis of disability, and that **children** with disabilities are not excluded from free and compulsory primary education, or from secondary education, on the basis of disability;

b   Persons with disabilities can access an inclusive, quality and free primary education and secondary education on an equal basis with others in the communities in which they live;

c   Reasonable accommodation of the individual's requirements is provided;

d   Persons with disabilities receive the support required, within the general education system, to facilitate their effective education;

e   Effective individualized support measures are provided in environments that maximize academic and social development, consistent with the goal of full inclusion.

Article 25 – Health

States Parties recognize that persons with disabilities have the right to the enjoyment of the highest attainable standard of health without discrimination on the basis of disability. States Parties shall take all appropriate measures to ensure access for persons with disabilities to health services that are gender-sensitive, including health-related rehabilitation. In particular, States Parties shall:

a   Provide persons with disabilities with the same range, quality and standard of free or affordable health care and programmes as provided to other persons, including in the area of sexual and reproductive health and population-based public health programmes;

b   Provide those health services needed by persons with disabilities specifically because of their disabilities, including early identification and intervention as appropriate, and services designed to minimize and prevent further disabilities, including among **children** and older persons;

Article 26 – Habilitation and rehabilitation

1   States Parties shall take effective and appropriate measures, including through peer support, to enable persons with disabilities to attain and maintain maximum independence, full physical, mental, social and vocational ability, and full inclusion and participation in all aspects of life. To that end, States Parties shall organize, strengthen and extend comprehensive habilitation and rehabilitation services and programmes, particularly in the areas of health, employment, education and social services, in such a way that these services and programmes:

a   Begin at the **earliest possible stage**, and are based on the multidisciplinary assessment of individual needs and strengths;

b   Support participation and inclusion in the community and all aspects of society, are voluntary, and are available to persons with disabilities as close as possible to their own communities, including in rural areas.

Article 28 – Adequate standard of living and social protection

1   States Parties recognize the right of persons with disabilities to an adequate standard of living for themselves and their families, including adequate food, clothing and housing, and to the continuous improvement of living conditions, and shall take appropriate steps to safeguard and promote the realization of this right without discrimination on the basis of disability.

2   States Parties recognize the right of persons with disabilities to social protection and to the enjoyment of that right without discrimination on the basis of disability, and shall take appropriate steps to safeguard and promote the realization of this right, including measures:

a   To ensure equal access by persons with disabilities to clean water services, and to ensure access to appropriate and affordable services, devices and other assistance for disability-related needs;

b   To ensure access by persons with disabilities, in particular women and **girls** with disabilities and older persons with disabilities, to social protection programmes and poverty reduction programmes;

c   To ensure access by persons with disabilities and their families living in situations of poverty to assistance from the State with disability-related expenses, including adequate training, counselling, financial assistance and respite care;

d   To ensure access by persons with disabilities to public housing programmes;

e   To ensure equal access by persons with disabilities to retirement benefits and programmes.

Article 30 – Participation in cultural life, recreation, leisure and sport

5   With a view to enabling persons with disabilities to participate on an equal basis with others in recreational, leisure and sporting activities, States Parties shall take appropriate measures:

d   To ensure that **children** with disabilities have equal access with other children to participation in play, recreation and leisure and sporting activities, including those activities in the school system.

Glossary

All names used in the book are aliases unless the case is in the public media or the person agreed to be named.

alternative care	Care for children away from their birth parents
BNU	Beijing Normal University
carer	Informal carers, including family, kin, friends
CDPF (DPF)	China Disabled Persons' Federation and DPFs at each level of government
child/children with disabilities	The book adopts person first language consistent with the CRPD
CRC	United Nations Convention on the Rights of the Child 1989
CRPD	United Nations Convention on the Rights of Persons with Disabilities 2006
inclusive education	The book refers to inclusive education as supported education within a mainstream classroom or school. It contrasts with special education in a segregated environment.
institutional care	Residential care in institutions, approximately 50–500 children in each institution. See also State Child Welfare Institution
MCA	Ministry of Civil Affairs. Provincial and local levels of Civil Affairs are referred to as a department or bureau
MLS	Minimum living security – social security for low-income households. *Dibao*
NGO	Non-government organization
Orphans allowance	Basic living security allowance for orphans
SCNSSD	Second China National Sample Survey on Disability (2006)

State Child Welfare Institution	Local government organization responsible for orphans, including organizing adoption and usually provides institutional care, and sometimes also other forms of alternative care in the community, such as foster care
therapy	The book refers to therapy rather than rehabilitation for consistency with social rather than medical understandings of disability, unless rehabilitation it is in a proper noun
Yuan (RMB)	Chinese dollar (Yuan) 10 yuan = UK£1.1

References

Ali, Z., Fazil, Q., Bywaters, P., Wallace, L. and Singh, G. (2001) Disability, ethnicity and childhood: a critical review of research. *Disability & Society* 16(7): 949–968.

Baker, K. and Donelly, M. (2001) The social experiences of children with disabilities and the influence of environment: a framework for intervention. *Disability and Society* 16(1): 71–85.

Banks, M.E. (2003) Disability in the family: a life span perspective. *Cultural Diversity and Ethnic Minority Psychology* 9(4): 367–384.

Beijing Family Planning Committee (2012) *Methods of Collection and Management of Social Support Fee in Beijing*, www.bjfc.gov.cn/web/static/articles/catalog_ff8080813 678bee3013678cd20c70015/article_ff80808136880dd601368b020e7a0050/ff8080813 6880dd601368b020e7a0050.html [21 May 2012].

Bell, M., Franklin, A., Greco, V. and Mitchell, W. (2009) Working with children with learning disabilities and/or who communicate non-verbally: research experiences and their implications for social work education, increased participation and social inclusion. *Social Work Education* 28(3): 309–324.

Beresford, B. (2004) On the road to nowhere? Young disabled people and transition. *Child: Care, Health and Development* 30(6): 581–587.

Bickenbach, J. (2009) Disability, culture and the UN convention. *Disability & Rehabilitation* 31(14): 1111–1124.

Blaxland, M., Shang, X. and Fisher, K.R. (2014) People oriented: a new stage of social welfare development in China. *Journal of Social Service Research* 10.1080/ 01488376.2014.923801

Braithewaite, J. and Mont, D. (2008) Disability and poverty: a survey of World Bank poverty assessments and implications. *Social Protection Discussion Paper 0805*, Washington: World Bank.

Bronfenbrenner, U. (1979) *The Ecology of Human Development*, Cambridge: Harvard University Press.

Bureau of Statistics of County H (2007) *Statistical Yearbook of County H, Jiangxi*, unpublished.

Bureau of Statistics of County H (2008) *Overview of Socioeconomic Development of County H, Jiangxi Province in 2007*, unpublished.

Callaway, A. (1999) Considering sign bilingual education in cultural context: a survey of deaf schools in Jiangsu Province. *China Deafness Education International* 1: 34–46.

Case, S. (2000) Refocusing on the parent: What are the social issues of concern for parents of disabled children? *Disability & Society* 15(2): 271–292.

CDPF, China Disabled Persons' Federation (2006) *A Notice of Issuing the Speech of Senior Officials in the Workshop of Rehabilitation work for Children with Disabilities*, www.cdpf.org.cn/2008old/kangf/content/2006-10/27/content_75604.htm [10 September 2011].

CDPF, China Disabled Persons' Federation (2007) *Handbook of Main Data from the Second National Sampling Survey on Disability (2006-2007)*. Office of the Second China National Sample Survey on Disability, Beijing: Huaxia Press.

CDPF, China Disabled Persons' Federation (2008) *Data Analysis of the Second China National Sample Survey on Disability*. Office of the Second China National Sample Survey on Disability and the Institute of Population Studies (IPS) Peking University, Beijing: Huaxia Press.

CDPF, China Disabled Persons' Federation (2013) www.cdpf.org.cn/english/aboutus/aboutus.htm [3 December 2013].

CDPF, China Disabled Persons' Federation (2015) *Statistical Communique on the Development of the Work for Persons with Disabilities in 2014* www.cdpf.org.cn/zcwj/zxwj/201503/t20150331_444108.shtml [3 May 2015].

CEDAW, United Nations Convention on the Elimination of all Forms of Discrimination against Women (1979) www.un.org/womenwatch/daw/cedaw/text/econvention.htm [3 May 2015].

Chan, C.K., Ngok, K.L. and Phillips, D. (2008) *Social Policy in China: Development and Wellbeing*, Bristol: The Policy Press, University of Bristol.

Chen, X. and Chen, Y. (2008) *The Status Analysis and Strategies of Children with Disabilities in China*, Beijing: Huaxia Press.

Chen, J., Liao, C. and Zou, G. (2009) Thinking about the main problems of the minimum living security system for urban residents. *Socioeconomic System Comparison* [Chinese] 4: 76–81.

Chen, L., Wehmeyer, M.L. and Zhang, D. (2005) Parent and teacher engagement in fostering the self-determination of students with disabilities: a comparison between the United States and the People's Republic of China, *Remedial and Special Education* 26(1): 55–64.

Chen, J., Yang, Z. and Wang, Y.P. (2014) The New Chinese Model of Public Housing: A Step Forward or Backward? *Housing Studies* 29: 534–550.

China News Agency (2012) *Statistics given by the Statistical Bureau show that more people lived in rural areas in China than in urban areas in China*, http://finance.chinanews.com/cj/2012/01-17/3610120.shtml [11 July 2014].

Chiu, M.Y.L., Yang, X., Wong, F.H.T., Li, J.H. and Li, J. (2013) Caregiving of children with intellectual disabilities in China – an examination of affiliate stigma and the cultural thesis. *Journal of Intellectual Disability Research* 57: 1117–1129.

Chung, E.Y.-H., Packer, T. and Yau, M. (2011) When East meets West: community-based rehabilitation in Chinese communities. *Disability & Rehabilitation* 33(8): 697–705.

Clarke, H. (2006) Preventing social exclusion of disabled children and their families: literature review. *Research Report RR782*, paper for the National Evaluation of the Children's Fund, Institute of Applied Social Studies University of Birmingham.

Compulsory Education Law (1986, 2006) www.gov.cn/flfg/2006-06/30/content_323302.htm [9 July 2012].

Connors, C. and Stalker, K. (2007) Children's experiences of disability: pointers to a social model of childhood disability. *Disability & Society* 22(1): 19–33.

Cotton, J., Edwards, C., Zhao, W. and Gelabert, J. (2007) Nurturing care for China's orphaned children. *Young Children* 62: 58–63.

CRC, United Nations Convention on the Rights of the Child (1989) www.ohchr.org/en/professionalinterest/pages/crc.aspx [2 May 2015].

CRPD, United Nations Convention on the Rights of Persons with Disabilities (2006) www.un.org/disabilities/default.asp?id=150 [1 February 2012].

Dauncey, S. (2007) Screening disability in the PRC: the politics of looking good. *China Information* 21: 481–506.

Dauncey, S. (2012) Three days to walk: a personal story of life writing and disability consciousness in China. *Disability & Society* 27: 311–323.

de Boer, A., Pijl, S.J. and Minnaert, A. (2011) Regular primary schoolteachers' attitudes towards inclusive education: a review of the literature. *International Journal of Inclusive Education* 15(3): 345–346.

Deng, M., Farnsworth, E. and Poon-McBrayer, K.F. (2001) The development of special education in China. *Remedial & Special Education* 22(5): 288–298.

Deng, M. and Holdsworth, J.C. (2007) From unconscious to conscious inclusion: meeting special education needs in West China. *Disability & Society* 22(5): 507–522.

Dowling, M. and Dolan, L. (2001) Families with children with disabilities – inequalities and the social model. *Disability & Society* 16(1): 21–25.

Downing, J. and Peckham-Hardin, K. (2007) Supporting inclusive education for students with severe disabilities in rural areas. *Rural Special Education Quarterly* 26(2): 10–15.

Dyson, L. (2012) Strategies for and successes with promoting social integration in primary schools in Canada and China. *International Journal of Disability, Development and Education* 59: 157–172.

Edele, A. (2005) Non-governmental organizations in China. *CASIN Report.* Geneva: Programme on NGOs and Civil Society and Centre for Applied Studies in International Negotiations.

Ellsworth, N.J. and Zhang, C. (2007) Progress and challenges in China's special education development. *Remedial and Special Education* 28(1): 58–64.

Emerson, E. (2004) Poverty and children with intellectual disabilities in the world's richer countries. *Journal of Intellectual and Developmental Disability* 29(4): 319–338.

Fisher, K.R. and Li, J. (2008) Chinese disability independent living policy. *Disability & Society* 23(2): 171–185.

Fisher, K.R., Li, J. and Fan, L. (2011) Barriers to the supply of nongovernment disability services in China. *Journal of Social Policy* 41(1): 161–182.

Fisher, K.R. and Shang, X. (2013) Access to health and therapy services for families of children with disabilities in China. *Disability & Rehabilitation* 35(25): 2157–2163.

Fisher, K.R. and Shang, X. (2014) Protecting the right to life of children with disabilities in China. *Journal of Social Service Research*, 10.1080/01488376.2014.922521.

Fisher, K.R., Shang, X. and Blaxland, M. (2011) Review Article: Human rights based social policies – challenges for China. *Social Policy & Society* 10(1): 71–78.

Fisher, K.R., Shang, X. and Guo, P. (2012) Gender, social policy and older women with disabilities in rural China, in Sung, S. and Pascall, G. (eds) *Gender in East Asian Welfare States: Confucianism or Gender Equality*, Basingstoke: Palgrave MacMillan.

Fisher, K.R., Shang, X. and Guo, P. (2014) Gender, social policy and older women with disabilities in rural China', in Sung, S. and Pascall, G. *Gender and Welfare State in East Asia: Confucianism or gender equality?* Basingstoke: Palgrave, Chapter 5: 141–170.

Fisher, K.R., Shang, X. and Li, J. (2015) Accountability of children's services organizations in China. *Asian Social Work and Policy Review* 9: 94–107.

Fisher, K.R., Shang, X. and Li, Z. (2011) The absent role of the state: analysis of social support to older people with disability in rural China. *Social Policy and Administration* 45(6): 633–648.

Fisher, K.R., Shang, X. and Xie, J. (2011) Support for social participation of children and young people with disability in China, in Carrillo, B. and Duckett, J. (eds) *China's Changing Welfare Mix: Local perspectives*, London and New York: Routledge.

Funder, K. (ed) (1996) *Citizen Child: Australian Law and Children's Rights*, Melbourne: Australian Institute of Family Studies.

Gao'an City Disabled Persons' Federation (2009) *Annual Report of the Gao'an City Disabled Persons' Federation 2008*, Gao'an: Gao'an City Disabled Persons' Federation.

Gao'an Government (2010) *Entering Gao'an*, Gao'an City Municipal Party Committee, www.gaoan.gov.cn/system/2011/12/22/011859232.shtml [11 July 2014].

Goodley, D. and Runswick-Cole, K. (2011) Problematising policy: conceptions of 'child', 'disabled' and 'parents' in social policy in England. *International Journal of Inclusive Education* 15(1): 71–85.

Gu, X. (2011) The most difficult task is in cities, not in rural areas for comprehensive coverage of medical insurance, www.zgylbx.com/hvyfuahsnew31230_1/ [11 May 2012].

Guo, B., Bricout, J.C. and Huang, J. (2005) A common open space or a digital divide? A social model perspective on the online disability community in China. *Disability & Society* 20(1): 49–66.

Hua, G. (2003) The situation and development of inclusive education for children with disabilities. *Education Studies* [Chinese] 24(2): 65–69.

Hampton, N.Z. (2001) An evolving rehabilitation service delivery system in the People's Republic of China. *Journal of Rehabilitation* 67(3): 20–25.

Hernandez, V.T. (2008) Making good on the promise of international law: the Convention on the Rights of Persons with Disability and Inclusive Education in China and India. *Pacific Rim Law and Policy Journal* 17(2): 497–527.

Holroyd, E. (2003) Chinese cultural influences on parental caregiving obligations toward children with disabilities. *Qualitative Health Research* 13(4): 4–19.

Howell, J. (2009) Government-organised nongovernment organisations, in Pong Dea (ed.) *Encyclopedia of Modern China.* Detroit: Gale.

Hu, X., Wang, M. and Fei, X. (2012) Family quality of life of Chinese families of children with intellectual disabilities. *Journal of Intellectual Disability Research* 56: 30–44.

Huang, Y.-P., Chen, S.-L. and Tsai, S.-W. (2012) Father's experiences of involvement in the daily care of their child with developmental disability in a Chinese context. *Journal of Clinical Nursing* 21: 3287–3296.

Huang, Y.T., Fried, J.H. and Hsu, T.H. (2009) Taiwanese mothers' attitude change toward individuals with disabilities. *Journal of Social Work in Disability and Rehabilitation* 8: 82–94.

Irwin, L.G., Siddiqi, A. and Hertzman, C. (2007) *Early Child Development: A Powerful Equalizer*, Commission on the Social Determinants of Health, World Health Organisation.

Jenks, E.B. (2005) Explaining disability: parents' stories of raising children with visual impairments in a sighted world. *Journal of Contemporary Ethnography* 34 (2): 143–169.

Johnson, K. (1996) The politics of the revival of infant abandonment in China, with special reference to Hunan. *Population and Development Review* 22(1): 77–98.

Johnson, K., Huang, B. and Wang, L. (1998) Infant abandonment and adoption in China. *Population and Development Review* 24(3): 469–510.

Kang, X. and Feng, L. (2014) *Observation Report on the Third Sector of China*. Beijing: Social Sciences Academy Press.

Katz, I., Shang, X. and Zhang, Y. (2011) Missing elements of a child protection system in China: the case of LX. *Social Policy & Society* 10(1): 93–102.

Kayess, R. and French, P. (2008) Out of darkness into light? Introducing the Convention on the Rights of Persons with Disabilities. *Human Rights Law Review* 8(1): 1–34.

Kelly, S.E. (2005) 'A different light': examining impairment through parent narratives of childhood disability. *Journal of Contemporary Ethnography* 34: 180–205.

Kohrman, M. (2005) *Bodies of Difference: Experiences of Disability and Institutional Advocacy in the Making of Modern China*, Berkeley: University of California Press.

Law on the Protection of Persons with Disabilities (1990, 2008) China Disabled Persons Federation, www.cdpf.org.cn/english/laws1documents/200804/t20080410_267460. html [2 May 2015].

Lim, F., Downs, J., Li, J., Bao, X.-H. and Leonard, H. (2013) Caring for a child with severe intellectual disability in China: the example of Rett syndrome. *Disability and Rehabilitation* 35: 343–351.

Lin, H.-C., Knox, M. and Barr, J. (2014) A grounded theory of living a life with a physical disability in Taiwan. *Disability and Society* 29: 968–979.

Lister, R. (2006) Children (but not women) first: New Labour, child welfare and gender. *Critical Social Policy* 26, 315–335.

Liu, F. (2010a) A girl breaking her palm in a lift, her mother killed her and committed suicide, but was rescued, http://news.sina.com.cn/s/2010-05-11/043120243838.shtml [25 July 2012].

Liu, F. (2010b) Jinmen woman killed a 3 years sick daughter and facing homicide prosecution, http://news.qq.com/a/20100721/000142.htm [25 July 2012].

Liu, G. (2011) Caring for twin children with cerebral palsy for thirteen years, a desperate suicided mother who drowned two sons was rescued, http://dg.oeeee.com/a/20110516/991351.html [25 July 2012].

Liu, G. and Zhao, Q. (2011) The court open day decided, thousands of mothers pleading for her, http://dg.oeeee.com/a/20110531/994990.html [25 July 2012].

Lo, L. (2008) Perceived benefits experienced in support groups for Chinese families of children with disabilities. *Early Child Development and Care* 180: 405–415.

Lu, S. (2005) *The System of China's Policies on Children and Protecting Minors*, www.china-ccaa.org/site per cent5Cinfocontent per cent5CETFY_20050907113342718.htm [28 July 2011].

Lu, Y.Y. (2009) NGO-state relations in contemporary China: the rise of dependent autonomy. *Development Issues* 11: 23–25.

Lygnegard, F., Donohue, D., Bornman, J., Granlund, M. and Huus, K. (2013) A systematic review of generic and special needs of children with disabilities living in poverty settings in low- and middle-income countries. *Journal of Policy Practice* 12(4): 296–315.

Ma, H.L. (ed.) (2002) *Social Welfare for China's Disabled Persons*, Beijing: China Social Press.

MacKay, M.E. and Covell, K. (2013) What about the rights of the infant with disabilities? Responses to infanticide as function of infant health status. *Canadian Journal of Disability Studies* 2(2): 35–57.

Mak, W.W.S. and Kwok, Y.T.Y. (2010) Internalization of stigma for parents of children with autism spectrum disorder in Hong Kong. *Social Science & Medicine* 70: 2045–2051.

Marriage Law of People's Republic of China (1980, 2001) www.npc.gov.cn/englishnpc/Law/2007-12/13/content_1384064.htm [2 May 2015].

Maternal and Child Health Law of People's Republic of China (2005) www.gov.cn/banshi/2005-08/01/content_18943.htm [31 January 2012].

MCA, Ministry of Civil Affairs (2003) *Temporary Methods for Managing Foster Care*, www.mca.gov.cn/article/zwgk/tzl/200711/20071100004024.shtml [3 May 2015].

MCA, Ministry of Civil Affairs (and 14 government organizations) (2006) *Opinions on Strengthening the Work of Orphan Assistance*, www.china. com.cn/chinese/PI-c/1183979.htm [11 February 2013].

MCA, Ministry of Civil Affairs (2011) *Social Service Development Statistical Report 2010*, www.mca.gov.cn/article/zwgk/mzyw/201106/20110600161364.shtml [1 January 2012].

MCA, Ministry of Civil Affairs (2013a) *Notice of Improving Works about Abandoned Babies*, www.mca.gov.cn/article/zwgk/fvfg/shflhshsw/201305/20130500460312.shtml [4 November 2013].

MCA, Ministry of Civil Affairs (2013b) *Statistical Report of the Development of Social Services in China, Ministry of Civil Affairs, China 2013*, www.mca.gov.cn/article/zwgk/mzyw/201306/20130600474640.shtml [3 May 2015].

McCabe, H. (2003) The beginnings of inclusion in the People's Republic of China. *Research and Practice for Persons with Severe Disabilities* 28: 16–22.

McCabe, H. (2007) Parent advocacy in the face of adversity: autism and families in the Peoples Republic of China, *Focus on Autism and Other Developmental Disabilities* 22(1): 39–50.

McCabe, H. (2008a) The importance of parent-to-parent support among families of children with autism in the People's Republic of China. *International Journal of Disability, Development and Education* 55: 303–314.

McCabe, H. (2008b). Two decades of serving children with autism in the People's Republic of China: achievements and challenges of a state-run mental health center. *Disability & Society* 23(3): 271–282.

McCabe, H. (2010) Employment experiences, perspectives, and wishes of mothers of children with autism in the People's Republic of China. *Journal of Applied Research in Intellectual Disabilities* 23(2): 122–131.

McCabe, H. (2013) Bamboo shoots after the rain: development and challenges of autism intervention in China. *Autism* 17: 510–526.

McCabe, H. and Barnes, R.E. (2012) Autism in a family in China: an investigation and ethical consideration of sibling issues. *International Journal of Disability, Development and Education* 59: 197–207.

McCabe, H. and McCabe, K. (2013) Disability and family in the People's Republic of China: implementation, benefits, and comparison of two mutual support groups. *Journal of Intellectual and Developmental Disability* 38: 12–22.

McLoughlin, C.S., Zhou, Z. and Clark, E. (2005) Reflections on the development and status of contemporary special education services in China. *Psychology in Schools* 42(3): 273–283.

Meekosha, H. (2004) Drifting down the gulf stream: navigating the cultures of disability studies. *Disability & Society* 19(7): 721–723.

Miles, M. (2000) Disability on a different model: glimpses of an Asian heritage, *Disability & Society* 15(4): 603–618.

Miles, M. and Huberman, A. (1994) *Qualitative Data Analysis: An expanded sourcebook* 2nd edn, Beverley Hills: Sage Publications.

Miles, S. and Singal, N. (2010) The Education for All and inclusive education debate: conflict, contradiction or opportunity? *International Journal of Inclusive Education* 14(1): 1–15.

Ministry of Finance (2012) *Report of Revenue and Expenditure*, http://gks.mof.gov.cn/zhengfuxinxi/tongjishuju/201301/t20130122_729462.html [2 May 2015].

Ministry of Health (2002) *Notice on Printing and Distributing China Action Plan of Promoting the Quality of Newborn Population and Reducing Birth Deficiencies and Disabilities (2002-2010)*, www.cjr.org.cn/zcfg/GuoJiaFaGui/24216.html [6 July 2010].

Mop (mop.com) (2010) *Discussion on the Baby with Aproctia in Tianjin*, http://dzh.mop.com/default.jsp?url=http://dzh.mop.com/topic/readSub_10931212_0_0.html [6 July 2010].

Muir, K. and Goldblatt, B. (2011) Complementing or conflicting human rights conventions? Realising an inclusive approach to families with a young person with disabilities and challenging behaviour. *Disability & Society* 26(5): 629–642.

National Bureau of Statistics (2007) *China City Statistics Year Book 2006*, Department of Urban and Social Economic Survey, Beijing: China Statistic Press.

National Bureau of Statistics (2011) Communiqué of the Sixth National Census Data in 2010 No. 1. 2011, www.stats.gov.cn/tjfx/jdfx/t20110428_402722253.htm [10 July 2012].

National Education Commission (2001) *Measures for Implementing Learning in Regular Class for Children with Disabilities*, National Education Commission and CDPF www.cdpf.org.cn/jiaoy/content/2001-07/19/content_75922.htm [29 October 2010].

Oliver, M. (1996) *Understanding Disability: From theory to practice*, Hampshire: Palgrave.

Pearson, V., Wong, Y.C. and Pierini, J. (2002) The structure and content of social inclusion: voices of young adults with learning difficulties in Guangzhou. *Disability & Society* 17(4): 365–382.

PED JICA, Planning and Evaluation Department, Japan International Cooperation Agency (2002) *Country Profile on Disabilities, People's Republic of China*, Tokyo: Japan International Cooperation Agency.

Peters, S., Johnstone, C. and Ferguson, P. (2005) A disability rights in education model for evaluating inclusive education, *International Journal of Inclusive Education* 9(2): 139–160.

Petersen, C. (2010) Population policy and eugenic theory: implications of China's ratification of the United Nations Convention on the Rights of Persons with Disabilities. *China: An International Journal* 8(1): 85–109.

Porter, T. and Gavin, H. (2010) Infanticide and neonaticide: a review of 40 years of research literature on incidence and causes. *Trauma, Violence, and Abuse* 11(3): 99–112.

Qiao, D.P. and Chan, Y.C. (2005) Child abuse in China: a yet-to-be-acknowledged 'social problem' in the Chinese mainland. *Child and Family Social Work* 10(1): 21–27.

Quinn, G. and Degener, T. (2002) Human rights and disability: the current use and future potential of United Nations Human Rights Instruments in the context of disability, United Nations.

Rajivan, A. and UNDP Team (2010) *Power, Voice and Rights: A Turning Point for Gender Equality in Asia and the Pacific*. New Delhi: Macmillan Publishers India Ltd.

Rao, D. and Liu, Z. (2011) Families with children with cerebral palsy urge the government to build additional rehabilitation agencies, http://dg.oeeee.com/a/20110519/992292.html [25 July 2012].

Rao, D., Wei, W., Li, M. and Chen, Y. (2011) The case of Han Qunfeng: most net users pleading for leniency, http://dg.oeeee.com/a/20110603/995895.html [25 July 2012].

Research Team of Anti-Infant Abandonment, Nankai University (2006a) *Survey of Public Opinion on Child Abandonment*, Beijing: UNICEF.

Research Team of Anti-Infant Abandonment, Nankai University (2006b) *Survey and Policy Suggestions of Families with Children with Disabilities*, Beijing: UNICEF.

Runswick-Cole, K. (2011) Time to end the bias towards inclusive education? *British Journal of Special Education* 38: 112–119.

Ryan, S. and Runswick-Cole, K. (2008) Repositioning mothers: mothers, disabled children and disability studies. *Disability & Society* 23(3): 199–210.

SCNSSD, Second China National Sample Survey on Disability (2006) see CDPF (2007, 2008).

SEU, Social Exclusion Unit (2001) *Preventing social exclusion*, Report by the Social Exclusion Unit to the UK Cabinet Office, March, London.

Shakespeare, T. (2006) *Disability Rights and Wrongs*, New York: Routledge.

Shang, X. (2001a) Moving towards a multi-level and multi-pillar system: institutional care in two Chinese cities. *Journal of Social Policy* 30(2): 259–281.

Shang, X. (2001b) *Orphans and Disabled Children in China and Alternative Care*, Report to the Ministry of Civil Affairs and UNICEF, Beijing: UNICEF.

Shang, X. (2002) Looking for a better way to care for children: cooperation between the state and civil society. *Social Service Review* 76(2): 203–228.

Shang, X. (2008) *The System of Social Protection for Vulnerable Children in China*, Beijing: Social Sciences Academic Press.

Shang, X. (2012) Looking for best practice in caring for disabled children: a case of socialized foster care in China. *Asia Pacific Journal of Social Work and Development* 22(1–2): 127–138.

Shang, X. and Fisher, K.R. (2013) *Caring for Orphaned Children in China*, Lanham: Lexington Books.

Shang, X. and Fisher, K.R. (2014) Social support for mothers of children with disabilities in China. *Journal of Social Service Research* 10.1080/01488376.2014.896849.

Shang, X., Fisher, K.R. and Xie, J. (2011) Discrimination against children with disability in China: a case study in Jiangxi Province. *International Journal of Social Welfare* 20(3): 298–308.

Shang, X., Saldov, M. and Fisher, K.R. (2011) Informal kinship care of orphans in rural China. *Social Policy & Society* 10(1): 103–116.

Shang, X. and Wang, X. (2012) *Discovery Report: Emerging Issues and Findings for Child Welfare and Protection in China (2011)*, Beijing: Social Sciences Academic Press.

Shang, X. and Wang, X. (2013) *Leading Research on Child Welfare and Protection in China: 2013*, Beijing: Social Sciences Academic Press.

Shang, X. and Wu, X. (2003) Protecting children under financial constraints: the case of Datong. *Journal of Social Policy* 32: 549–570.

Shang, X. and Wu, X. (2004) Changing approaches of social protection: social assistance reform in urban China. *Journal of Social Policy and Society* 33: 259–271.

Shang, X. and Wu, X. (2011) Care regime in China. *Journal of Comparative Social Welfare* 27(2): 123–131.

Shang, X., Wu, X. and Li, H. (2005) Social policy, gender and child abandonment in China. *Youth Studies* 4: 1–5.

Shang, X., Wu, X. and Wu, Y. (2005) Welfare provision to vulnerable children: the missing role of the state. *The China Quarterly* 18(1): 122–136.

Stake, R. (2000) Case studies, in Denzin NK and Lincoln YS. (eds) *The Handbook of Qualitative Research*, 2nd edn, Thousand Oaks: Sage Publications.

State Council (2005) *China's second periodic report on CRC implementation*, www.ohchr. org/english/bodies/crc/docs/AdvanceVersions/CRC.C.RESP.89(I)_C.pdf.

State Council (2008) *Opinions on the development of welfare for persons with disabilities*, www.gov.cn/jrzg/2008-04/23/content_952483.htm [28 January 2012].

State Council (2009) *Opinions regarding further accelerating the development of special education*, www.gov.cn/zwgk/2009-05/08/content_1308951.htm [28 January 2011].

State Council (2010) *Opinions on strengthening the work of protection orphans*, www.gov. cn/ zwgk/2010-11/18/content_1748012.htm [14 May 2012].

State Council (2013) *Opinions of the Office of the State Council on the government purchasing services from social forces*, www.mca.gov.cn/article/zwgk/fvfg/ mjzzgl/201310/20131000525921.shtml [4 December 2013].

Stein, M.A. (2010) China and disability rights. *Loyola of Los Angeles International and Comparative Law Review* 33(7): 7–26.

Sun, Y. (2004) Welfare demand analysis on China's children with special difficulties and the due intervention strategies, *Youth Study* [Chinese] 1: 9–13.

Sun, X., Allison, C., Auyeung, B., Baron-Cohen, S. and Brayne, C. (2013a) A review of healthcare service and education provision of Autism Spectrum Condition in mainland China. *Research in Developmental Disabilities* 34: 469–479.

Sun, X., Allison, C., Auyeung, B., Matthews, F.E., Murray, S., Baron-Cohen, S. and Brayne, C. (2013b) Service provision for autism in mainland China: A service providers' perspective. *Research in Developmental Disabilities* 34: 440–451.

Tan, Y. (2010) *'Hope' event fading out: mother wishes not to be disturbed*, http://news. enorth.com.cn/system/2010/02/11/004494951.shtml [6 July 2010].

Tang, H., Zhou, R. and Huang, J. (2011) *Court announcement of the case of 'Mother who drowned her twin children with cerebral palsy', husband said the punishment was too heavy*, http://baobao.sohu.com/20110629/n311982183.shtml [25 July 2012].

Tengxun Forum (2010) *Young mother killed 3 year old sick daughter, claimed to alleviate suffering of the child*, http://comment5.news.qq.com/comment.htm?site=newsandid =24931015 [25 July 2012].

Tianya Laiba Milk Powder (2010) *Story about a baby girl with aproctia in Tianjin*, http:// laiba.tianya.cn/laiba/CommMsgs?cmm=43194andtid=2718017910248651052 [2 July 2010].

Tianya Laiba Women (2010) *Follow-up story about the baby with aproctia*, http://laiba. tianya.cn/laiba/CommMsgs?cmm=876andtid=2717672208334590140 [6 July 2010].

UNCRC, United Nations Committee on the Rights of the Child (2005) Fortieth session Consideration of Reports submitted by states parties under article 44 of the convention Concluding observations: China.

UNCRC, United Nations Committee on the Rights of the Child (2006a) *Excluded and invisible, the state of the world's children 2006*, UNICEF.

UNCRC, United Nations Committee on the Rights of the Child (2006b) *General comment no. 9 the rights of children with disabilities*, Forty-third session, Geneva, 11–29 September.

UNDP, United Nations Development Programme (2013) 2013 Human Development Report: The Rise of the South: Human Progress in a Diverse World, New York: UNDP.

UNESCO, United Nations Educational, Scientific and Cultural Organization (1994) *Salamanca Statement and Framework for Action on Special Needs Education*, www. unesco.org/education/pdf/SALAMA_E.PDF [3 May 2015].

UNESCO, United Nations Educational, Scientific and Cultural Organization (2004) *EFA Flagship Initiative, The Right to Education for Persons With Disabilities: Towards Inclusion* http://unesdoc.unesco.org/images/0013/001378/137873e.pdf [3 May 2015].

UNESCO, United Nations Educational, Scientific and Cultural Organization (2014) *Education For All Global Monitoring Report 2013/4*, 11th EFA, UNESCO. www. efareport.unesco.org [4 August 2014].

UNESCO Bangkok, United Nations Educational, Scientific and Cultural Organization Bangkok (2014) Barriers to inclusive education, www.unescobkk.org/education/inclusive-education/what-is-inclusive-education/barriers-to-inclusive-education/   [6 August 2014].

Unger, J. (2008) *Associations and the Chinese State: Contested Spaces*, Armonk: M. E. Sharpe.

UNGACC, United Nations Guidelines for the Alternative Care of Children (2009) www. unicef.org/aids/files/UN_Guidelines_for_alternative_care_of_children.pdf   [13   July 2014].

UNICEF, United Nations Children's Fund (2006) *An Investigation of Families with Children with Disabilities and Relevant Policies.* Unpublished internal document.

UNICEF, United Nations Children's Fund (2013) *The State of the World's Children 2013: Children with disabilities*, www.unicef.org/sowc2013 [2 May 2015].

Wang, P., Fang, H. and Li, X. (2006) A comparison of poverty standard between China and International. *China Rural Economy* 12: 62–65.

Wang, P. and Michaels, C.A. (2009) Chinese families of children with severe disabilities: Family needs and available support. *Research and Practice for Persons with Severe Disabilities* 34: 21–32.

Wang, P., Michaels, C.A. and Day, M.S. (2011) Stresses and coping strategies of Chinese families with children with autism and other developmental disabilities. *Journal of Autism and Developmental Disorders* 41(6): 783–795.

Wang, X., Wang, L. and Wang, Y. (2012) *The Quality of Growth and Poverty Reduction in China*, Beijing: Social Sciences Academic Press.

Watson, S. and Griffiths, D. (2009) Right to life, in Owen F and Griffiths D. (eds) *Challenges to the Human Rights of People with Intellectual Disabilities*, London: Jessica Kingsley Publishers.

Western Net (2011) *The court announcement of the case of Yao Jiaxin: Yao was sentenced to death*, http://news.163.com/11/0422/11/7286SHQR00011229.html [25 July 2012].

White, G., Howell, J. and Shang, X. (1996) *In Search of Civil Society: Market Reform and Social Change in Contemporary China*, Oxford: Clarendons Press.

Wong, S.Y., Wong, T.K.S., Martinson, I., Lai, A.C., Chen, W.J. and He, Y.S. (2004) Needs of Chinese parents of children with developmental disability. *Journal of Learning Disabilities* 8: 141–158.

WHO, World Health Organisation (2011) *World Report on Disability 2011.* WHO Press, Geneva whqlibdoc.who.int/publications/2011/9789240685215_eng.pdf [2 May 2015].

Xinhua News (2010) 2013 dependency ratio of population in China is at the turning point, still has 25 year dividend, http://news.xinhuanet.com/politics/2010-05/18/c_12115988. htm [3 May 2015].

Xiong, N., Yang, L., Yu, Y., Hou, J., Li, J., Li, Y., Liu, H., Zhang, Y. and Jiao, Z. (2011) Investigation of raising burden of children with autism, physical disability and mental disability in China. *Research in Developmental Disabilities* 32: 306–311.

Yang, W. (2010) One child with disability was born in China in every 30 Seconds, can we prevent the disability at birth? *Renmin Daily*, 13 September 2010, http://health.people.com.cn/GB/12703109.html [9 September 2011].

Yin, Z., Dai, H., Xiao, Z. and Xue, H. (2007) A research study into the requirements of disabled residents for rehabilitation services in Beijing. *Disability & Rehabilitation* 29(10): 825–833.

Yin RK. (2003) *Case study research*, 3rd edn, Thousand Oaks: Sage Publications.

Zhang, X., Rao, D. and Wei, X. (2011) *The track of the thirteen years of a mother who drowned her twin children with cerebral palsy*, http://dg.oeeee.com/a/20110517/991813.html 25 July 2012.

Zhongguo Jiaoyuwang (2009) *Members of Political Consultant Committee Proposes the Establishment of Funding for the Treatment of Children with Leukaemia*, www.chinaedunet.com/yejy/ziyuan/2009/content_163759.shtml [20 January 2010].

Zhou, G. (2000). *Niuniu: The Notes by a Father*, Guilin: Publishing House of Guangxi Normal University.

Ziyou (2005) *Whose Youth Is As Mad As Mine?* Shanghai, Children's Publishing House.

Index

abandonment issues 48, 53–70, 182–3, 197
abortion 54
absolute poverty 104–6, 113
absolute right to life 58
abuse 15, 197
access issues 100, 107–28, 148–9
ACWF *see* All China Women's Federation
additional children, penalties 37
advertisements 122–3, 149
agencies: abandonment issues 56–7, 62, 68–9; welfare provision 39–40, 42, 44–5
age variations: foster care 93–4; incidence differences 25, 28–32; mothers' gendered experiences 75–86; social participation rights 160–78; welfare provision 34–7
All China Women's Federation (ACWF) 42
alternative family care 88–99
attendance, education 147–59
autism 55, 117–18, 121, 123–4, 137, 144
availability issues 124–5
awareness-raising 20–1, 196–7

barriers to: education experiences 147–59; social participation rights 160
basic living protection allowances 47
birth rates 53–5
blind/visual impairment: age group variations 28–9; education experiences 150, 153–4, 158; right to life and protection 56, 66; social exclusion 182; social participation rights 161, 164, 166, 169; support for mothers 76–7, 83; welfare provision 38

capacity issues, education 148
care & protection rights 14–18, 22, 53–70, 73–99, 181–3, 192
case studies: abandonment issues 55–69; care & protection rights 73–87; child development rights 118, 121–5; discrimination/exclusion 181–9; economic security 100, 103–6, 108–11; education 136–8, 149–51, 153–8; health & therapy services 118, 121–5; mothers' gendered experiences 73–87; poverty 100, 103–6, 108–11; social participation rights 161–78; support for mothers 73–87
CDPF *see* China Disabled Persons' Federation
CEDAW *see* Convention on the Elimination of All Forms of Discrimination against Women
cerebral palsy: alternative family care 96; economic security 103–5, 109; education policy 137, 144; health & therapy services 118, 121–2, 125–6; right to life & protection 57–9, 62–4; support for mothers 76, 80
certificate of disability 107–8, 149
Child Development in China, National Programme (1992–99, 2001–10, 2011–20) 38
child development rights 18–22, 115–29, 193–4; cost issues 115–28; discrimination 184–8; education 19–20, 22, 130–59; health & therapy services 115–28; inclusion/education 130–44; mothers' gendered experiences 73, 75, 77, 80–1, 85–6; poverty 125–6; social

exclusion 184–8; welfare provision 115–29

children's rights 11–24, 34, 38–42, 47, 50, 53–72, *see also individual rights*

children's voices 60–3, 93

China Disabled Persons' Federation (CDPF) 40–3, 116

China National Committee for the Well-being of Youth 42

citizen opinions, right to life & protection 64–5

citizenship rights 160

city education policies 138–9

communication, social participation rights 161, 165–7, 176–7

Communist Party of China (CPC) 39

Communist Youth League of China 42

community inclusion 97

community members: abandonment issues 56–7, 61–3, 65; mothers' gendered experiences 73, 81–5; social exclusion/discrimination 189; social participation rights 161, 167–9, 171–3, 176–7

compulsory education 130–44

conditional enrolment, education 149–51

conditional right to life 58

Constitution 38–9

Convention on the Elimination of All Forms of Discrimination against Women (CEDAW 1979) 12

Convention on the Rights of the Child (CRC) 12–13, 38–9, 195–6

Convention on the Rights of Persons with Disabilities (CRPD) 12–21, 25, 38–9, 54, 64, 196–200

Cooperative Medical Care (NRCMC) 116

costs: abandonment issues 53–4, 58–9, 63, 65–9; child development rights 115–28; economic security 100–4, 106, 108–14; education experiences 156–7; health & therapy services 115–28; life & protection rights 53–4, 58–9, 63, 65–9; social exclusion/discrimination 183–4; therapy services 115–28; welfare provision 34–5, 43–4

CPC *see* Communist Party of China

CRC *see* Convention on the Rights of the Child

CRPD *see* Convention on the Rights of Persons with Disabilities

cultural life recreation 21–2, 200

daily care 73–86

deaf/hearing impairment: age group variations 28–9; economic security 101; education 137, 140–3, 149–51, 153, 157–8; social participation rights 162, 164–75; welfare provision 38

debt, mothers' experiences 79–80

decision-making processes, abandonment 59–69

demographic changes 28–32, 34–7

development rights *see* child development rights

differences in incidence of disability 25–32, 102–6, 113

Disabilities: Convention on the Rights of Persons (CRPD) 12–21, 25, 38–9, 54, 64, 196–200; Law on the Protection of Persons with (1990, 2008) 33, 137

disability certificates 107–8, 149

disability community participation rights 161, 167–9, 171–3

Disabled Persons Federation (DPF) 127, 138, 162, 167, 171–5, 177–8

discrimination 53, 61–3, 66–9, 73–4, 81–2, 85–6, 109–10, 147, 154–5, 160, 177, 180–90; abandonment issues 53, 61–3, 66–9, 182–3; case studies 181–9; child development rights 184–8; community members 189; definitions 180; economic security 109–10, 183–4; education 147, 154–5, 183–6; exclusion 180–90, 192, 194; extended families 182–3; families 180–90; life & protection rights 53, 61–3, 66–9, 181–3; mothers' gendered experiences 73–4, 81–2, 85–6; participation rights 160, 177, 186–7; social participation 160, 177, 186–7; social security 109–10

DPF *see* Disabled Persons Federation

earnings 100–1, 111–12, 114, 163, 168–9, 173–4

ecological models, social participation rights 160–1

economic development/revenue 34–5

economic security 16–18, 22, 100–14, 183–4, 193
education 19–22, 97, 117–25, 130–59, 183–6, 193, 199; life & protection rights 54, 56, 65, 68, 70; mothers' gendered experiences 79–80, 84–5; social participation rights 163–5, 168–72, 174–7
emotional support 95
employment 100–1, 111–14, 163–5, 168–9, 173–4, 176–8
enrolment, education 149–51
ethnicity, social participation 162–4
exclusion 130–5, 140–4, 148–54, 158, 160–1, 177, 180–94
exploitation, freedom from 15, 197
extended families: abandonment issues 56, 58–60, 65, 68–9; discrimination/exclusion 182–3; economic security 100–1, 104; life & protection rights 56, 58–60, 65, 68–9; mothers' gendered experiences 76, 79–80, 83–6; orphans/alternative family care 89; poverty 100–1, 104
extreme rural poor 47

families 11–22; abandonment issues 53–70; alternative care 88–99; care and protection rights 73–99; child development rights 115–28; discrimination/exclusion 180–90; economic security 100–14; education experiences 117–25, 147–59; health & therapy services 115–28; life and protection rights 53–70; mothers' gendered experiences 73–87; poverty 100–14; respect 15–16, 198; social participation rights 160–78; structure differences 25; welfare provision 37–8, *see also* extended families
Family Planning Commission 41
fathers, mothers' experiences of caring 74, 76–7, 79, 82, 84–6
financial revenue, welfare provision 34–5
financial security: foster care 92–4; mothers' gendered experiences 73, 75, 77–81, 84–6, *see also* economic security
five-year plans 13, 116

foster care 48, 88–98
freedom from violence 14–18, 22, 197
free education, rights to 130–44
free public health care 115
friend's support 83–5, 169–71
funding *see* costs

Gao'an City Special School 139–44
gendered roles, mothers' experiences 73–87, 160
geographical distribution, incidence differences 25–32
government support: abandonment issues 54–9, 63–5, 69–70; care & protection rights 88–99; child development rights 115–17, 119, 121, 124–7; economic security 107–10; education 131, 133–44, 148, 153, 156–8; health & therapy 115–17, 119, 121, 124–7; life and protection rights 54–9, 63–5, 69–70; mothers' gendered experiences 73, 75–6, 81–2, 84–6; poverty 107–10; therapy 115–17, 119, 121, 124–7; welfare provision 34–5, 39–50
grandparents 56, 58–60, 65, 68–9
Greenwood State Child Welfare Institution foster care 88–91, 94–5, 97
Guangdong Disabled Persons Federation 64

habilitation 19, 199–200
hair salons 171–2, 174–5
health 18–19, 22; foster care 89, 93, 95–8; insurance 115–17, 125; tests 54; and therapy services 89, 93, 95–8, 115–29; welfare provision 33–52, 199
historical overviews, education policy 133–5
home, respect for 15–16, 198
household status 30–2
housing 106–7

implementation challenges, mainstream schools 136–7
incidence differences/rates 25–32, 102–6, 113
inclusion 20–2, 90, 96–8, 130–44, 160
income poverty 100–14

income support 73, 75, 77–81, 84–6
infanticide 56–7, 59, 62–4
informal social groups 174–5, 177
information access 117–28, 148–9
institutional care 88–99, *see also*
    government support
insurance 107, 109, 113–17, 125
intellectual disabilities: age group
    variations 28–9, 32; economic security
    104, 109; education policy 135, 137–40,
    144; health & therapy services 118–19,
    123–4; right to life & protection 56, 58;
    social exclusion 185–6; social
    participation rights 163–4; support for
    mothers 75–6; welfare provision 38–9
interest representation 161, 173–7
international children's rights 11–22
Internet 56–7, 61–3, 123, 171
interrelated rights, social exclusion 180–90
isolation 160

land security 100–1, 106
Law on the Protection of Persons with
    Disabilities (1990, 2008) 33, 137
laws: education 133–5; right to life &
    protection 54; welfare provision 38–9
learning support access 148–9
leisure activities 21, 200
leukaemia 116
levels of education 132–3
liberty of movement and nationality 15,
    197
life and freedom from violence 14–15, 197
life and protection rights 14–15, 53–72,
    181–3, 197
lifesaving treatment 56–8
living standards 102–6, 108, 200
local school capacity 148
local State Child Welfare Institution foster
    care 88–91, 94–5, 97

mainstream state schools 135–7, 151–2
management: foster care 91–3; special
    education schools 141–4
Medical Care (NRCMC) 116
medical insurance 109, 113–17, 125
medical treatment: abandonment issues
    54–70; child development rights
    115–29; economic security/poverty 101,

104, 109–11, 113–14; life & protection
    rights 54–70; mothers' gendered
    experiences 76, 78–85, *see also* health
Mental Health Research Center, Nanjing
    117
minimum living security (MLS) 46, 79,
    84–5, 107, 109, 111
Ministry of Civil Affairs 41
Ministry of Education 41
Ministry of Human Resources and Social
    Security 41
misdiagnosis issues 121–2
MLS *see* minimum living security
mortality rates 115–16
mothers' gendered experiences of caring
    73–87, 160
motivation, education 134–5
movement and nationality liberty 15, 197
multidirectional relationships, economic
    security 100–2
multiple disabilities 28–9, 32, 56, 76, 119,
    189
murder 56–7, 59, 62–5, 67

Nanjing Child Mental Health Research
    Center 117
National Health and Family Planning
    Commission 41
nationality liberty 15, 197
National Minors Protection Committee
    (NMPC) 42
National Programme of Action for Child
    Development in China (1992–99,
    2001–10, 2011–20) 38
neighbourhood factors 161
New Rural Cooperative Medical Care
    (NRCMC) 116
NGO *see* non-government organizations
NMPC *see* National Minors Protection
    Committee
non-government organizations (NGO):
    abandonment issues 56–7, 62, 68–9;
    education experiences 142–4, 148;
    foster care 95; health & therapy services
    116, 125; life and protection rights
    56–7; social participation rights 175,
    178; welfare provision 42, 44–5
NRCMC *see* New Rural Cooperative
    Medical Care

orphans 39, 41, 44–9, 88–99
Outline of the Twelfth Five-Year Plan for the Disabled in China (2011–15) 13

parental reasons for abandoning children 53–70
parental responsibilities 73–86
parent-less children 39, 41, 44–9, 88–99
participation rights 160–79, 186–7, 194
peer relationships 155, 161–2
penalties, additional children 37
People's Republic of China, formation 34
physical disabilities: age group variations 28–9, 32; discrimination 182–9; education policy 97, 135, 137, 139, 144; health and therapy services 118–19, 125; right to life & protection 58, 182–3; social exclusion 181–9; support for mothers 75–7
policies: reforms 191–4; welfare provision 38–9
political organizations 39–44, *see also* government support
positive impacts, education experiences 157–8
poverty 17–18, 100–14, 125–6, 173–4, 183–4
preventing/protecting child abandonment 48, 53–70
private schools 142–4, 150, 153
professional support 63, 65, 88–93, 95–6, 98
protection rights 14–18, 22, 48, 53–99, 181–3, 192, 197, 200
provincial finances 34–5
provincial population structures 34, 36–7
public health care 115

recreation 21–2, 200
recruitment, foster care 91–2
reforms, social policy 191–4
regional finances 34–5
regional incidence differences 25–32
regulations: education policy 133–5; welfare provision 38–9
rehabilitation 19, 199–200
relative poverty 104–6, 113
relief funds 47, 107–10
respect issues 15–16, 198

responsibilities, mothers' gendered experiences 73–86
rights of: children 11–24, 34, 38–42, 47, 50; social participation 160–79, *see also individual rights*
rights to children's development 18–22, 115–59, 184–8, 193–4; mothers' gendered experiences 73, 75, 77, 80–1, 85–6
right to: care & protection 14–18, 22, 53–70, 73–99, 181–3, 192; economic security 16–18, 22, 100–14, 183–4, 193; free education 130–44; life & protection 14–15, 53–72, 181–3, 197
rural areas: child development rights 115–20, 124–6; discrimination 181–9; economic security 101–14; education 132–41, 149, 156–7; exclusion 181–9; health & therapy services 115–20, 124–6; incidence differences 25–8, 30–2; Minimum Living Security 46; mothers' gendered experiences 73–9, 85–6; poverty 101–14; welfare provision 46–7

school conditions 147–53
Second China National Sample Survey on Disability (SCNSSD 2006): economic security 100, 102–3, 108–9; education policy 130, 133, 138; health & therapy services 118; incidence distribution 25–32; social participation rights 160
segregation 130–5, 140, 142, 144, 148–54, 158, *see also* exclusion
service support rights 117–28
sex variations: alternative family care 90, 94; economic security 100, 102–3, 107–8, 111–13; education 132; health & therapy services 118–19, 126; incidence differences 25, 28, 32; life & protection rights 55, 57; social participation rights 160, 162–78
shared care responsibilities 73, 81–5
siblings 81, 168
size, household status 30–2
social assistance provision 45–9
social attitudes 147, 154–5, 160
social exclusion 160, 177, 180–90, 192, 194

social inclusion 20–2, 90, 96–8, 160
social institutions of support, participation rights 160–79
social insurance 107–9, 113–14
social interdependence 12
social networks 12, 75, 83
social participation rights 160–78, 186–7, 194
social policy 73–4, 86, 191–4
social protection 17–18, 200
social relationships, social participation rights 161–2, 167–73
social relief 47, 107–10
social security 41, 45–8, 100, 107–14
social support 39–50, 53–70, 73–86
socio-economic factors 147, 155–7
special education schools 137–44, 151–3, 169–71, 177
specialized foster care 88–99
speech disabilities: age group variations 28–9; economic security 103; education experiences 155–6; education policies 135, 142–3; health & therapy services 118–19, 126; right to life & protection 56, 76; social participation rights 164–7, 169–76
sports activities 21, 200
standard of living protection 17–18, 200
State Child Welfare Institution foster care 88–91, 94–5, 97
state responsibility, children's rights 12–22
suicides 56–7, 59
supervision, foster care 91–2
support services 18–19, 22; education 130–1, 133–44, 147–59; for mothers 73–87; social participation rights 160–79, *see also individual support services*
survival rates 56–7

teachers 148–58
temporary social relief 47
therapy services 89, 93, 95–8, 115–29
training: foster care 91–2, 96; social participation rights 171–2, 174–5
treatment *see* medical treatment

United Nations (UN) Conventions 12–22, 195–200
universal free education 130–44
urban areas: discrimination 181; economic security 102–14; education 132–9, 141–2, 144, 149; exclusion 181; health & therapy services 115–20, 124; incidence differences 25, 28, 30–2; Minimum Living Security 46; mothers' gendered experiences 73–6, 79, 82, 85; poverty 102–14

violence, protection from 14–18, 22, 197
vision disabilities *see* blind/visual impairment
vocational training 171–2, 174–5

welfare provision 33–52, 73–5, 115–29
women's rights 73–86

young people's employment status 111–14

Taylor & Francis eBooks

Helping you to choose the right eBooks for your Library

Add Routledge titles to your library's digital collection today. Taylor and Francis ebooks contains over 50,000 titles in the Humanities, Social Sciences, Behavioural Sciences, Built Environment and Law.

Choose from a range of subject packages or create your own!

Benefits for you

>> Free MARC records
>> COUNTER-compliant usage statistics
>> Flexible purchase and pricing options
>> All titles DRM-free.

 REQUEST YOUR FREE INSTITUTIONAL TRIAL TODAY

Free Trials Available
We offer free trials to qualifying academic, corporate and government customers.

Benefits for your user

>> Off-site, anytime access via Athens or referring URL
>> Print or copy pages or chapters
>> Full content search
>> Bookmark, highlight and annotate text
>> Access to thousands of pages of quality research at the click of a button.

eCollections – Choose from over 30 subject eCollections, including:

Archaeology	Language Learning
Architecture	Law
Asian Studies	Literature
Business & Management	Media & Communication
Classical Studies	Middle East Studies
Construction	Music
Creative & Media Arts	Philosophy
Criminology & Criminal Justice	Planning
Economics	Politics
Education	Psychology & Mental Health
Energy	Religion
Engineering	Security
English Language & Linguistics	Social Work
Environment & Sustainability	Sociology
Geography	Sport
Health Studies	Theatre & Performance
History	Tourism, Hospitality & Events

For more information, pricing enquiries or to order a free trial, please contact your local sales team:
www.tandfebooks.com/page/sales

 Routledge
Taylor & Francis Group

The home of
Routledge books

www.tandfebooks.com